Practical Meditations

By
Paramhansa Yogananda

Alight Publications
2008

Practical Meditations
(Volume 2 from the Collected Works of Yogananada)

By Paramhansa Yogananda

First Edition Published in May 2008

Alight Publications
PO Box 930
Union City, CA 94587
http://www.alightbooks.com

ISBN 1-931833-29-X

Printed in the United States of America

Dedicated
to
Sincere Seekers
of
the Way

Contents

Practical Meditations

Editors's Note

Metaphysical Meditations / 1

Whispers From Eternity / 78

Super Advanced Course I / 257

Editors's Note

Paramhansa[1] Yogananda was one of the first Indian Masters to stay and teach in the United States. His teachings have reached millions throughtout the World and his influence is still very strong among all sincere spiritual seekers. He passed away in 1952, after ceaselessly teaching everyone who came to him as well as travelling extensively during his thirty-two years of ministry.

In the first volume of his collected works called **The Essence of Kriya Yoga**, we included two complete works (The Science of Religion and Songs of the Soul,) as well as extensive extracts from the Autobiography of a Yogi and articles from the 1930's.)

The focus in this second volume is Yogananda's teachings on the practical aspects of Meditation. We have included three complete works. It is our sincere hope that this will give the reader a unique insight into the practical methods taught by this great Master of Yoga.

---

[1] *Paramhansa was a title conferred on Yogananda by his Master, Shri Yukteswar and literally means Great Swan. It is given to a Great Soul who has acheived Self-Realization and is teaching others to reach spiritual heights. There is some contraversy about the spelling of the title -- we have adopted the spelling used by Yogananda himself.*

METAPHYSICAL MEDITATIONS

Contents

Foreword /1

Devotion and Worship /2

Meditations on God /13

Expansion of Consciousness /24

On Finding God /34

On Material Concerns /44

On Self-Improvement /58

Christmas Meditations /72

FOREWORD

Most people would want to meditate if they understood how to do so. The purpose of meditation is to know God, to connect the little joy of the soul with the vast joy of the Spirit.

Meditation is not the same as concentration. Concentration consists in freeing the attention from objects of distraction and focusing it on one thing at a time. Meditation is that special form of concentration in which the attention has been liberated from restlessness and is focused on God. A man *may concentrate* on the thought of Divinity or of money; but he may not meditate on money or on any other material thing. Meditation is focused only on thoughts of God and His holy prophets.

Meditation consists in certain physical, psychological, and metaphysical processes by which the "static" of restlessness may be removed from man's mental "radio," which may then be tuned in with the Infinite.

All forms of meditation involve the one who meditates, the process of meditation, and the Object of the meditation. The aim is to attain a consciousness of Spirit by calm, continuous, one-pointed attention, until the soul is merged in everlasting bliss. The meditator should therefore know a definite method of meditation and should choose a definite spiritual thought or experience on which to meditate.

This book offers certain definite metaphysical methods of meditation for the student who has already struggled through the mobs of rowdy thoughts and has entered the portals of silence. Instructions for the devotee will be found preceding each group of meditations in the various sections of the book.

The meditations given are of three types: prayers or demands addressed to God, affirmations about God, and those spoken to the individual consciousness. Select one that meets your need and audibly or mentally repeat the words slowly and purposefully until you become absorbed in the inner meaning

DEVOTION AND WORSHIP

To Begin a Meditation

LOCK the eyelid-doors and shut out the wild dance of tempting scenes. Drop your mind into the bottomless well of your heart. Hold the mind on your heart that is bubbling with life-giving blood. Keep your attention tied to the heart, until you feel its rhythmic beat. With every heartbeat feel the pulse of almighty Life. Picture the same all-pervading Life knocking at the heartdoor of fifteen hundred million human bodies and of billions of other creatures. The heart-throb constantly, meekly announces the presence of Infinite Power behind the doors of your awareness. The gentle beat of all-pervading Life says to you silently, "Do not receive only a little flow of My life, but expand the opening of thy feeling-powers. Let Me flood thy blood, body, mind, feelings, and soul with My throbs of universal life."

To Awaken Mental Freedom

Sit still with a straight spine. Cover up your fidgety eyeballs with the sheets of your eyelids. Hold them still. Then loosen your mind from the consciousness of body-weight. Relax the nerve-strings that are attached to the heavy muscles and bones of your body. Forget the consciousness of carrying a heavy bundle of bones tied in the thick cloth of flesh. Rest. Free your mind from the consciousness of a beast of burden. Do not think of your body-load, but feel your soul untied from the constant material quality of heaviness. Mentally race in your fancy's airplane above, beneath, left, right, in infinity, or wherever you want to go. Feel and meditate on this, your mental freedom from *your* body. Dream, dwell, and feel this body-aboveness when sitting still; the consciousness of freedom will constantly increase.

Meditations on Devotion

May Thy love shine forever on the sanctuary of my devotion, and may I be able to awaken Thy love in all hearts.

O Father, receive Thou the fervor of my soul, the devotion of incarnations, the love of ages that I have kept locked in the vault of my heart.

Divine Father, in my temple of silence I have made a garden for Thee, decorated with the blossoms of my devotion.

With aspiring heart, with zealous mind, with flaming soul, I lay at Thy feet of omnipresence all the flowers of my devotion.

O God, I will worship Thee as beauty and intelligence in the temple of Nature. I will worship Thee as power in the temple of activity, and as peace in the temple of silence.

I Will Wait for Thee

In the corner of my heart I have a mystic throne for Thee. The candles of my joys are dimly lighted in the hope of Thy coming. They will burn brighter when Thou appearest. Whether Thou comest or not, I will wait for Thee until my tears melt away all material grossness.

To please Thee my love-perfumed tears will wash Thy feet silence. The altar of my soul will be kept empty until Thou comest.

I will talk not; I will ask naught of Thee. I will realize that Thou knowest the pangs of my heart while I wait for Thee.

Thou dost know that I am praying; Thou dost know that I love no other. Yet whether Thou dost come to me or not, I will wait for Thee, though it be for eternity.

My Offering to Thee

Each morning I offer my body, my mind, and any ability that I possess, to be used by Thee, O Infinite Creator, in whatever way Thou dost choose to express Thyself through me. I know that all work is Thy work, and that no task is too difficult or too menial when offered to Thee in loving service.

Divine Mother, with the language of my soul I demand realization of Thy presence. Thou art the essence of everything. Make me see Thee in every fiber of my being, in every wisp of thought. Awaken my heart!

Beloved Father, my wordless chants of yearning for Thee will sing in cadence with my heart-throbs. I shall feel Thy presence in all hearts. I shall watch Thy hands working in the law of gravitation and in all other natural forces. In the tread of all living creatures I shall hear Thy footsteps.

As I radiate sympathy and good will to others I open the channel for God's love to come to me. Divine love is the magnet that attracts all blessedness.

I will not become too much attached to things, as this will cause me to forget God. We lose things, not as a punishment, but as a test to see if we love little things more than the Infinite Lord.

Thou unseen Charmer of Souls, Thou art the fountain flowing from the bosom of friendship. Thou art the rays of secret warmth that unfolds buds of feeling into blossoms of endearing, soulful words of poetry and loyalty.

Into the shrine of devotion, come Thou, O Bliss God!

Father, enter Thou into my soul through the portals of my heart's devotion and through my prayers.

Beloved God, no more with words but with the burning flame of my heart's love I worship Thee.

> I obey Thee in the temple of discipline.
>
> I love Thee in the temple of devotion.
>
> I worship Thee in the temple of my love.
>
> I touch Thy feet in the temple of stillness.
>
> I behold Thine eyes in the temple of delight.
>
> I feel Thee in the temple of emotion.
>
> I fight for Thee in the temple of activity.
>
> I enjoy Thee in the temple of peace.

I will rise with the dawn and rouse my sleeping love to waken in the light of true devotion for the peace-God within.
Into the invisible church of my prayer, built with strong white blocks of devotion, come Thou to receive the humble offerings of my heart, renewed by love.

Divine Mother, open wide the bud of my devotion and release Thy fragrance that it may spread from my soul to the souls of all others, ever whispering of Thee.

I Have Heard Thy Voice

Divine Mother, I have heard Thy voice whispering in the fragrance of the rose. I touched Thy tenderness in the softness of the lily. In the whispers *of my* devotion, it was Thy love that answered.

Undying Devotion

O Thou Great Lover, Thou art Life, Thou art the Goal, Thou art my Desire. Deliver me from Thy *maya* of delusion. Tempt me with Thy presence instead. Beloved God, fill my heart with undying devotion to Thee alone.

Christ is risen from the sepulcher of my indifference, and I behold him in the light of my devotion. I, a sleeping son of God, am coming out of my bodily prison into the vast freedom of Spirit.

Teach me to drink the everlasting nectar of joy found in the fountain of meditation.

My Well of Silence

His laughter caught my heart. His joy invaded my sorrowful heart as I swung in a hammock beneath the pines under the blue.

I felt the sky astir and His presence moving through me. My body became still; my power of silence dug into my bosom until a bottomless well sprang up.

The bubbling waters of my well clamored and called all thirsty things around me to come and drink of my inspirations. Suddenly the vast blue pouted and plunged its blue lips into the well of my heart. The pines, the sailing clouds, the mountains, earth, planets, everything, put their mouths into my well of bliss. All things drank of me. Then, satisfied, they plunged into the waters of my immortality. Their gross bodies touched the transmuting pool of my soul and became purified and luminous. Just as grains of sugar dissolve in a pot of sparkling water, so the cloudlets, tall hills, scenic beauties, stars, lakes, worlds, brooklets of laughing minds, long winding rivers of ambitions of all creatures traveling along many trails of incarnations - all melted in the ocean of my all-dissolving silence.

O Divine Shepherd of Infinite Perception, rescue the lambkins of my thoughts, lost in the wilderness of restlessness, and lead them into Thy fold of silence.

Beloved Father, let the embers of my devotion glow with Thy presence evermore.

Beloved God, pluck the lotus of my devotion from the mire of earthly forgetfulness and wear it on Thy breast of ever-awake memory.

I bow to Thee, O God, in the temple of the skies, in the temple of Nature, and in the soul-temples of human brothers.

I Worship God Everywhere

I bow to the one infinite Father, differently manifesting in the many churches and temples that have all been erected in His honor. I worship the one God resting on the various altars of different teachings and religious faiths.

Today I will worship God in deep silence and wait to hear His answer through my increasing peace of meditation.

I will mingle my inner devotional whispers with the prayers of all saints, and continuously offer them in the temple of silence and activity until I can hear His whispers loudly, everywhere.

This day shall be the best day of my life. Today I will start with a new determination to dedicate my devotion forever at the feet of Omnipresence.

Expanding Love

(Meditate, dwell on, and feel this.)

My kingdom of love shall expand. I have loved my body more than anything else. That is why I am identified with and limited by it. With the love that I had given to the body, I will love all those who love me. With the expanded love of those who love me, I will love those who are mine. With the love for myself and the love for my own, I will love those who are strangers. I will use all my love to love those who do not love me, as well as those who love me. I will bathe all souls in my unselfish love. In the sea of my love, my family members, my countrymen, all nations, and all creatures will swim. All creation, all the myriads of tiny living things, will dance on the waves of my love.

I saturate myself with the perfume of Thy presence, and I wait to waft with the breeze the aroma of Thy message of love to all.

In the temple of my earthly mother's love I will worship the incarnated love of the Divine Mother.

All desire for love I will purify and satisfy in sacred divine love for God.

Beloved Infinite, I will keep Thee ever imprisoned behind the strong walls of my undying love.

Whether or not Thou answerest my demands and prayers, I shall go on loving Thee.

O Father, teach me to *vivify* my prayers with Thy *love*. May I realize Thy nearness behind the *voice* of my prayer.

I know that just behind the screen of my love-demands Thou art listening to the silent words of my soul.

I will behold God Himself bestowing on me His divine love through the hearts of all.

MEDITATIONS ON GOD

Meditate on God's Light

Look at a light and close your eyes. Forget the darkness around you and watch the bright red color within your eyelids. Try to look intently into that violet-red color before you. Meditate on it and imagine that it is becoming bigger and bigger. Behold around you a dimly shining sea of violet light. You are a wave of light, a ripple of peace floating on the surface of the sea.

Now watch carefully. You, the little wave, are tossing on an ocean of light. Your tiny life is a part of the all-pervading Life. As your meditation deepens, you, a little shallow wave of peace, are becoming the deep, wide ocean of peace.

Meditate on the thought, "I am a wave of peace." Feel the vastness just beneath your consciousness. The wave should feet the sustaining life of the vast ocean beneath it.

God's Protecting Presence

Teach me to feel that I am enveloped always in the aureole of Thine all-protecting omnipresence, in birth, in sorrow, in joy, in activity, in meditation, in ignorance, in trials, in death, and in final emancipation.

Teach me to open the gate of meditation that alone leads to Thy blessed presence.

Behind the wave of my consciousness is the sea of Cosmic Consciousness. Under the ripple of my mind is the supporting ocean of Thy vastness. I am protected by Thy Divine Mind.

Naughty or good, I am Thy child. Sinner or saint, I am Thine own.

Thy light of goodness and Thy protective power are ever shining through me. I saw them not, because my eyes of wisdom were closed. Now Thy touch of peace has opened my eyes; Thy goodness and unfailing protection are flowing through me.

I Will Extol Thee

O Heavenly Father, I will extol Thy glory, the beauties of Thy paradise within us. May I live in the garden of soul-happiness and noble thoughts and be filled with the aroma of Thy love evermore.

O Spirit, make my soul Thy temple, but make my heart Thy beloved home where Thou wouldst dwell with me in ease and everlasting understanding.

Wilt Thou not open Thy lips of silence and whisper constant guiding thoughts to my soul?

Teach me to behold Thy face in the mirror of my stillness within.

Beloved Lord, teach me to feel that Thou art the sole activating power, and that in recognition of Thee as the Doer lies the value of all my life's experiences. Teach me to behold Thee as the only Friend, helping and encouraging me through my earthly friends.

Heavenly Father, from today I will strive to know Thee; I will make the effort to cultivate Thy friendship. All my duties will be performed with the thought that I am realizing Thee through them, and thus am pleasing Thee.

Life is a struggle for joy all along the way. May I fight to win the battle on the very spot where I now am.

When pain or anger or any kind of suffering comes to me, I will view it as a spectator. I will separate myself from my experiences. At all costs I will endeavor to retain my peace and happiness.

Beloved Father, I realize that praise does not make me any better, nor blame worse. I am what I am before my conscience and Thee. I shall travel on, doing good to all and seeking ever to please Thee, for thus shall I find my only true happiness.

Take This Darkness Away

Heavenly Father, take this darkness away! When I sit with closed eyes surrounded by my own darkness, cause to blaze upon me in splendor the aurora of intuition, that in its light I may watch Thee with worshiping eyes.

Mother Divine, draw aside Thy glittering veil of cosmic motion pictures and show me Thy delusion-dispersing face of mercy.

Heavenly Father, awaken my heart, awaken my soul, ignite my darkness, tear the veil of silence and fill my temple with the fragrance of Thy glory.

Heavenly Father, destroy in us the wrong thought of ages-that we are frail human beings. Manifest Thyself as the light of inner reason, the deep blaze of wisdom.

Thy love, O God, flowing through human hearts hath lured me to find the source of perfect love in Thee.

Teach Me To Worship Thee

Beloved Father, teach me the mystery of my existence! Teach me to worship Thee in breathlessness, in deathlessness. In the fire of devotion, consume my ignorance. In the stillness of my soul, come, Father, come! Possess me and make me feel, in and around me, Thine immortal presence.

In the solitude of my mind my devotion is bursting to hear Thy voice. Take away the dreams of earthly sounds that yet lurk in my mind. I want to hear Thy quiet voice ever singing in the silence of my soul.

As Thou art omnipresent, Thou canst but be present in me. Omnipresence presupposes omnipotence and omniscience. These also are attributes of my soul. O Spirit! may I be able to unfold even a fragment of That which my inner Self contains.

Divine Father, teach me to worship Thee on the altar of silence within and on the altar of activity without.

I Will Drink Thy joy

I will drink vitality from the golden fountains of sunshine; I will drink peace from the silver fountain of mooned nights; I will drink Thy power from the mighty cup of the wind; I will drink Thy consciousness as joy and bliss from all the little cups of my thoughts.

In Thy blessed light I shall remain awake forever, watching Thy precious omnipresent face with ever-vigilant eyes through all the eons of eternity.

I had been seeking God's love in the barren dryness of mortal affection. After wandering through the desert of undependable human sympathy, at last I have found the inexhaustible oasis of divine love.

With folded hands, bowed head, and heart laden with the myrrh of reverence, I come to Thee to obey the silent command of Thy voice.

O divine Friend! though the darkness of my ignorance be as old as the world, still make me realize that with the dawn of Thy light the darkness will vanish as though it had never been.

What is this life coursing in my veins? Could it be other than divine?

Heavenly Father, descend within me. Make me feel that Thou art present in my brain, in my spine, and in my deepest thoughts. I bow to Thee.

I am lost, Father, in the wastelands of wrong beliefs; I cannot find my home. Rise on the darkness of my mental sky and be the polestar of my groping mind. Lead me to Thyself who art my Home.

Teach me to redeem my matter-sold mind and brain that I may give them to Thee in prayer and ecstasy, in meditation and reverie.

Reveal Thyself

Come Thou, O Father, reveal the vast kingdom of Thy presence! Reveal Thyself! Teach my heart to pray; teach my soul to feel that all doors may open and Thy presence be revealed.

Every day I see Thee paint the sky with bright colors. I watch Thee clothe the bare soil with green grass. Thou art in the sunshine. Oh, Thou art so plainly present everywhere! I bow to Thee.

Divine Spirit, I will seek Thee until I find Thee. Finding Thee I will reverently receive whatever gifts it is Thy desire I should have. But I ask nothing throughout eternity but the complete gift of Thyself.

Divine Beloved, make me know, at once and forever, that Thou hast always been mine, ever mine. My error-dreams are past, buried in the sepulcher of oblivion. I am awake, basking in the sunlight of life in Thee.

The ocean of God's abundance flows through me. I am His child. I am the channel through which all divine creative power flows. Bless me, Father, that above all things I seek Thee first, as befits Thy true child.

Beloved God, let the flowers *of my* devotion blossom in the garden of my heart while I await the dawn of Thy coming.

Dear Father, open all the windows of faith that I may behold Thee in the mansion of peace. Fling open the doors of silence that I may enter Thy temple of bliss.

Beloved God, protect the celestial temple of my mind against the entry of tenacious warriors of evil thoughts.

I know that I am responsible for my own welfare. Therefore I will discard all useless pursuits and idle thoughts, that daily I may find time for God.

Divine Father, teach me to dive again and again into meditation, deeper and deeper, until I find Thine immortal pearls of wisdom and divine joy.

My Heavenly Father is Love, and I am made in His image. I am the cosmic sphere of Love in which I behold all planets, all stars, all beings, all creation as glimmering lights. I am the Love that illumines the whole universe.

I want Thee, O God, that I may give Thee to all!

O Fountain of Love, make me feel that my heart is flooded by Thine omnipresent love.

Father, teach me to reclaim my birthright and to live as an immortal.

Father of hearts, awaken the consciousness of Thy loving presence within me.

On the throne of silent thoughts the God of peace is directing my actions today. I will usher my brothers into the temple of God through the door of my peace. *By my* example I will try to help others. I will serve all through my spiritual happiness.

I will think until I find the ultimate answer. I will turn the power of thought into a searchlight whose brightness will reveal the face of Omnipresence.

Whether I am a small or a big wave of being, the same Ocean of Life is behind me.

Teach me to think of Thee until Thou dost become my only thought.

O Father, no matter what my tests may be, may I bear them joyously by feeling Thy presence always in my heart. The knowledge of Thy presence will make all the tragedies and comedies of life naught but dramas of ecstatic entertainment.

Father, transfer my consciousness from my limitations, suggested by others and by my own weak thoughts, to the realization that I, Thy child, am the owner of Thy Kingdom of infinite possessions.

O Father, show me the highway that leads to Thee. Give me bursting aspirations of the heart. In the echo of devotion teach me to hear Thy voice.

O Fountain of Flame, let Thy light be established within me, about me, everywhere.

Father, Mother, beloved Spirit, reveal Thyself unto me.

A true yogi feels the throb of his heart in all hearts; his mind in all minds; his presence in all motion. I will be a true yogi.

In the stillness of my soul I humbly bow before Thine omnipresence, knowing that Thou art ever leading me onward and upward on the path of Self-realization.

EXPANSION OF CONSCIOUSNESS

Tune in With the Cosmic Sound

LISTEN to the cosmic sound on the sensitive right side of your head. Feel it spreading through the brain. Hear its continuous pounding roar. Now hear and feel it spreading over the spine and bursting open the doors of the heart. Feel it resounding through every tissue, every feeling, every cord of your nerves. Every blood cell, every thought is dancing on the sea of roaring vibration.

Observe the spread of the volume of the cosmic sound. It sweeps through the body and mind into the earth and the surrounding atmosphere, into the airless ether, and into millions of universes of matter.

Meditate on the marching spread of the cosmic sound. It has passed through the physical universes to the subtle shining veins of rays that hold all matter in manifestations.

The cosmic sound is commingling with millions of multicolored rays. The cosmic sound has entered the realm of cosmic rays. Listen to, behold, and feel the embrace of the cosmic sound and the eternal light. The cosmic sound now pierces through the heartfires of cosmic energy and they both melt within the bosom of cosmic consciousness and cosmic joy. The body melts into the universe. The universe melts into the soundless voice. The sound melts into the all-shining light. And the light enters the bosom of infinite joy.

The Cosmic Sea

When you find that your soul, your heart, every wisp of inspiration, every speck of the vast blue sky and its shining star-blossoms, the mountains, the earth, the whippoorwill, and the bluebells are all tied together with one cord of rhythm, one cord of joy, one cord of unity, one cord of Spirit, then you shall know that all are but waves in His cosmic sea.

I Go Within

I was a prisoner carrying a heavy load of bones and flesh, but I have broken the chains of my muscle-bound body by the power of relaxation. I am free. Now I shall try to go within.

I am sitting on the altar of my throbbing heart. I watch the roaring, shouting torrent of life-force moving through the heart into the body. I turn backward to the spine. The beat and roar of the heart are gone. Like a sacred hidden river my life-force flows in the gorge of the spine. I enter a dim corridor through the door of the spiritual eye, and speed on until at last the river of my life flows into the ocean of life and loses itself in bliss.

I am the macrocosm and the microcosm. My body is the universe; I am the astral breath that enlivens all things. I am the vast life that is throbbing as the little life in my heart.

O Holy OM!

Holy Ghost, sacred Om vibration, enlarge my consciousness as I listen to thine omnipresent sound. Make me feel that I am both the cosmic ocean and the little wave of body-vibration in it.

Teach me to hear Thy voice, O Father, the cosmic voice that commanded all vibration to spring forth. Manifest to me as Om, the cosmic song of all sound.

O omnipresent cosmic sound of Om, reverberate through me, expanding my consciousness from the body to the universe, and teach me to feel in Thee the all-permeating perennial bliss.

O cosmic sound of Om, guide me, be with me, lead me from darkness to light.

Expansion in Eternity

Eternity yawns at me below, above, on the left and on the right, in front and behind, within and without.

With open eyes I behold myself as the little body. With closed eyes I perceive myself as the cosmic center around which revolves the sphere of eternity, the sphere of bliss, the sphere of omnipresent, omniscient, living space.

I feel Him like a gentle breath of bliss breathing in my body of universes. I perceive Him shining through the bright twinkles of all luminosity and through the waves of cosmic consciousness.

I behold Him as the light of solar inspiration holding the luminaries of my thoughts in the rhythms of balance.

I feel Him as a bursting voice, leading, guiding, teaching secretly in the soul-temples of all men and all creation.

He is the fountain of wisdom and of radiant inspiration flowing through all souls. He is the fragrance oozing from the incense vase of all hearts. He is a garden of celestial blossoms and bright thoughtflowers. He is the love that inspires our love-dreams.

I feel Him percolating through my heart, as through all hearts, through the pores of the earth, through the sky, through all created things. He is the eternal motion of joy. He is the mirror of silence in which all creation is reflected.

My earthly experiences serve as a process of destruction of my limiting mortal delusions. In God the wildest dreams are realized. ("I will give him the morning star" - Revelations *2:28.*)

The reality of my life cannot die, for I am indestructible consciousness.

I am submerged in His eternal light. It permeates every particle of my being. I am living in that light, for the divine Spirit has filled me within and without.

I will close my physical eyes and dismiss the temptations of matter. I will peer through the darkness of silence until my eyes of relativity open into the one inner eye of light. When my two eyes that behold both good and evil become single, and behold in everything only the divine goodness of God, I shall see that my body, mind, and soul have become filled with His omnipresent light.

All the veils of my ignorant outer life are burned in the light of my awakening in Christ, and I behold the intelligence of the baby Jesus cradled in the petals of roses, in the weaving of lights, and in the love-thoughts of all true hearts.

I am infinite, I am spaceless, I am tireless; I am beyond body, thought, and utterance; beyond all matter and mind. I am endless bliss.

The ocean of Spirit has become the little bubble of my soul. Whether floating in birth, or disappearing in death, in the ocean of cosmic consciousness the bubble of my life cannot die, for I am indestructible consciousness, protected in the bosom of Spirit's immortality.

I am no longer the wave of consciousness thinking itself separated from the sea of cosmic consciousness. I am the ocean of Spirit that has become the wave of human life.

Like a silent invisible river flowing beneath the desert flows the vast dimensionless river of Spirit, through the sands of time, through the sands of experience, through the sands of all souls, through the sands of all living atoms, through the sands of all space.

O infinite Energy, infinite Wisdom, recharge us with Thy spiritual vibration.

Outer Lures, Away!

Bewitching scenic beauties, stop your dance before my eyes! Lure not my attention away!

Enchanting melodies, keep not my mind enthralled in the revels of material songs!

Haunting sirens of sweet sensations, paralyze not my sacred intuitions by your enticing touch! Let my meditation race for the sweet bower of eternal divine love.

Luring aroma of lilacs, jasmine, and roses, stop not my homeward marching mind!

These tempting enchantresses of the senses are now gone. The cords of flesh are broken. The grip of the senses is loosened. I exhale and stop the storm of breath; the ripples of thought melt away.

O Father, Thou art sacred perennial joy, Thou art the joy I seek, Thou art the joy of the soul. Teach me to worship Thee through the joy born of meditation.

I Am Flying Home

Goodbye, blue house of heaven. Farewell, stars and celestial celebrities and your dramas on the screen of space. Goodbye, flowers with your traps of beauty and fragrance. You can hold me no longer. I am flying Home.

Adieu to the warm embrace of sunshine. Farewell, cool, soothing, comforting breeze. Goodbye, entertaining music of man.

I stayed long reveling with all of you, dancing with my variously costumed thoughts, drinking the wine of my feelings and my mundane will. I have now forsaken the intoxications of delusion.

Goodbye, muscles, bones, and bodily motions. Farewell, breath. I cast thee away from my breast. Adieu, heart-throbs, emotions, thoughts, and memories. I am flying home in a plane of silence. I go to feel my heart-throb in Him.

I soar in the plane of consciousness above, beneath, on the left, on the right, within and without, everywhere, to find that in every nook of my space-home I have always been in the sacred presence of my Father.

I Am in All Places

Meditate: I am beholding through the eyes of all. I am working through all hands, I am walking through all feet. The brown, white, olive, yellow, red, and black bodies are all mine.

I am thinking with the minds of all, I am dreaming through all dreams, I am feeling through all feelings. The flowers of joy blooming on all heart-tracts are mine.

I am eternal laughter. My smiles are dancing through all faces. I am the waves of enthusiasm in all God-tuned hearts.

I am the wind of wisdom that dries the sighs and sorrows of all humanity. I am the silent joy of life moving through all beings.

God's vastness I glimpsed in the skies of quietness. His joy I tasted in the fountains of my existence. His voice I heard in my unsleeping conscience.

Heavenly Father, teach me to find freedom in Thee, that I may know nothing on earth belongs to me; all belongs only to Thee. Teach me to know my home is Thine omnipresence.

O Cosmic Silence, I hear Thy voice through the murmur of brooks, the song of the nightingale, the sounding of conch shells, the beat of ocean-waves, and the hum of vibrations.

Teach me to behold Thy vastness, Thy changelessness behind all things, that I may perceive myself as a part of Thy changeless Being.

O Father, break the boundaries of the little waves of my life that I may join the ocean of Thy vastness.

In the hall of creation, O Divine Mother, everywhere I hear the rhythm of Thy footsteps, dancing wildly in the booming thunder and softly in the song of atoms.

I will conflagrate all space and roll over its bosom, unburnt and deathless. I will dive into infinity, never reaching the end. I will run and race and spread my laughter in all things, in all motion, and in the motionless void.

I will consciously receive the light of the omnipresent Father constantly passing through me.

Let me behold naught but beauty, naught but good, naught but truth, naught but Thine eternally immortal fountain of bliss.

Awaken me, O heavenly Father, that I may arise from the confining tomb of flesh into the consciousness of my cosmic body.

Unite my love with Thy love, unite my life with Thy joy, and my mind with Thy cosmic consciousness.

O mighty Ocean, I pray that the rivers of my desires, meandering through many deserts of difficulties, may merge in Thee.

ON FINDING GOD

On Spreading Ripples of Peace

Fix your mind in between the eyebrows on the shoreless lake of peace. Watch the eternal circle of rippling peace around you. The more you watch intently, the more you will feel the wavelets of peace extending from the eyebrows to the forehead, from the forehead to the heart, and on to every cell in your body. Now the waters of peace are overflowing the banks of your body and laving the vast territory of your mind. Now the flood of peace overflows the boundaries of your mind and moves on around you in infinite directions.

With the sword of peace, O Lord, let me fight through the thick skirmish of trials.

I am the prince of perpetual peace playing in a drama of sad and happy dreams on the stage of experience.

Peace

Peace flows through my heart, and blows
    through me as a zephyr.
Peace fills me like a fragrance.
Peace runs through me like rays.
Peace stabs the heart of noise and worries.
Peace burns through my disquietude.
Peace, like a globe of fire, expands and fills
    my omnipresence.
Peace, like an ocean, rolls on in all space.
Peace, like red blood, vitalizes the veins of
    my thoughts.
Peace, like a boundless aureole, encircles my
    body of infinity.
Peace-flames blow through the pores *of my*
    flesh, and through all space.
The perfume of peace flows over the gardens
    of blossoms.
The wine of peace runs perpetually through
    the winepress of all hearts.
Peace is the breath of stones, stars, and sages.
Peace is the ambrosial wine of Spirit flowing
    from the cask of silence,
Which I quaff with my countless mouths of atoms.

Meditation on Silence

My silence, like an expanding sphere, spreads everywhere.

My silence, spreads like a radio song, above, beneath, left and right, within and without.

My silence spreads like a wildfire of bliss; the dark thickets of sorrow and the tall oaks of pride are all burning up.

My silence, like the ether, passes through everything, carrying the songs of earth, atoms, and stars into the halls of His infinite mansion.

May I not dope myself with the opiate of restlessness. Behind the throb of my heart, I shall feel the throb of God's peace.

I will fill my heart with the peace of meditation. I will pour heartfuls of my joy into peace-thirsty souls.

All spiritually successful people, such as Jesus, Babaji, Lahiri Mahasaya, Sri Yukteswar, Swami Shankara, and other masters are manifestations of our one Father, God. I am happy in the realization that my spiritual ambition to realize unity with God is one that has already been attained by all great masters.

Each day I will meditate more deeply than yesterday. Each tomorrow I will meditate more deeply than today. I will meditate during most of my leisure hours.

Today, with the soft touch of intuition, I will tune my soul-radio and rid my mind of static restlessness, that I may hear

Thy voice of cosmic vibration, the music of atoms, and the melody of love vibrating in my superconsciousness.

I will find perpetual celestial happiness within. Peace will reign in silence or in the midst of activities. Let me hear Thy voice, O God, in the cave of meditation.

God's Flaming Presence

I will seek Thee as the ever-increasing bliss of meditation. I will feel Thee as boundless joy throbbing in my heart. I will seek to know Thee first, last, and all the time. Finding Thee first, I shall find through Thee all things I crave.

Teach me to find Thy presence on the altar of my constant peace, and in the joy that springs from deep meditation.

Bless me, that I may find Thee in the temple of each thought and activity. Finding Thee within, I shall find Thee without, in all people and all conditions.

Teach me to feel that it is Thy smile that manifests in the dawn, on the lips of roses, and on the faces of noble men and women.

I will do away with the mockery of parroting prayer. I will pray deeply until the darkness of meditation burns with Thy flaming presence.

Heavenly Father, I will not wait until tomorrow for Thy song. From today I will broadcast my soul-call into the ether and Thou must respond through the receiver of my silence.

Take away from my mind the weight of indifference and forgetfulness; make me drink the nectar of Thine ever-blessed presence.

With the deepening of inner and outer silence, Thy peace comes. I will try always to move about quietly, ever listening for Thy footsteps.

Having Thee as the deepest joy of deepest meditation, I know that all things, prosperity, health, and wisdom, will be added unto me.

In the temple of silence I found Thine altar of peace. On the altar of peace I found Thine ever-new joy.

Teach me to fish for Thee in the deepest waters of my soul.

Find God in Joy

No matter what causes it, whenever a little bubble of joy appears in your invisible sea of consciousness, take hold of it, and keep expanding it. Meditate on it and it will grow larger. Watch not the limitations of the little bubble of your joy, but keep expanding it until it grows bigger and bigger. Keep puffing at it with the breath of concentration from within, until it spreads all over the ocean of infinity in your consciousness. Keep puffing at the bubble of joy until it breaks its confining walls and becomes the sea of joy.

Within my soul is the joy that my ego is seeking. I suddenly become aware of His bliss honeycombed in the hive of silence. I will break the hive of secret silence and drink the honey of unceasing blessedness.

In the voice of the viol, the flute, and the deep-toned organ I hear God's voice.

With flowers, with bright skies, with the divine manna of joy in happy minds, with souls full of wisdom, with songs of the birds, with divine melodies in the hearts of men, my Beloved is calling me to retrace my footsteps to His home of peace within.

I will drive away all despondency in order to make a mighty effort to feel God by meditating, until He finally appears.

I will meditate more and more deeply until I feel His presence.

I wilt seek the kingdom of God in the joy arising from constant, long, deep, continuous meditation. I will conscientiously seek to contact God within, and will not be satisfied with the little imaginary inspirations that come from short, restless silences.

By contacting God I will be reclaimed as His child. Without asking or begging I shall receive all prosperity, health, and wisdom my share, as His divine child.

O Thou Perfume of all hearts and all roses, I mind not how many days of scalding sorrow cross the threshold of my life to search and test me. Through Thy blessing may they remind me of my errors that have kept me away from Thee.

I care not if all things are wrested away from me by my self-created destiny, but I shall demand of Thee, my Own, to guard the slender taper of my love for Thee.

O glorious Omnipresence, let not the fire of memory for Thee be blown out by the gusts of oblivion arising from the whirlwinds of my worldliness.

Every star of heaven, every pure thought, every good act shall be a window through which to behold Thee.

Through meditation I will stop the storm of breath, mental restlessness, and sensory disturbances raging over the lake of my mind. Through prayer and meditation I will harness my will and activity to the right goal.

My Omnipresent Throne

I came down from my omnipresent throne of love in the bosom of space and in the hearts of twinkling lights to find a cozy place in the heart of man. I stayed there long, shut out from my large, large home.

I was everywhere; then I hid myself away in the small places. Now I come out of my hiding places and I open the gates of the human limitations of family, caste, color, and creed. I am racing everywhere to feel again my consciousness of omnipresence.

Through the transparency of my deepest meditation I shall receive the light of the omnipresent Father passing through me.

I shall be a son of God, even as Jesus was, by receiving God fully through my sacred, meditation-expanded consciousness.

The moment I am restless or disturbed in mind I will retire to silence and meditation until calmness is restored.

Meditations on the Christ

I will follow the shepherds of faith, devotion, and meditation, who will lead me through the star of inner wisdom to the Christ.

I will behold the "only begotten," the only reflection of transcendental God the Father, born in the womb of finite vibratory matter as the Christ Intelligence that shepherds all creation to an intelligent divine end.

I will break the chains of restlessness and limitlessly expand the power of my meditation until the universal Christ Consciousness is able to manifest fully through me.

Bless me, Father, that the single eye of realization lead me to behold through all the veils of matter the infinite presence of Christ.

I Will Meditate

Beloved God, since no earthly engagement is possible without using powers borrowed from Thee, I will renounce everything that interferes with my daily engagement to meditate on Thee in living silence.

Today I will meditate no matter how tired I think I feel. I will not allow myself to be a victim to noise while trying to meditate. I will transfer my consciousness to the inner world.

Through the gateway of meditation I shall enter God's temple of peace everlasting. There I will worship Him at the altar of ever-new contentment. I will kindle the fire of happiness to illuminate His temple within.

I will meditate regularly that the light of faith may usher me into the immortal kingdom of my Heavenly Father.

Divine Mother, I will pull away the starry veil of the blue, I will tear away the cover of space, I will melt away the magic carpet of thoughts, I will shut off the diverting motion pictures of life, that I may behold Thee.

I know God can be realized through meditation, by intuitional perception, but not by the restless mind.

I will open my eyes to the joy of meditation; then I shall see that all darkness will vanish.

I will make my inner environment perfect through meditation, that it be impervious to all adverse outside influences.

I will begin each day with meditation on the Supreme Being.

I will bathe in the sacred pool of God's love hidden behind the ramparts of meditation.

ON MATERIAL CONCERNS

Never Lose Hope

If YOU have given up hope of ever being happy, cheer up. Never lose hope. Your soul, being a reflection of the ever-joyous Spirit, is, in essence, happiness itself.

If you keep the eyes of your concentration closed, you cannot see the sun of happiness burning within your bosom; but no matter how tightly you close the eyes of your attention, the fact nevertheless remains that the happiness-rays are ever trying to pierce the closed doors of your mind. Open the windows of calmness and you will find a sudden burst of the bright sun of joy within your very Self.

The joyous rays of the soul may be perceived if you interiorize your attention. These perceptions may be had by training your mind to enjoy the beautiful scenery of thoughts in the invisible, tangible kingdom within you. Do not search for happiness only in beautiful clothes, clean houses, delicious dinners, soft cushions, and luxuries. These will imprison your happiness behind the bars of externality, of outwardness. Rather, in the airplane of your vizualization, glide over the limitless empire of thoughts. There behold the mountain ranges of unbroken, lofty, spiritual aspirations for improving yourself and others.

Glide over the deep valleys of universal sympathy. Fly over the geysers of enthusiasm, over the Niagara Falls of perpetual wisdom, plunging down the hoary crags of your soul's peace. Soar over the endless river of intuitive perception to the kingdom of His omni-presence.

There, in His mansion of bliss, drink from His fountain of whispering wisdom, and quench the thirst of your desire. Dine with Him on the fruits of divine love in the banquet hall of eternity. If you have made up your mind to find joy within yourself, sooner or later you shall find it. Seek it now, daily, by steady, deeper and deeper meditation within. Make a true effort to go within and you will find there your longed-for happiness.

The Light of Smiles

(Meditate, dwell on, and practice this in daily life.)

I will light the match of smiles. My gloom-veil will disappear. I shall behold my soul in the light of my smiles, hidden behind the accumulated darkness of ages. When I find myself, I shall race through all hearts with the torch of my soul-smiles. My heart will smile first, then my eyes and my face. Every body-part will shine in the light of smiles.

I will run amid the thickets of melancholy hearts and make a bonfire of all sorrows. I am the irresistible fire of smiles. I will fan myself with the breeze of God-joy and blaze my way through the darkness of all minds. My smiles will convey His smiles and whoever meets me will catch a whiff of my divine joy. I will carry fragrant purifying torches of smiles for all hearts.

I will make the weeping ones smile, by smiling myself even when it is difficult.

In the cheer of all hearts I hear the echo of Thy bliss. In the friendship of all true hearts I discover Thy friendship. I rejoice as much in the prosperity of my brothers as I do in my own prosperity. In helping others to be wise I increase my own wisdom. In the happiness of all I find my own happiness.

Nothing shall blight my smiles. Grim death, disease, or failure cannot daunt me. Disaster cannot really touch me, for I possess the unconquerable, unchangeable, ever new bliss of God.

I will burn candles of smiles in the bosoms of the joyless. Before the unfading light of my cheer, darkness will take flight from the hearts of my brothers.

First and foremost, I will try to be a joy-billionaire and thus satisfy my needs for spiritual and material prosperity at the same time.

Spreading Divine joy

Beginning with the early dawn, I will radiate my cheer to everyone I meet today. I will be the. mental sunshine for or all who cross my path.

Let my love spread its laughter in all hearts, in every person belonging to every race. Let my love rest in the hearts of flowers, of animals, and of little specks of star-dust.

O Infinite One, forever show Thy glowing face in all my joys and in the flaming light of my love for Thee.

O divine silent Laughter, be enthroned beneath the canopy of my countenance and smile through my soul.

I will try to be happy under all circumstances. I will make up my mind to be happy within myself right now, where I am today.

Let my soul smile through my heart and let my heart smile through my eyes that I may scatter Thy rich smiles in sad hearts.

Healing Light of God

Thy perfect light is divinely present in all my body-parts. Wherever that healing light is manifest, there is perfection. I am well, for perfection is in me.

Thy healing light has been shining within me, around me, but I kept the eyes of my inner per-ceptions closed so that I beheld not Thy transmuting light.

I will plunge the gaze of my faith through the window of the spiritual eye and baptize my body in the healing light of Christ Consciousness.

Lord, teach me to remember and be grateful for the years of health that I have enjoyed.

Heavenly Father, teach me to remember Thee in poverty or prosperity, in sickness or health, in ignorance or wisdom. Teach me to open my closed eyes of unbelief and behold Thine instantaneously healing light.

For Health and Vitality

Today I will seek God's vitality in the sun, bathing my body in its light to appreciate the life-giving, disease-destroying gift of the ultraviolet rays, from God.

God's power is moving through my digestive muscles. My stomach is well, for I know His healing life is there.

The light of Thy perfect health shines in all the dark nooks of my bodily sickness.

In all my body-cells Thy healing light is shining. They are entirely well, for Thy perfection is in them.

I will recognize all disease as the result of my transgression against health laws and I will try to undo the evil by right eating, by less eating, by fasting, by more exercise, and by right thinking.

Father, help me, that I may naturally, spontaneously, and easily form the habit of proper eating. May I never become a victim of greed and thus cause myself suffering.

With faith in my Father I behold the shadows of sickness obliterated now and forever. I fully realize that His light exists always; I may not be overwhelmed by my self-created darkness except when I wilfully close my eyes of wisdom.

I will always behold in my life the perfect, healthy, all-wise, all-blissful image of God.

Heavenly Father, charge my body with Thy vitality, charge my mind with Thy spiritual power, charge my soul with Thy joy, Thine immortality.

Heavenly Father, fill my veins with Thine invisible rays, making me strong and tireless.

The all-seeing eye is behind my eyes. They are strong, for Thou dost see through them.

Beloved God, purify the dross in me. Banish disease and poverty from the world evermore. Banish ignorance from the shores of men's souls.

I Am Not the Body

Beloved God, I know that I am not the body, not the blood, not the energy, not the thoughts, not the mind, not the ego, not the astral self. I am the immortal soul that illumines them all, remaining unchangeable in spite of their changes.

I am a spark from the Infinite. I am not flesh and bones. I am Light.

Eternal youth of body and mind, abide in me forever, forever, forever.

Help me to learn, O Spirit, to live more and more by direct cosmic energy and less and less by gross food.

O Father, Thine unlimited and all-healing power is in me. Manifest Thy light through the darkness of my ignorance.

O Spirit, teach me to heal the body by recharging it with Thy cosmic energy; to heal the mind by concentration and smiles.

To Broadcast to Others

Fix the gaze of your restless eyes on the spot between the eyebrows. Dive into the sacred star of meditation. Keep broadcasting love-thoughts to your dear ones of this world and to those who have gone ahead of you in robes of light. There is no space between minds and souls, though their physical vehicles may be far apart. In thought our loved ones and all else we cherish are really ever near.

Keep broadcasting, "I am happy in the happiness of my loved ones who are on earth or who are in the great beyond."

I will seek to make others truly happy, in gratitude for the divine happiness Thou hast given me. I will serve all through my spiritual happiness.

In helping others to succeed I shall find my own prosperity. In the welfare of others I shall find my own well-being.

I will seek the kingdom of God first, and make sure of my actual contact with Him. Then, if it be His will, all things — wisdom, abundance, and health — will be added unto me as part of my divine birthright, since He made me in His image.

Father, I have been like the prodigal son. I have wandered away from Thy home of all power, but now I am back in Thy home of Self-realization. I want the good things that Thou hast, for they all belong to me. I am Thy child.

Teach me to know that Thou art the power that keeps me healthy, prosperous, and seeking Thy truth.

I am an image of the supreme Spirit. My Father possesses everything. I and my Father are one. Having the Father, I have everything. I own everything that He owns.

Though our efforts be crowned with utmost fulfillment, all ordinary pursuits of life offer only partial joy; but in seeking God, we tap the reservoir of unending bliss.

Friendship and Service

I will abide in receptive hearts - an unknown friend, ever rousing them to sacred feelings, silently urging them through their own noble thoughts to forsake their slumber of earthliness. In the light of wisdom I will dance with all their joys in the unseen bower of silence.

I will behold the person who now considers himself as my enemy to be in truth my divine brother hiding behind a veil of misunderstanding. I will tear aside this veil with a dagger of love so that, seeing my humble, forgiving understanding, he will no longer spurn the offering *of my* good will.

The door *of my* friendliness will ever be open equally for those brothers who hate me and for those who love me.

I will feel for others as I feel for myself. I will work out my own salvation by serving my fellow man.

I know that if I offer my friendship to all, as Christ did, I shall begin to feel the cosmic love, which is God. Human friendship is the echo of God's friendship. The greatest thing that Jesus Christ demonstrated was giving love in return for hatred. To give hatred for hatred is easy, but to give love for hatred is more difficult and far greater. Therefore I will burn hatred in the roaring conflagration of my spreading love.

I will take the best from every people: the Americans, Hindus, Germans, English, French, Italians, Swedes, Chinese, Japanese, and all others. I will admire the good qualities of all nationalities and turn away my attention from their errors.

This day I will break the boundaries of self-love and of family loves and make my heart big enough for all God's children. I will kindle a fire of universal love, beholding my Heavenly Father dwelling in the temple of all natural ties. All desire for affection I will purify and satisfy in attaining the sacred love of God.

I Will Serve All

I want no monuments on the mountains of human fame. I want secretly to remain in the caves of divine love in God-tuned souls and silently to serve them with invisible thoughts of helpfulness.

Namelessly and formlessly, I would like to be a silent divine messenger, visiting the dark corners of all minds and kindling candles of peace on altars of silence.

Today I forgive all those who have ever offended me. I give my love to all thirsty hearts, both to those who love me and to those who do not love me.

I will be a fisher of souls. I will catch the ignorance of others in a net of my wisdom and offer it for transmutation to the God of all gods.

Wherever people appreciate my efforts to do good, I shall know that there is the place where I can be of greatest service.

Divine Prosperity

I will not be a beggar, asking limited mortal prosperity, health, and knowledge. I am *Thy* child, and as such I demand, without limitations, a divine son's share of Thine illimitable riches.

Falling into a forgetful state of mortal beggary, I have failed to claim my divine birthright.

I want prosperity, health, and wisdom without measure, not from earthly sources but from Thine all-possessing, all-powerful, all-bountiful hands.

Teach me to feel that Thou art the power behind all wealth, and the value within all things. Finding Thee first, I will find everything in Thee.

The kingdom of the planets and all the opulence of the earth belong to Thee, my divine Father. I am Thy child; therefore I am the owner of all things even as *Thou* art.

Father, teach me to include the prosperity of others in the pursuit of my own prosperity.

Father, let me feel that I am Thy child. Save me from beggary! Let all good things, including health, prosperity, and wisdom, seek me instead of my pursuing them.

Since all affairs are directly or indirectly guided by Thy laws, I will bring Thy presence consciously into my mind through meditation, in order to solve the problems life has sent me.

I will spend less and less, not like a miser, but as a man of self-control. I will spend less that I may save more, and with those savings bring security to myself and my family. I will also liberally help my needy human brothers.

The king of the universe is my Father. I am the prince-successor to all His kingdom of power, wealth, and wisdom.

The One in All

I will behold the Invisible in the visible forms of my father, mother, and friends, sent here to love and help me. I will show my love for God by loving them all with divine love. In their human expressions of love I will recognize only the One Divine Love.

I am the servant ready to serve all needy minds with my simple advice, with my gifts of healing truth, and with my humble wisdom gathered in the shrine of silence. My highest ambition is to establish a temple of silence in every person I meet.

I know I am one with the light of Thy goodness. May I be a lighthouse for those who are tossed on the sea of sorrow.

I bow to the Christ in the temples of all human brothers, in the temple of all life.

I will radiate love and good will to others that I may open a channel for God's love to come to all.

ON SELF-IMPROVEMENT

Meditating on the Moonbeams

Mix your mind with the moonbeams at night. Wash your sorrows in their rays. Feel the mystic light spreading silently over your body, over trees, over vast lands. Standing in an open space with still eyes, behold, beyond the limits of the moonbeam-revealed scenery, the bedimmed fringe of the shining horizon. Let your mind, by steady wing-beats of meditation, spread beyond the lines of visible scenes and over the horizon. Let your meditation run past the rim of the visible to the lands of fancy.

Spread your mind from the moonbeam-visible objects to the dim stars and distant skies lying beyond in the eternal stillness of the ether, all throbbing with life. Watch the moonbeams spread, not only on one side of the earth, but everywhere in the eternal region of your spacious mind. Meditate until, in the cool moonbeams of *your* calmness, you race over trackless skies and, in realization, behold the universe as Light.

Attaining Freedom

Why tie the infinite soul to a bony post of flesh? Let go! Cut the cords of flesh-consciousness, attachment to the body, hunger, pleasure, pain, and bodily and mental involvements. Relax. Loosen the soul from the grip of the body. Let not the heaving breath remind you of physical bars. Sit still in breathless silence, expecting every minute to make the dash for freedom into the Infinite. Love not your earthly prison.

Free mind from body with a keen-edged knife of stillness. Cut loose your consciousness from the body. Use it no more as an excuse to accept limitations. Turn away your consciousness from the binding body-post. Rush your consciousness beyond the body, sweeping through the minds, hearts, and souls of others. Switch on your light in all lives. Feel that you are the One Life that shines in all creation.

Creative Activity

I will use my creative thinking ability to gain success in every worth-while project that I undertake. I will help myself that I may bring into proper use all my God-given powers. He will help me if I help myself, praying to Him to bring success to my efforts.

I have buried dead disappointments in the cemeteries of yesterday. Today I will plow the garden of life with my new creative efforts. Therein I will sow seeds of wisdom, health, prosperity, and happiness. I will water them with self-confidence and faith, and will wait for the Divine to give me the rightful harvest.

If I reap not the harvest, I will be thankful for the satisfaction of having tried my best. I will thank God that I am able to try again and again, until with His help I do succeed. I will thank Him when I have succeeded in fulfilling my heart's worthy desire.

I will try to perform only dutiful, noble actions to please God.

I am the captain of my ship of good judgment, will, and activity. I will guide my ship of life, ever beholding the polestar of His peace shining in the firmament of my deep meditation.

I will be calmly active, actively calm. I will not be lazy and become mentally ossified. I will not be overactive, able to earn money but unable to enjoy life. I will meditate regularly to maintain true balance.

Today I open the door of my calmness, that the angel of silence may gently enter the temple of all my activities. I will perform all duties serenely, saturated with peace.

I am the prince of peace sitting on the throne of poise, directing the kingdom of activity.

As I work and create I will remember that it is God who is working through me.

Working for God

I will acquire divinely deep concentration and then use its unlimited power to meet all God-given demands of my life.

I will do everything with deep attention. My work at home, in the office, in the world, all duties great and small, will be performed well, with my deepest attention.

Instead of being absent-minded, I will think of Thee.

On the throne of silent thoughts the God of peace is directing my actions today.

After contacting God in meditation I will go about my work, whatever it may be, knowing that He is with me, directing me and giving me power to bring forth that for which I am striving.

I will use my money to make the world-family better and happier, according to the measure of my ability.

Overcoming Fear and Worry

God is within me, around me, protecting me, so I will banish the gloom of fear that shuts out His guiding light and makes me stumble into ditches of error.

I will wipe away, with the soothing veil of Divine Mother's peace, the dream fears of disease, sadness, and ignorance.

Teach me to be tenaciously and cautiously courageous instead of often being afraid.

I am protected behind the battlements of my good conscience. I have burned my past darkness. I am interested only in today.

I will fear nothing except myself, when I try to deceive my conscience.

Today I will burn the faggots of worries and fears, and kindle the fire of happiness to illumine God's temple within.

Father, teach me not to torture myself and others with the ugly fires of jealousy. Teach me to accept with satisfaction the measure of kindness and friendship from my loved ones that I deserve. Teach me not to moan for what I may not receive. Teach me to use love instead of jealousy to rouse others to do their duty toward me.

With the spreading of the vital rays of the sun, I will spread the rays of hope in the hearts of the poor and forsaken. I will kindle courage in the hearts of the despondent. I will light a new strength in the hearts of those who think they are failures.

I will seek divine safety first, last, and all the time in the constant inner thought of God-peace.

Heavenly Spirit, bless me that I may easily find happiness instead of becoming worried at every test and difficulty.

Overcoming Anger

I make up my mind never more to wear anger on my face. I will not inject the poison of anger in the heart of my peace and thus kill my spiritual life.

I will be angry only with anger and with nothing else. I cannot be angry with anyone because the good and the bad both are divine brethren, born of my one divine Father.

I will calm the wrath of others by the good example of my tranquility, especially when I see my brothers suffering from the delirium of anger.

Teach me not to kindle anger and thus devastate with the conflagration of wrath the green oasis of peace within me and in others. Teach me rather to extinguish anger with the torrents of my unceasing love.

Heavenly Father, command the lake of my kindness ever to remain undisturbed by the storms of misery-making anger.

On Criticism and Misunderstanding

I will not waste my time in talking about the faults of others. If I find myself inclined to enjoy criticizing others I will first talk loudly against myself before others.

I will criticize no one unless asked by him to do so, and then only with a desire to help.

I will try to please everyone by kind, considerate actions, ever striving to remove any misunderstanding knowingly or unknowingly caused by me.

I will spread the sunshine of my good will wherever the darkness of misunderstanding lies.

I will always hold aloft an unfading torchlight of continuous kindness to guide the hearts of those who misunderstand me.

I wipe away my tears of sorrow, finding it does not matter to Thee whether I play a big or a small part, so long as I play it well.

On Humility and Pride

All my powers are but borrowed powers from Thee. No one is greater than Thee, O my Father. I would cease to live and express without Thy wisdom and strength. Thou art so big; I am so little.

Teach me not to be proud. Thou art the Guru-Preceptor, teaching in the temple of all souls. I bow to Thee at the feet of everyone.

I will conquer pride by humility, wrath by love, excitement by calmness, selfishness by unselfishness, evil by good, ignorance by knowledge, and restlessness by the ineffable peace acquired in the stillness of inner silence.

I will take pride in being humble. I will feel honored when chastised for doing God's work. I will rejoice for any opportunity to give love when hated.

I will seek God first; then all my desires will be satisfied. Whether I live in a palace or a hut will make no difference.

I will use my honestly acquired money to live simply, doing away with luxury.

I make up my mind that nobody can excite me by insulting words or deeds, and that nobody can influence me by praise so that I shall think that I am greater than I am.

I will cultivate calmness of mind, knowing God is ever with me. I am Spirit!

I will care nothing for cruel, false criticism nor for garlands of praise. My sole desire is to do Thy will, to please Thee, my heavenly Father.

I will speak the truth, but I will at all times avoid speaking unpleasant or harmful truths. I will offer no criticism that is not motivated by kindness.

On Worldly Pleasures

Wisdom's fire is burning. I am feeding the flame. No use sorrowing more! All perishable pleasures, all temporary aspirations I am using as faggots to feed the eternal fire of knowledge. The old cherished logs of desire that I had saved to fashion furniture of pleasures, I cast into the hungry flames.

Ah, my myriad ambitions are crackling joyously at the touch of God's flame. My ancient home of passions, of possessions, of incarnations, of many kingdoms of my fancy, of many air castles of my dreams - all are being consumed by this fire of my own kindling.

I am beholding this blaze not with sadness but with joy, for that fire has not only burned my home of matter but all the sorrow-haunted buildings of my fancy. I am glad beyond the wealth of kings.

We are Thy heedless children and the playthings of the world allure us. Teach us to play only with the divine flames of Thy spirit.

Overcoming Temptation

Teach me, O Spirit, to distinguish between the soul's lasting happiness and the temporary pleasures of the senses.

Teach me not to engross myself in passing sense-pleasures. Teach me to discipline my senses that they may always make me really happy. Teach me to substitute for flesh temptation the greater allurement of soul-happiness.

I laugh at all fears, for my Father-Mother, beloved God, is attentively awake and present everywhere with the deliberate purpose of protecting me from the temptations of evil.

I am king of myself, not a fancy-enslaved king of possessions. I own nothing, yet I am the ruler of my own imperishable kingdom of peace. I am no longer a slave serving my fears of possible losses. I have nothing to lose. I am enthroned in perennial satisfaction. I am a king indeed.

O King of kings, train Thou in the camp of discipline the nobilities of self-control and calmness in me. Be Thou their divine General against the invading hordes of darkness, passion, and greed.

O Father, train the children of my senses to wander not away from Thy home. Turn my eyes within to gaze upon Thine ever-changing beauty; train my ears to listen to Thine inward song.

Divine Mother, teach me to be so much attached to Thee that I cannot become bound to material pleasures. Teach me by Thy love to conquer all desire for a worldly life.

Divine Teacher, discipline my unwise wayward senses; spiritualize their pleasures, that they ever look beyond the illusion of glittering visible forms to find the divine joys of simplicity.

To Develop Will

Today I will make up my mind to succeed in whatever I do. Will power is a tremendous factor in all activities. It can start motions in cosmic energy.

O eternal Energy, awaken in me conscious will, conscious vitality, conscious health, conscious realization.

Teach me, O Spirit, to cooperate with Thy will until all my thoughts shall conform to Thy harmonious plans.

There is hidden strength within me to overcome all obstacles and temptations. I will bring forth that indomitable power and energy.

O Spirit, teach me to make my will unceasing in its performance until the little light of my will burns as the cosmic blaze of Thine all-powerful will.

Strengthen my will power, O Father. Teach me not to be enslaved by bad habits.

Beloved Father, I know that by strong will power I can overcome disease, failure, and ignorance, but the will vibration must be stronger than the vibration of physical or mental disease. The more chronic the disease, the stronger, steadier, and more unflinching must be my determination, faith, and effort of will.

Divine Father, this day I will make an effort to understand the great importance of wisely using my will power at all times.

I will use His wisdom-guided will to direct my habit-guided will.

I will tune my free will with the infinite will of God, and my only desire shall be to do the will of Him who sent me. .

Today I will cultivate initiative. The man of initiative creates something from nothing; he makes the impossible possible by the great inventive power of Spirit.

Wisdom and Understanding

Since Thine indelible image of perfection is in me, teach me to wipe away the superficial stains of ignorance and to know that Thou and I are, and always have been, one.

I am an immortal child of God, living for a little while in the caravanserai* of this body. I am here to behold the tragedies and comedies of this changeable life with an attitude of unchangeable happiness.

May all demoniac noisy thoughts take flight, that Thy silent song-whispers of guidance may be audible to my forgetful soul.

I will behold wisdom in ignorance, joy in sorrow, health in weakness; for I know that God's perfection is the only reality.

*A caravanserai or inn where Oriental caravans rest on their journeys here means a temporary stopping place on man's journeys through incarnations.

Since God has given me all I need, I will know Him first and then use His counsel to desire and to do only what He wills. Being endowed with free choice, I am a son of God in reality. I have been dreaming that I am a mortal man. I am now awake. The dream that my soul is imprisoned in a bodily cage has vanished. I am all that my heavenly Father is.

Each morning I will rouse the judge of my impartial introspection and ask it to try me before the tribunal of conscience. I will direct the district attorney of discrimination to prosecute the rowdy errors that steal the peace-wealth of my soul.

I will build mansions of wisdom in the unfading garden of peace, resplendent with blossoms of beautiful soul-qualities.

I will strive to make myself and all others rich with God, first and last.

God the transcendental Father, God the immanent Christ Consciousness, and God the holy creative Vibratory Force, grant me wisdom to know the truth! And through my self-effort and knowledge of the law, let me climb the precious ladder of realization, to stand at last on the shining summit of attainment, face to face with the one Spirit.

I am here before Thee, O Father, throwing again and again the shafts of my prayer to pierce the bulwark of Thy dark silence. I invoke Thee to send a searchlight of true wisdom, that I may find Thee in the broken castle of my ignorance.

Dear Father, whatever conditions confront me, I know that they represent the next step in my unfoldment. I will welcome all tests because I know that within me is the intelligence to understand and the power to overcome.

CHRISTMAS MEDITATIONS

Meditation For Christmas Eve

Lift your eyes and concentrate within. Behold the astral star of divine wisdom and let the wise thoughts in you follow that telescopic star to behold the Christ everywhere.

In that land of everlasting Christmas, of festive, omnipresent Christ Consciousness, you will find Jesus, Krishna, the saints of all religions, the great guru-preceptors waiting to give you a divine floral reception of everlasting happiness.

Prepare for the coming of baby Christ by decorating an inner Christmas tree. Around that sacred tree lay gifts of calmness, forgiveness, nobility, service, kindness, spiritual understanding, and devotion, each one wrapped in a golden covering of good will and bound with a silver cord of your pure sincerity.

May the Lord, on the Christmas morn of your spiritual awakening, unwrap the gorgeous presents of your heart-offerings that have been sealed with tears of your joy and bound with cords of your eternal fidelity to Him.

He accepts only the gifts of sacred soul-qualities. His acceptance will be His greatest gift to you; f or it means that, in return, the gift He will bestow on you shall be nothing less than Himself. In giving Himself He shall make your heart big enough to hold Him. Your heart shall throb with Christ in everything.

Enjoy this festivity, the birth of Christ, in your mind and soul and in every living atom.

By daily meditation you will prepare the cradle of your consciousness to hold the infinite baby Christ. Every day will become a true Christmas of divine communion.

A Christmas Vow

I will prepare for the coming of the Omnipresent Baby Christ by cleaning the cradle of my consciousness, now rusty with selfishness, indifference, and sense attachments; and by polishing it with deep, daily, divine meditation, introspection, and discrimination. I will remodel the cradle with the dazzling soul-qualities of brother love, humbleness, faith, desire for God-contact, will power, self-control, renunciation, and unselfishness, that I may fittingly celebrate the birth of the Divine Child.

Meditation For Christmas Morn

Celebrate the birth of Christ in the cradle of your consciousness during the Christmas season. Let His vast perception in Nature, in space, and in universal love be felt within your heart.

Break the limitations of caste, color, race, religious prejudice, and inharmony, that the cradle of your heart be big enough to hold within you the Christ-love for all creation.

On every Christmas morn of your inner perception, prepare precious packages of divine qualities and deliver them to the beloved souls who gather around the Christmas tree of inner awakening* to commemorate His birth in understanding, truth, and bliss.

---

* I.e., the spine, with its six chakras or centers of light and life-energy.

Celebrating the birth of omniscient, omnipresent Christ Consciousness on the joyous Christmas festivity of your inner awakening, you will find the unbroken happiness of your dreams.

Let the omniscient Christ Consciousness[+] come to earth a second time and be born in you, even as it was manifested in the mind of Jesus.

[+]*In Sanskrit, Kutastha Chaitanya, the blissful consciousness in all creation that remains ever unchanged.*

Christmas Meditation

All my thoughts are decorating the Christmas tree of meditation with the rare gifts of devotion, sealed with golden heart-prayers that Christ may come and receive my humble gifts.

I will mentally join in the, worship in all mosques, churches, and temples; and perceive the birth of the universal Christ Consciousness as peace on the altar of all devotional hearts.

O Christ, may the birth of Thy love be felt in all hearts this Christmas and on all other days.

The Transfiguring Christ

Christ has ever abided in me. He has preached through my consciousness to my rowdy and hypocritical thoughts. By the magic wand of meditative intuition, He has stopped the storms in the sea of my life and of many other lives. I was mentally blind, my will was lame; but I was healed by the awakened Christ in me.

Christ walked on the restless waters of my mind, yet the Judas of restlessness and ignorance, deluded by the Satan of sense lures, betrayed in me the Christ calmness, the Christ joy, and crucified Him on the cross of forgetfulness.

He commanded my dead wisdom to come forth from its sackcloth of delusion, and raised my wisdom to new life.

At last my will, faith, intuition, purity, hope, meditation, right desires, good habits, self-control, sense-aboveness, devotion, wisdom — all these disciples obeyed the commandments of the Christ who appeared on the high mountain of my meditation.

After waiting for me through many incarnations, Christ is being born anew in me. All the boundaries of my little mind are broken that the Christ-child may wake on the lap *of* my consciousness.

O living Christ, present in the body of Jesus and in all of us, manifest Thyself in the essence of Thy glory, in the strength of Thy light, in the power of Thy wisdom.

O Christ, bless Thy children that they inwardly cooperate with Thy laws. Make us realize that Thou art the best shelter from harm.

Teach us, O Christ, to be devoted to our Father as Thou art.
Christ Consciousness in me is the shepherd to lead my restless thoughts to my home of divine peace.

O Lord! make my heart big enough to hold Thee; then shall it throb with the Christ Consciousness in everything. Then shall I enjoy the festivity of Thy birth in my mind, my soul, and in every living atom.

WHISPERS FROM ETERNITY

Contents

Key to Demands / 80
Hints to the Reader / 82
Watching the Cosmic Motion Picture of Life / 90
Demands for developing Cosmic Consciousness / 95
Prayers at Dawn, Noon, Evening & Night / 103
Invocation to the Manifestation of God / 109
Prayers for Universality / 116
Miscellaneous Demands / 118
Prayers of Devotion / 159
Prayer-Demands for the Use of Children / 204
Chants /207
Poems /210
Dreams of God /241
Conquering the Fear of Death / 250
Glossary /254

WHISPERS FROM ETERNITY*

I was deaf, but Eternity whispered to me unceasingly. My wisdom's hearing-power slowly left its slumber, and I heard the Whispers of Eternity becoming ever clearer and clearer, in response to my sacred demands.

I asked Eternity: "What do Thy whispers mean?"

The whispers grew stronger and stronger until at last, suddenly, Eternity loudly answered: "Hear, thou, God's voice of guidance, unceasingly. I am His spokesman—Eternity. I have whispered through thy slumber of ages: 'Wake thyself!' Now, thou art awake, and yet My whispers will never cease to say: 'Wake thy brothers!' In the nooks of sleeping minds, everywhere, My whispers are constantly working. Work thou with Me, through living, eternal whispers—that all may hear His voice."

I replied to Eternity: "I will send whispers to all sleeping brothers, saying: 'Awake! Get ready! Come home where He gives perennial peace!" And I will borrow Thy voice, Eternity, when my earthly voice can be heard no more, and then I will still utter through Thee: 'O! hear His all-solacing song-whispers!"

---

* The word "Eternity," as used herein, is meant to symbolize God as manifested in nature and human souls. This hook endeavors to show how a practical communion can he established between Eternity and the human mind. Communion with the Intangible God is possible only through the tangible manifestations of Eternity.

Man's demands to God and Eternity for guidance must he made through effectual secret whispers, in deep meditation; these will be answered through helpful whispers. The demands should be unceasingly uttered to the ears of living Eternity in the human soul; then God and Eternity will respond with mysterious, silent help—changing one's entire being and environment.

I will wait for all, just to utter Eternity's whispers. As my countless human brothers, as well as beasts and atom-sparks, slowly travel toward the chamber of final freedom, in a seemingly endless train, I will softly say, through these *Whispers from Eternity*: "Awake! Let us all go home together, following His ever-calling voice."

KEY TO DEMANDS

(Please Read Carefully)

Spiritualizing a Prayer or a Demand. Just as a wet match, when struck, does not produce fire, so a mind saturated with restlessness is unable to produce the fire of concentration, even when prodigious efforts are made to strike the cosmic spark.

The flame of inspiration is hidden within the lines of the prayers and demands in this book; but since they are saturated with the diverting waters of printer's ink, paper, and intellectual meanings, one has to do away with these distractions in order to bring forth the flame of wisdom from within them. Different minds reading the same prayer will interpret it differently, and feel it differently. The vast ocean of truth can be measured only according to the capacity of one's own cup of intelligence and perception. So will the inspiration behind the prayers and demands be felt according to the depths of one's intuition and feeling.

In order to benefit by all the God-warmth within any of these prayers or demands, one should take only one paragraph at a time from any demand, mentally picture the meaning, visualize the imagery of the figure of speech, and meditate deeply on it, until the fiery meaning emanates, free from word limitations.

A word is like a drunken, dumb man, who *feels* what kind of liquor is in him but who is unable to *express* himself clearly about it. He may, by merely a cry or a little gesture, indicate the kind of wine he drank. So are the words in these demands drunk with God, but they would never be able fully to express and explain the quality of the wine of inspiration within them, except by way of a little gesture and a mumbled cry of suggestion.

One may wish to read a complete prayer or demand, to get a quick view of its entire meaning. But if he will read it over and over again, many times, and then, with closed eyes, repeatedly try to *feel* the deep inspiration behind and within it, he will thus *spiritualize* it—that is, rouse the inspiration slumbering beneath the thick, silken quilt of words.

Prayers and demands are like plants which daily grow new blossoms: the flowers change, but the plants remain. Similarly, a prayer-plant may have the same branches and leaves of words, but every day will yield new roses of God-feeling and inspiration, if one regularly waters the plant with meditation. The prayer-plant should be protected from the storms of doubt, distraction, mental idleness, leaving-meditation-until-tomorrow (the morrow that never comes), absent-mindedness, and thinking-of-something-else while imagining the mind is wholly on the soul of a prayer.

Such parasites on the prayer-plants should be destroyed by the germicides of self-control, determination, and loyalty to a teaching. Thus, daily the glowing, immortal roses of inspiration may be gathered from the plants of these *prayer-demands*.

Be still, and let God answer through you. Learn to know Him by knowing your Self. Visualize Him as formless but with form, silent but with voice as well. For example, when God is described as a visible Cosmic Idol, worshipped with drum-beats of ocean-roar, one should actually try mentally to visualize the entire concept behind the Cosmic Idol. And when the Almighty is spoken of as the Divine Mother, one should feel the same devotion to God, the Universal Mother, as a loving child feels toward its mother.

O! seeker after soul-awakening! Every day, dry with the heat of concentration the form-wet matchsticks of words in a demand; then repeatedly strike them on the tinder of your mind, and at last you will see the divine flames leap out.

HINTS TO THE READER

Please select a demand from the contents according to your need, and then calm your mind by sitting motionless on a straight chair, with spine erect. With eyes closed, or lifted (if open), meditate on the meaning of the demand selected by you, until it becomes a part of you. Then saturate the demand with devotion and meditate upon it. As your meditation becomes deeper, increase your devotion, and mentally offer the demand as your own heart's outburst. Imbue yourself with the faith that your heart's craving, expressed through this specific demand, is being felt by God.

Feel that just behind the screen of your devotional demands, God is listening to the silent words of your soul. Feel this! Be *one* with your heart's demand—and be thoroughly convinced that He has listened to you. Then go about your duties, seeking not to know whether God will grant your demand. Believe absolutely that your demand has been heard, and you will know that what is God's is yours also. Unceasingly meditate on God, and when you *feel* Him, you will acquire dominion over all things.

Resurrect words from the sepulcher of hollow, intellectual concepts, by the Christ-command of your deepest perception.

Since these demands were given to me by the Universal Father, they are not mine. I only felt them and gave them expression through the avenue of words, in order that I might share them with you. My blessing goes with them, and I pray that they may strike an answering note on the living harp-strings of your heart, so that you may feel them just as I have felt them.

We should, as Children of God, Demand and not beg or pray as Beggars.

God made man in His image. All those who know how to receive Him, can realize the sleeping divinity by expanding the powers of the mind. Being children of God, we have dominion over all His things in the universe, even as He has.

Why does Man, an image of God, suffer?

The question arises, why is it that many of our wishes are not fulfilled, and that many of God's children suffer intensely? God, with His divine impartiality, could not make one child better than another. He originally made all souls alike, and in His image. They also received the greatest gifts of God: freedom of the will, and power to reason and to act accordingly.

Man suffers because of his Actions in the Past.
Somewhere, sometime in the past, men have broken the various laws of God, and accordingly have brought about lawful results.

All men have been given absolute liberty to use human reason wrongly or rightly. Misuse of God-given reason leads to sin, which is suffering; the right use leads to joy and to happiness. God, with His infinite nobility, would not punish us; we punish ourselves through our own unreasonable actions, and reward ourselves through our own good conduct. This alone explains why God's responsibility ended when He endowed man with reason and with freewill.

The Law of Cause and Effect governs the actions of man.
Man has misused this God-given independence and thus has brought ignorance, physical suffering, pre-mature death and other ills upon himself. He reaps what he sows. The law of cause and effect applies to all lives. All the todays in one's life are determined by the actions of all the yesterdays, and all the tomorrows of one's life depend upon the way in which all the todays are handled and lived.

Thus it is that man, although created in the image of God and potentially endowed with His powers, loses his claim and birthright to dominion over his Father's universe, through his own faults and self-imposed limitations. The misuse of reason, and the identification of the soul with the transitory body, or with environmental or hereditary or world influences, are responsible for man's despairs and miseries.

How a sleeping Son of God may become an awakened Son of God. Yet the fact remains that a soul, however wrong outwardly, is potentially a sleeping son of God. The greatest of all sinners is but an un-awakened son of God, a sleeping immortal, who refuses fully to receive His light by clarifying his consciousness. That is why in *John* 1:12 we find written: "But as many as *received* Him, to them gave He power to become the sons of God, even to them that believe on His name."

The ocean cannot be received in a cup unless the cup is made as large as the ocean. Likewise, the cup of human concentration and human faculties must be enlarged in order to comprehend God. *Receiving* denotes capacity acquired by self-development; it is different from mere belief.

How the Belief of being a Son of God can become a Realization. The purport of the St. John quotation is, that those sleeping sons of God, who awake by following the law of spiritual discipline, receive or feel God by developed intuition, and thus regain their latent powers as sons of God. It is ignorance which prompts man to imagine his littleness and limitations. *Ignorance is the sin of all sins.*

It is the sleeping man who acknowledges and emphasizes his dream of human weaknesses. It is wrong for a soul to believe itself limited by the body, instead of *knowing* itself as a part of the unlimited Spirit. It is good and right to believe that one is a son of God, rather than the son of a mortal only, for it is metaphysically true that man is essentially made in the image of God. It is wrong, therefore, for one to imagine that he is a perishable creature. Even by *belief,* alone, one may some day *realize* his own soul to be a son of God. Hence, a wayward child must start by *believing* that he is a son of God, as belief is the initial condition for testing and knowing a truth.

When in trouble, one automatically prays to an unknown God and expects relief. If freed, even accidentally, from trouble, he believes his prayers were heard and responded to by God. But should his prayers remain unanswered, he becomes confused and begins to lose faith in God.

God, though all-powerful, does not act unlawfully or arbitrarily merely because one prays. He gives independence to man, who does what he pleases with it. To forgive human shortcomings arbitrarily would mean that God contradicts Himself—disregards the law of cause and effect, as applied to the law of action, and handles human lives, not according to the laws created by Himself, but according to His whim. Nor can God be moved by flattery or by praise to change the course of His immutable laws.

There is a great deal of beggary and ignorance in ordinary prayer. People just pray. Few know how to pray and touch God with their prayers; nor do they know whether their prayers are responded to or not; or whether things happened, unaffected by prayers. Nor do we distinguish between things which we need and things which we want. Sometimes it is very good that we do not receive what we think we want. A child may want to touch a flame, but, to save it from harm, the mother does not grant the child's wish.

My purpose in presenting these *Sacred Demands*, received in the course of my various fruitful communions with our Father, is to enable my fellow-beings to contact Him effectually. I prefer the word "demand" to "prayer," because the former is devoid of the primitive and medieval conception of a kingly tyrant-God whom we, as beggars, have to supplicate and flatter.

We should not ask God to be partial to us, because of our prayers, nor to break the laws of cause and effect governing our actions, by way of forgiveness for our wrong-doing. Must we then inevitably face the fruits of our actions as if by preordination or so-called fate?

No! There is a way out. The best of all ways is not to ask favors or amnesty from evil results, nor to be resigned and sit idle, inviting the law of action to take its course. We must remember that what is done by ourselves can be undone by ourselves. We must adopt the antidotes for our poisonous actions. Ill health can and must be overcome by obeying laws of good health. But what about chronic diseases and sufferings which are beyond the control of human care? When the power of human methods for curing ills, physical and mental, fails, revealing its limitations, then we must ask God, who is unlimited in power, to help, and must demand as sons of God and not as beggars.

Every begging prayer, no matter how sincere, limits the soul. As sons of God, we must believe that we *have* everything the Father has. This is our birthright. Jesus realized the truth, "I and my Father are One." That is why He had dominion over everything, even as His Father had. Most of us beg and pray without first establishing, in our own minds, our divine birthright; that is why we are limited by the law of beggary. We do not have to beg, but to *reclaim* and *demand* from our Father that which we, through our human imagination, thought to be lost.

It becomes necessary at this stage to destroy the wrong thought of ages—that we are frail human beings. We must think, meditate, affirm, believe and realize daily that we are sons of God. This realization may take time, but we must begin with the right method, rather than gamble with the unscientific beggary of prayers and consequently be subject to disbelief, doubts or the jugglery of superstition. It is only when the slumbering ego perceives itself not as a body, but as a free soul or son of God, residing in and working through the body, that it can rightfully and lawfully demand its divine rights.

These *sacred demands* reveal a few of the attitudes of the soul that have met with successful response from God. However, it is better not to demand in another's language. One should not consult a book on love when one meets his beloved, but should use the spontaneous language of his heart. If one uses another's language of love, in demands addressed to God, one must make the words his own, by thoroughly understanding and dwelling upon their meaning, and applying to them the utmost concentration and love; as when a lover addresses his beloved in the language of a great poet, with love and feeling, it is not amiss.

Blind repetition of demands or affirmations, without concomitant devotion or spontaneous love, makes one merely a "praying victrola," which does not know what its prayer means. Grinding out prayers vocally and mechanically, while inwardly thinking of something else, does not bring response from God. A blind repetition, taking the name of God in vain, is fruitless. Repeating a demand or prayer over and over again, mentally or orally, and with deepening attention and devotion, spiritualizes the prayer, and changes conscious, believing repetition into super-conscious experience.

The Divine Being cannot be deceived by the mockery of a prayer, because He is the fountain of thoughts. He cannot be bribed at any time, yet it is easy to move Him with sincerity, persistency, concentration, devotion, determination and faith. Furthermore, repeating a long, intellectual prayer with the mind absent, develops hypocrisy; and to pray or demand without understanding, develops ignorance, fanaticism and superstition. Repeating a demand with deepening concentration and faith is not mechanical repetition, but a changing, progressing power and mental preparation which, step by step, scientifically reaches God.

These *sacred demands* are logical, devotional, deep soul-outbursts. If one prepares the mind by concentration, and then deeply, with ever-increasing faith and devotion, mentally (or aloud, in congregations), affirms these scientific divine demands, one is bound to receive results. To re-establish your unity with the Divine Father as a son of God is your greatest demand. Realize this, and you have received everything.

In order to examine, do not dig up the *demand-seed* now and then, after sowing it in the soil of faith, or it will never germinate to fulfillment. Sow your *demand-seed* in faith, and water it by repeated daily practices in demanding rightly. Never be discouraged if results are not forthcoming immediately. Stand firm in your demands, and you will regain your lost divine heritage; and then, and then only, will the Great Satisfaction visit your heart. Demand until you establish your divine rights. Demand unceasingly that which belongs to you, and you will receive it.

In demanding rightly, there is no room for superstition, disappointment or doubt. Once you learn to operate the right chain of causation which effectually moves God, you will know that He was not hiding from you, but that you were hiding from Him behind the shadow of self-created darkness. Once you feel that you are a son of God, then by the steady effort of mental discipline and devotional meditation you will have dominion over all things

If your demand remains unfulfilled, unanswered, you can blame only yourself and your past actions. Do not become despondent. Do not say that you have resigned yourself to fate, or the preordained commands of a whimsical God, but try, with increased effort after each failure, to get what you have not: what you did not receive because of your own fault, but what is yours already in Spirit. You should demand with sacred devotion the recognition of your divine birthright as a son of God.

To know how and when to pray exactly according to the nature of our own demands is what brings the desired results. When the right method is applied, it sets in motion the proper laws of God, and the operation of these laws alone can scientifically bear results. God thus abides by the laws which He has made.

WATCHING THE COSMIC MOTION PICTURE OF LIFE

In this hall of life, we are all motion picture actors as well as movie fans. We entertain, inspire and instruct others with the show of our experiences; and we ourselves watch the ever-changing, interesting pictures of other lives.

The pictures of current events are filmed in the east, west, north and south. The various nations with their strange and colorful actings of diverse customs, traditions and occupations amid varying scenic and climatic environments, offer infinitely rich and inexhaustible material for producing life-films of ever-new interest.

Educational, sensational, comical, saddening and inspiring pictures are taken by the mind-camera of the average man, every day, any time, anywhere. There are many comic films in life. Inspiring scenes help us when we behold the unrolled film of the lives of great men and great adventurers such as Lincoln, Gandhi, Mme. Curie, Byrd, Emerson and thousands of other unique personalities, as well as the heroic world figures of religious teachers, such as Jesus, Buddha, Zoroaster, Confucius, Mohammed, Krishna and others.

We watch, moved and entertained, the mental motion pictures as filmed in Shakespearean tragedies and other great dramatic writings, in the house of our imagination. The pictures of world events, daily facts, evoked by our newspapers, hold our passing interest. The pictures of the sufferings of others bring a tear, a determination to help them. Through their sorrow, we find our own joy in helping them.

Sympathetic higher beings entertain themselves with the joy of helping mortals. If they cried, and became identified with the tears of others, they could not render help. For sorrow increases sorrow, which can only be diminished and healed through contact with the potent salve of unshakably happy minds. Hence, in watching the tragic mistakes or misfortunes of other lives, or of our own, we should feel only tears of joy because of our ability and absolute power to help. There cannot be room for the dark disturbing emotion of grief in children made in the likeness of God.

Individuals who are highly nervous, or who are suffering with the malady of melancholia, or anaemic pessimism, or who are stricken with spells of despair at the approach of the least difficulties of life—these do not profit by watching the pictures of tragedy in other lives. They will have fainting spells; they cannot thus learn the lesson of the result of wrong behavior and thus desist from error, nor can they render help to those who are suffering, since they themselves are not free from pain.

Thus, one must be thoroughly prepared mentally to watch profitably the motion picture of the tragedy of trying experiences in the lives of others, in order to be able to render help in making others look upon life as only a picture for their entertainment and instruction.

The great wars of Europe and Asia, the natural cataclysms of earthquakes and floods, the famines, prosperous eras, influence of world-saints, statesmen, and villains, the work of the colossal geniuses of the ages—the poets, business men, writers, courageous reformers, great lovers, and heroes—these events and these natures have all played their parts in the studio of the centuries.

Everything took time; to the consciousness of man everything seemed to last long. Each life seemed almost unending, each great event was all-absorbing, but when the Director of Life called "Cut!" the film was finished. The greatest lives, the complex knotted existences, the whole history of nations, your life and mine, past, present, and future (if we could but see), which seem to drag on minutely, could nevertheless be filmed and each life shown in a couple of hours. One's life, lived through a hundred years, seems so long-drawn-out when taken through the slow mental camera, but with the telescopic lens of retrospection, one sees the whole panorama at a glance.

Is this life a movie show? The millions of geologic years, the constellations of heaven, the floating vapors, atomic combinations, earth materials, oceans, continents, nations and their histories, millions of births and the almost complete change by death every hundred years of all the earth's inhabitants, the various great intellectual, spiritual, and material civilizations, their rise and fall—with this background, we can see all life as a vast, ever-changing, ever-new, ever-entertaining mighty film in the hall of introspection. This life is a picture shown in serials and by installments, infinitely interesting, ever-fresh, ever-stirring, ever-complex. The master minds and world-changing men such as Jesus, Buddha, Socrates, Asoka, Mohammed, Caesar, William the Conqueror, Darwin, Copernicus, Galileo, Newton, and other outstanding pioneers and leaders are the great stars of the motion picture productions, who command universal attention from their audiences.

The pictures of life must always be different to be interesting. One does not want to see, again and again, the same comedies of lives or the same news of prosaic facts, or the same tragedies of harrowing or gruesome experiences. One wants variety, and can hardly bear to see the same picture twice. That is why the Great Director of the motion picture of life keeps everything changing. You can not drink twice from the same running water; you can not watch the same event twice. The water passes by;

the events change; you are not now the same man that you were a second ago—your thoughts have changed, your sum total is in a different proportion.

Why not then take life simply as a motion picture? To do that, you must steel your mind against sorrow. You must be prepared for variety. You must be a motion picture player, an entertainer, as well as one of the audience, in watching your own pictures and the pictures of others. While playing the part of combating disease, or fighting failures, or undergoing accidents, or enduring the trials of life, you must know that you are just playing a part.

Just as an actor in the moving pictures is untouched by the sorrow he has to depict in his characters, so must you remain untouched by the changing pictures of inevitable misfortune, sickness, sudden failure and unforeseen obstacles in life. Sickness, failure and grief are so, simply by the relative standards of human consciousness. A disciplined consciousness, united to cosmic consciousness, never inwardly experiences sickness, or suffering, or failure. As God's children, we are always perfect, and we must recover that consciousness by wisdom and true understanding of the meaning of life and its problems.

Care not if you are not the principal player in the movies of life. No motion picture is made up of only one player, or one event. Your part in playing, if short or obscure, is yet very important, for without you the "plot" of life is incomplete. In the Universal Director's eyes, he who plays his life's part well, whatever that may be, is made a star to shine in His immortal galaxy.

Most of our troubles spring from not knowing what our parts are. This results from not developing our innate intuitive soul faculties. Rouse the all-feeling, all-seeing wisdom by regular meditation, and find your part. Then you must play and watch your own playing, or the playing of others—be it the news of plain facts, or a comedy of errors, or the tragedy of trying experiences—with an inwardly entertained mind. There is no room for pain, grievance, or boredom in watching the movies of our own lives. The retrospective consciousness of man can play all the noble parts of life joyously, untouched by suffering. These cosmic movies are all for our entertainment.

The Great Director of the Motion Picture Company of Life is made of joy. We, as His children, are made in His image of joy. From joy we came, in joy we live, in joy we melt. He brought out this cosmic motion picture to keep Himself entertained. Having come out of His being, we are endowed with the same quality of super-consciousness, by which we can watch the pictures of life, of birth, death and world events with the same divinely enjoying spirit.

You watch a tragedy in a motion picture house, and when it is over, you say: "O, it was a fine picture!" So must you be able to look upon the pictures of trials of your own life and say: "O, my life is interesting, with troubles and difficulties to be overcome. These are all my stimulants to show me my errors, and help me assume the right mental attitude by which I can watch with joy the fascinating spectacle of life."

The consciousness of man is made of God and is pain-proof. All physical and mental sufferings come by identification, imagination, and wrong human habits of thinking. We have to travel along the labyrinthine path of life, visiting many motion picture houses of varied experiences, entering them with the consciousness of being entertained and instructed.

Then life and death will be watched with an unchangeable, joyous consciousness. We will find our consciousness to be one with cosmic consciousness, unchanged by the human waking of birth or the sleep of death. Thus we will watch the cosmic motion picture with perennial, ever-new joy.

SACRED DEMANDS TO THE INFINITE

DEMANDS FOR DEVELOPING COSMIC CONSCIOUSNESS*

O! You who have come to the portals of these prayers: Pass not by in haste. Enter and bathe in the sacred pool of God-Love, hidden behind the ramparts of meditation.

Every day, take one prayer-demand at a time, and read it carefully. First, get the *intellectual* concept, then *concentrate* upon it, addressing it to God by deep, unceasing, forceful, mental whispers.

At last, the demand will become individualized. Fragrant flower-thoughts will blossom from the original prayer-plant, thoughts born of concentration and watered by the divine dew of meditation.

Each word, if it is a word, shall wear, *for you*, a garment of burning flame. Each word will be a guiding torchlight in the procession of prayer-thoughts marching to God. Each word will spread flames to light the path of some lost brother on the way. Each word-flame will sing a song that He has sung. Each word-flame will reveal some lost gem of truth. Each word-flame will illumine some dark corner of the mind. Each thought-flame will, in silence, pour forth sermons of His sacredness. Each feeling-flame will hum with the presence of His love, everywhere, and will wake the sleeping ones to hear His ever-calling voice, saying: "Come home!"

---

*see glossary

1
Cosmic Salutation.
(Inspired by the Bhagavad Gita, the Hindu Bible)

O Spirit, I bow to Thee, in front of me, behind me, on the left, and on the right. I bow to Thee above and beneath. I bow to Thee all around me. I bow to Thee, within and without me. I bow to Thee everywhere, for Thou art omnipresent.

2
We demand as Thy Children.

Thou art our Father. We are made in Thine own image. We are sons of God. We neither ask nor pray like beggars, but *demand* as Thy children, wisdom, salvation, health, happiness, eternal joy. Naughty or good, we are Thy children. Help us to find Thy will in us. Teach us to use independently the human will (since Thou gavest that to us to use freely), in tune with Thy wisdom-guided will.

3
Demand for Recharging Body-Battery.

O Spirit, teach us to heal the body by recharging it with Thy cosmic energy, to heal the mind by concentration and smiles, and the soul by meditation-born intuition.

4
Spiritual Interpretation of the Lord's Prayer.

O Heavenly Father, Mother, Friend, Beloved God, may the halo of Thy presence spread over all minds.

May the kingdom of matter-worship be changed into worship of Thee. Because we cannot truly love anything without Thee, may we learn to love Thee first and above all. May the heavenly kingdom of bliss which is in Thy Spirit, manifest itself in all its divine qualities on earth, and may all lands be made free from limitations, imperfections, and miseries. Let Thy kingdom which is within, manifest itself without.

Father, leave us not in the pit of temptations, wherein we fell through our misuse of Thy gift of reason. When we are freer and stronger—if it be Thy wish to test us, to see if we love Thee more than temptation—then, Father, make Thyself more tempting than temptation. Father, if it be Thy desire to test us, help us that our wills grow strong to meet Thy tests.

Give us our daily bread: food, health, and prosperity for the body, efficiency for the mind, and above all, Thy wisdom and Thy love for our souls. Teach us to deliver ourselves, with Thy help, from the meshes of ignorance woven by our own carelessness.

5
Thou Art the best Bomb-Shelter.

When clouds of devastating war drop rain of fire and death, I will not forget that Thou, O God, art my best Bomb-Shelter. In life and death, in disease, famine, pestilence and poverty, I cling to Thee, who alone can show me that in all dualities of life's experiences I can remain unharmed. Thou wilt ever protect me, making me realize I am immortal, untouched by the changing conditions of childhood, youth, age, and of world upheavals.

6 Universal prayer of the Cosmic Temple

With a myriad of living thoughts of devotion, I have built for Thee a temple of awakened silence. I have brought the multi-colored lamps of wisdom from all good faiths. They all shine with the luster of Thy one truth.

The commingled incense of human cravings for Thee soars in spirals from the vase of our hearts. Thy sacred presence is glistening on altars everywhere.

All prayers of all temples, tabernacles, churches, and mosques are chanting to Thee in the one universal language of deep love. The orchestra of our feelings plays in tune with the chorus of all soul-songs, the cry of all tears, the bursting shout of all joys, and the anthem of all prayers.

In this wall-less cosmic temple of our souls, we worship Thee, our one Father. Be pleased to reveal Thyself thus, always. *Amen, Aum, Amin.*

7 Worshipping the Cosmic Idol

O Infinite Spirit, I shall worship Thee as finite, today. O Cosmic Silence, I shall hear Thine unheard voice through the murmur of brooks, the song of nightingales, the sound of blown conch-shells, the beat of oceans, and the hum of vibrations.

India-wise, in the cosmic temple of my mind, in ceremony I shall worship Thee, my Idol of Finitude. I shall behold in reverence Thy face, glowing red with vital power in the sun, and bestowing soothing moonbeam-glances to dispel my gloom.

I shall no more call Thee unseen, for during my worship I shall look straight through Thine infinite, starry eyes into Thy mystic heart. With Thy breath of the heaving wind I shall mix my borrowed breath. My wordless chants of yearning for Thee will sing in cadence with my heart-throbs. I shall feel Thy heart beating in all hearts. I shall watch Thy working hands in the law of gravitation and in all other cosmic forces. In the sound of the feet of all living creatures I shall hear Thy footsteps.

In my worship, I shall behold Thy vast, skiey body, adorned with the dark, twinkling veil of night, or the pale light of dawn, or the grey twilight. O, my Cosmic Idol, garlanded with the stringed beads of the milky way, diademed with the rainbow, wearing diamonds of glittering planets, I bow to Thee.

The pores of the sky perspire with Thy life, and Thy blood runs through Thy veins of rivers, streams, streamlets and the blood-cells of men. No more as unseen shall I worship Thee, but as my seen, Cosmic-bodied Idol.

The temple-bells of nature's harmony, the drumbeats of sea-roars, the myriad candles of minds and chants of all churches, devotion-flowers from the garden of souls, and the incense of loves—are all assembled by me for Thy worship, O visible Idol of my soul.

With opened eyes and the eye of my mind, I shall behold Thee, my living Idol-of-Nature God, and worship Thee with vocal or mental chants, with a bouquet of devotion, activity, and wisdom, with the language of love, heart-whispers, tearless tears of meditation, and silent sobs of intuition.

8
Salutation to the Great Preceptor.
(Sanskrit Scriptures).

Bearing the bliss of Brahma, happiness supreme; wearing the image of wisdom; beyond the dispute of quality; free as the soaring sky; Knower of all there is to be known; Thou perennial, taintless one; Witness of all happenings; beyond all conceptions' boundaries; uncolored by good, bad and active qualities: my ever-awake Preceptor—I bow to Thee!

9
Thou Mother of Flames, show Thy Face, hidden beneath the veil of Cosmic Motion Pictures

O Mother of time, space, form, and relativity, Thou hast taken a finite form—the Kali-Divine, colossal, symbol-idol of all-sheltering nature. The invisible Spirit took Thy shape—a visible Mother Divine, in whom throbs the heart of all-protecting, mothering kindness.

O Mother Divine! The beauty-mark of the moon is set between Thy two dark eyebrows of twilight and night. Clouds of eternity veil Thy face. Gusts of prophetic lives often have dared to blow fitfully away Thy veil of mystery, momentarily revealing Thy face hiding from our stares of ignorance.

O Mother Divine, in the dawn of creation I beheld Thee on the track of time, roaming in the rustic attire of primitive culture, crowned with wild nature, and wearing the garland of unpolished minds and opaque, finite things.

In the noon-day of creation, I beheld Thee, wearing a garment of sunny mentalities, scorching souls with the heat of their own material fire. Thy body of activity sweated with restlessness. All Thy children felt the strain of struggle, and implored Thee to send the cooling breeze of peace.

In Thy noon-hour of fulfillment, Thou didst equally attend the forsaken slums of misery, the halls of festive prosperity, and the shrines of peaceful wisdom.

In Thine attire of mid-day mentalities, Thou didst travel through the fiestas of centuries, beholding the dream of human life and death, of the evolution and dissolution of planets, of the birth and death of civilizations, of the drama of nebulae-molding worlds—the dream of new-born planets and earthquakes and partial dissolutions. Then the dark night approached, and Thou didst wear the grim, dark veil of mourning, to put creation through the terrible but purifying ordeal of destruction's fire. The sun burst and belched fire; the cosmic earthquake broke the vase of the sky, dropping embers of stars; and all creation was a furnace of flames. Everything was fire: matter, sin, darkness, all things were cast into Thy crucible, there to become pure, luminous.

Creation came from fire: beneath the ashes of matter, the embers of creation slept; and, rocked by Thy hands, O Mother Divine, creation awoke with its body of pure flames.

Thine one hand of power wakes unseen creative force to take many-hued, fair, finite forms. Another hand holds the astral sword of preservation, keeping all planets swinging in the rhythm of balance. Thy third hand clutches the severed head of cosmos, representing dissolution when all creation sleeps in Thee. Thy fourth hand stills the storms of delusion, bestowing the rays of salvation upon seeking devotees.

O Kali, Thou deep Mother of creative activity, wearing a garland of human minds; the rhythm of Thy wild dance of creation ceases only when Thy feet touch the transcendent breast of Thine Invisible Consort of Infinity—Shiva, in whom all creation has rest.

O Mother-Progress, the dance of Thy life I hear in the tinkling bells of little laughing, harmonious lives. On the floor of my tender thoughts, Thine inspirations softly dance in tune with the music of the spheres.

In the hall of creation, everywhere, O Kali, I hear the rhythm of Thy footsteps, dancing forcefully in the booming thunder, and softly in the song of atoms.

The Infinite sleeps beneath the shroud of magic delusion, and then, O Goddess of Forms, Thy fantastic dances of finitude begin on His bosom. Thou hast danced nearer than the throbs of my soul, and I have heard the symphony of Thy steps on the farthest horizon of my mind. Divine Mother, Thou mayest dance everywhere: but O, I pray Thee, do Thou ever play the music of Thy magic footsteps in the sacred sanctum of my soul!

O Goddess Kali, in Thy changing robes art woven the dreams of creation, preservation and destruction. Mother Divine, on the beauteous veil of Thy mind a million cinemas of cosmic dramas play. Thus dost Thou entertain and amuse Thy good children, and frighten Thy naughty ones.

Mother Divine, draw aside Thy glittering veil of cosmic motion pictures and show me Thy delusion-dispersing face of mercy.

10
Demand for the Opening of the Spiritual Temple Doors everywhere.

O Father, when I was blind I found not a door which led to Thee, but now that Thou hast opened my eyes, I find doors everywhere: through the hearts of flowers, through the voice of friendship, through sweet memories of all lovely experiences. Every gust of my prayer opens an unentered door in the vast temple of Thy presence.

PRAYERS AT DAWN, NOON, EVENING, AND NIGHT

**11
Prayer at
Dawn.**

With the opening of the earliest dawn and the lotus-buds, my soul softly opens in prayer to receive Thy light. Bathe each petal of my mind with Thy radiant rays! I saturate myself with the perfume of Thy presence, and I wait to waft with the breeze the aroma of Thy message of love to all. Bless me, that with the spreading dawn I may spread Thy love everywhere. Bless me, that with the awakening dawn I may awaken all souls with my own and bring them to Thee.

**12
Prayer at
Noon.**

The sun shines high in the heavens: everything is fully awake. Awaken Thou me, likewise! Thou art invisible, yet Thine energy flows through the rays of sunshine. Fill my veins with Thine invisible rays, making me strong and tireless. As the sun shines in the busiest streets, may I behold Thy rays of protecting love in the crowded places of my life's activities. As the light shines steadily, undisturbed, on the street, whether crowded or empty, so may I hold my calmness and my strength steadily, while I move through the crowded or empty streets of life. Give me strength; and what I receive, teach me to share with others.

**13
Prayer at
Eventide.**

The day is done. Refreshed and sanctified with the sunshine of the day, I pass through the portals of evening, dimly adorned with faint stars, to enter into the temple of silence and worship Thee. I worship Thy Spirit of approaching calmness. What prayers shall I offer, for I have no words to offer Thee? I shall light a little fire of devotion on the altar of my soul. Will that light suffice to bring Thee into my dark temple—my dimly lighted temple, dark with my ignorance? Come! I crave, I yearn for Thee!

14
Prayer at Night

With closed eyes, I sit in the temple of night and worship Thee. The sunlight, revealing a million alluring things, has vanished. One by one, I have closed the doors of my senses, lest the fragrance of the rose, or the song of the nightingale, distract my love from Thee. I am alone in this dark, dark temple. I have left everything, but where art Thou? Darkness is haunting; but, unafraid, I am groping, seeking, crying for Thee. Wilt Thou leave me alone? Come, show Thyself!

The door of my memory swings open. Throbbingly thrilled, my heart looks for Thee, but I find Thee not. Halt! Ye throng of a million thoughts and experiences past! Come not into my sacred temple. I close the bursting, thought-pressed door and run everywhere to find Thee. Where art Thou?

Darkness deepens, and as I sit still, in anguish of despair, I behold a little taper of concentration burning within me. I stand up, and madly rush through the dimly lighted temple—the farther I go, the deeper grows the gloom. I clasp the empty darkness in hope of seizing Thee. Finding Thee not, I return again, and see the taper dimly burning.

I sing outwardly a loud prayer. My large teardrops, and my strong gusts of prayer almost extinguish the taper. I will pray no more with words nor rush or run about in the temple of Stygian darkness, nor drown the taper with my tears. I will sit still, and command my breath to make no sound. I rebuke my boisterous love for Thee. The taper of meditation burns brighter now.

O, how maddening! I cannot worship Thee with words, but only with wistful yearning. Brighter the light grows: I behold Thee now. Thou art I. I worship Thee. As night hides everything, I will worship Thee in hidden silence.

I am glad with the joy of all minds. I will use the screen of the night to hide myself from the tempting things of the day.

O Night, when I am worried, throw thy veil of silent darkness around me. Create a dark temple for me wherever I go, that I may invoke and call Him, whom I love, at any time, anywhere, everywhere.

15 Prayer-demand before taking food.

Heavenly Father, receive this food. Make it holy. Let no impurity of greed ever defile it. The food comes from Thee. It is to build Thy temple. Spiritualize it. Spirit to Spirit goes. We are the petals of Thy manifestation, but Thou art the Flower, its life, beauty and loveliness. Permeate our souls with the fragrance of Thy presence.

16 Prayer-Demand for recharging of Body-Battery.

O Conscious, Cosmic Energy, it is Thou who dost directly support my body. Solid, liquid and gaseous foods are converted and spiritualized into energy by Thy cosmic energy—and it supports my body. Help me to learn, O Spirit, to live more and more by direct cosmic energy and less and less by food. Thine energy burns in the bulb of the senses. I recharge myself with Thine omnipresent cosmic energy.

17
Prayer before practicing Concentration.

Teach me, O Spirit, by meditation, to stop the storm of breath, mental restlessness and sensory disturbances raging in the lake of my mind. Let the magic wand of my intuition stop the gale of passions and unnecessary desires, and in the rippleless lake of my mind let me behold the undistorted reflection of the moon of my soul, glistening with the light of Thy presence.

18
Demand for Pearls of Wisdom to be obtained in the Sea of Meditation.

Father Divine, teach me to dive deep in the ocean of meditation for the pearls of wisdom. Teach me to plunge headlong, armored with the diving suit of conscience, that the sharks of passions may not destroy me. If I find not the wisdom-pearls by one or two divings, teach me not to call the sea of meditation devoid of the pearls of Thy wisdom. *Rather teach me to find fault with my diving.* Teach me to dive again and again in meditation, deeper and deeper always, until I find Thine immortal pearls of wisdom and divine joy.

19
Prayer for expanding Love from self to all brethren.

O Divine Mother, teach me to use the gift of Thy love in my heart to love the members of my family more than myself. Bless me, that I may love my neighbors more than my family. Expand me, so that I love my country more than my neighbors, and that I love *my world* and all human brethren more than my country, neighbors, family, and myself.

Lastly, teach me to love Thee more than anything else, for it is Thy love with which I love everything. Without Thee I cannot love anybody or anything. Father Divine, teach me to enter through the portals of family love, or through the love of my friends into the mansion of wider social love. Teach me, then, to pass through the doors of social love into the wider mansion of international love. Teach me to pass through the portals of international love into the endless territory of divine love, in which I may perceive all animate and inanimate objects as breathing and living by Thy love.

Teach me to tarry not at any of the fascinating, gorgeous gates of family, social or international love. Teach me to pass through all these portals, leading to smaller territories of love, until, passing through the last gate of human love, I can enter into the endless territory of divine love, in which I shall find all living, semi-living or sleeping things as my own.

20
A bouquet of all Loves of God.

O God the Father, teach me to make a bouquet of the variously hued flowers of filial, conjugal, friendly, parental, masterly loves, and to lay it on the altar of my heart, where Thou reignest. If I cannot make a bouquet, I will pluck the rarest love that grows in the garden of my devotion and will lay that before Thee. Wilt Thou receive it?

21
Prayer-Demand to the Holy Vibration for Omnipresence.

O Holy Vibration, boom on the shores of my consciousness. Break the limiting boundary of my consciousness in the body. Reverberate through my body, mind, soul, my surroundings, the cities, the earth, the planets, the universe, and every particle of creation. Unite my consciousness with cosmic consciousness.

22 Prayer-Demand for Self-Realization.

O cosmic vibration, reverberate through me as the cosmic, intelligent sound, and teach me to find in Thee the presence of the reflected Christ consciousness. O Holy Vibration, lead me to intuit the Christ consciousness in Thee.

O omnipresent, cosmic sound of Amen or *Aum*, reverberate through me, expanding my consciousness from the body to the universe, and teach me to feel in Thee the all-permeating, perennial bliss.

23 Prayer-Demand for removing the Cork of Ignorance.

No more shall my consciousness remain bottled in this phial of flesh, corked with ignorance. No more will I remain moving through the sea of cosmic consciousness, night and day, years, incarnations—so close, yet without contacting the sea. Through the bursting vibration of cosmic sound, and the surging of Thy holy name, I have removed the cork of ignorance, which so long separated Thee from me, though living so near. Now my consciousness within the body will meet the all-pervading consciousness without. No longer will I thoughtlessly walk in Thee, knowing and feeling Thee not. Thine image within shall meet Thine image which is everywhere. By releasing the "I-ness" in me, I know that I am Thou, and that it is Thou who art the little egos of all.

INVOCATIONS TO THE MANIFESTATION OF GOD IN THE TEMPLES OF GREAT LIVES

**24
My Guru.**
Thou light of my life—thou camest to spread wisdom's glow over the path of my soul. Centuries of darkness dissolved before the shafts of thy luminous help. As a naughty baby, I cried for my Mother Divine, and She came to me as my Guru—Swami Sri Yukteswar. At that meeting, O my Guru, a spark flew from thee, and the faggots of my God-cravings, gathered through incarnations, smouldered and blazed into bliss. All my questions have been answered through thy flaming, golden touch. Eternal, ever-present satisfaction has come to me through thy glory.

My Guru, thou voice of God, I found thee in response to my soul-cries. Slumbers of sorrow are gone, and I am awake in bliss.

If all the gods are displeased, and yet thou art pleased, I am safe in the fortress of thy pleasure. And if all the gods protect me by the parapets of their blessings, and yet I receive not thy benedictions, I am an orphan, left to pine spiritually in the ruins of thy displeasure. O Guru—thou didst bring me out of the bottomless pit of darkness into the paradise of peace.

Our souls met after years of waiting. They trembled with an omnipresent thrill. We met here, because we had met before.

Together we will fly to His shores, and then we will smash our planes of finitude forever and vanish into our infinite life.

I bow to thee as the spoken voice of silent God. I bow to thee as the divine door leading to the temple of salvation. I bow to thee—to thy Master, Lahiri Mahasaya, harbinger of Yoga in Benares; and I lay the flowers of my devotion at the feet of Babaji, our supreme Master!

25
Come to me, O Christ, as the Divine Shepherd of Souls.

O Christ—Thou rarest flower of hearts—Thou didst sail on the storm-tossed lake of prejudiced minds. Its evil-scented, gloomy thought-waves lashed Thy lily-tender soul. They crucified Thee with their evil. Yet Thou didst shed the aroma of goodness and forgiveness, and didst help them to be purified by remorse, so helping them to become attractively sweet-scented with Thine all-loving Flower-Soul.

O Thou Great Lover of error-torn brothers—an unseen monument of the mightiest miracle of love was established in each heart when the magic wand of Thy voice uttered: "Forgive them, for they know not what they do."

Thou hast healed the cataract of hatred, and now we have grown to see: "Love thine enemies as thyself, for they are thy brothers—though sick and sleeping."

Thou hast taught us not to increase their delirious kicks of hatred by battering them with the bludgeons of revenge. Thine undying sympathy hath inspired us to heal and wake our brothers, suffering from the delirium of anger, by the soothing salve of our forgiveness.

Thy crucifixion reminds us of the *daily* crucifixion of our fortitude by trials, of our wisdom by ignorance, of our self-control by the scathing hands of temptation, and of our love by misunderstanding.

Thy test on the cross proved the victory of Thy wisdom over ignorance, of Thy soul over flesh, of Thy happiness over pain, and of Thy love over hatred. So are we heartened to bear our crosses bravely and pleasantly. Teach us to pour out sweetness when crucified by harshness, to bear with calmness the assault of worries, and to give understanding unceasingly to those who unjustly hate us.

O Shepherd of Souls, wandering hearts are of themselves seeking the one fold of divine devotion. We have heard the ever-calling music of Thine infinite kindness. Our one desire is to be at home with Thee, to receive the Cosmic Father with joyous, open eyes of wisdom, and to know that we are all sons of our own One God.

Teach us to conquer the Satan of dividing selfishness, which prevents the gathering of all brother-souls into the one fold of Spirit.

Calling to one another by the watchword: "Love him who loves you, and love all who love you not," let us rally beneath the canopy of the universal sense of Christ-Oneness. Amen.

**26
Come to me,
0 Krishna, as
the Divine
Cowherd.**

O Krishna, Lord of Hindustan, I sorrowed by the lonely Jumna river bank, where Thy flute-notes thrilled the air and led the lost calves to their homes. O Lotus of Love, musing on the sad absence of Thy delusion-dispelling eyes, I saw Thine invisible Spirit take form, frozen by my devotion's frost.

Thy divine form of sky-blue rays, with feet of eternity, walked on the banks of my mind, planting lasting footprints of realization there. I am one of Thy lost calves which followed Thy flower-footprints on the shoals of time. Listening to the melody of Thy flute of wisdom, I am following the middle path of calm activity, by which Thou hast led many through the portals of the dark past into the light.

Since all of us are of Thy fold, whether moving, sidetracked, or held stationary by the fogs of disbelief, O Divine Christ-na, lead us back to Thy fold of everlasting freedom. O Krishna, Thou reignest on the heart-throne of each knower of Thy love.

27
Come to me as Swami Shankara.

Swami Shankara, thou dazzling star, soaring in wisdom's skies, thou hast shed thy light over many souls darkened by religious formalities.

Many sheep of human darkness have fled before the leonine roar of thy Self-realization. With Christ, thou hast sung: "I am He," "Thou art That," "I and my Father are One," and awakened us from our material sleep.

Thou first exponent of "matter exists not as it appears to be," we pay homage to thee.

O Swami of Swamis, thou didst teach us to behold the one ocean of Spirit, hidden beneath the dancing, melting waves of finite forms.

Thou didst tell us that our God is not gloomfaced nor revengeful, a seeker of faults, but that His face wears the aureole of all-alluring smiles. Thou hast shown us how to garner blossoming laughter of hearts, and how to adorn the vase of our souls with a bouquet of mighty, celestial laughter.

Our smiling lives were churned out of thy sea of light, and in thy oceanic joy our many lives dance; and at the lull of desire's storm, in thy vast laughter we will merge.

O Shankara, many have seen the sea of Spirit dancing in thy smile: We bow to thee!

**28
Come to me
as Moses.**

O Moses, thou blossom of prophets! Thy wisdom's power has led many out of the desert of sorrow to the smiling lands of joy.

The lips of thy life have whispered the secret way to set ablaze the bushes of soul-darkness with wisdom's fire, and in its glow to behold God's mercy-face.

In the "burning-bush" of love, He saw thee, wet with trickling tears of kindness to all, and behold, He said:

"Let My ten angels of heaven escort thee to earth, to blow in silence through the trumpets of all times, My Ten Commandments, declaring the march of Mine invisible army of divine qualities to fight the Satan of human darkness and his allies of sin, error, untruth, and their gloom-drunk soldiers."

O Moses, thou torch-bearer of salvation, many soldier-souls are seeking to join thee in thy ceaseless march through the dark night of time, to fight the forces of gloom.

O God-loving Moses, teach us to fight weakness with power, and to worship supremely the God of Gods reigning on the throne of all hearts—and no other God!

29
Come to me as Mohammed.

O Mohammed, thou flaming Son of God! In the bright luster of thy martial, celestial song, many have found solace in activity for their chivalrous souls, eager to rescue dame knowledge from the tyrant of darkness.

None but the divine warrior wins in battle between strong peace and weak lust-pleasure, so thy soldiers have dipped their rapiers of shining good into the poison hearts of evil and ebbed their lives away.

Mohammed, iconoclast of soul-shorn symbol-idols, thou didst teach the worship of the One Formless God, washed clean of all distorting dreams of symbols and forms.

Mohammed, thy voice warned thy fold not to stray in dry pastures of earth sense-lusts, but to browse on the rich harvests of immortal mind.

Thy followers know thou art the mortal enemy of sense-drugging, thought-devastating, God-banishing liquors and opiates. Thou didst teach that the lust for wine is the misguided craving for the real Wine, extracted from the winepress of sincere, regular prayer of *Namaz*.

Mohammed, thy lighthouse, the *Koran*, hath guided many stray soul-ships safely around the submerged rocks of sin and led them safely to His shore.

Thou didst teach by occasional fasting, or by dropping the company of gross food, to tempt the Spirit to descend upon the altar of refinement and partake of the nectar of souls.

Mohammed, with the beats of the war-drums of *Allah Ho Akbar*, or the Almighty, drive away the Satan of "matter-stick-to-itiveness."

May thy war-songs of spiritual power overcome the forces of frailty and limitation which invade our hearts.

30
Come to me as Buddha.

O Buddha, the gold vein of thy sermon of mercy ran through gloom-gorged, rocky hearts, and illumined their darkness.

Thou loftiest soarer of renunciation's skies, beneath thy God-lifted eyes, the kingdom of sense-comfort, the rivers of gross greed, the vast and lust-scorched deserts of desire, the tall trees of temporal ambition, the cactus plants of prickly world-worries—all melt into invisible smallness.

Buddha, the arc-light of thy sympathy sought to melt the hardness of cruel hearts. Once thou didst save a lamb by offering thyself in its stead.

Thy solemn thoughts still silently roam through the ether of minds, searching for ecstasy-tuned hearts. Seated beneath the banyan bodhi tree, thou didst make a solemn tryst with the Spirit:

"Beneath the banyan bough,
On the sacred seat I take this vow:
Let derma, bones, and fleeting flesh dissolve;
Until the mysteries of life I solve,
And receive the all-coveted Priceless Lore,
From this place I shall stir, never, nevermore."

Thou symbol of sympathy, incarnation of mercy, give us thy determination, that we may seek truth as doggedly as thou didst. Bless us, that we may be awakened, like thee, to seek remedy for the sorrow-throbs of others as we seek it for ourselves.

PRAYERS FOR UNIVERSALITY

**31
Prayer-
Demand
asking God
to be the
President of
the United
States of the
World.**

Our Father, President of the United States of planets, galaxies, worlds, universes, Thy democratic rule of self-evolution and free-choice is bringing Thy citizen-children nearer and nearer unto Thine ideals.

Born in Thy states of freedom of will, we received our celestial birthright of eternal, everlasting freedom. But, alas! we imprisoned and enslaved our omnipresence behind the bars of sense-enjoyment, evil, selfishness, and hide-bound, narrow-eyed patriotism.

Teach us, Father, to melt with the warmth of our love and understanding, the fancy-frozen boundaries of family, society and nationality.

Bless us, O all-wise Father, that we may live in the United States of the World, with Thee as our President, perennially elected by the free choice of all the good citizens of our hearts, ruling ourselves through our own self-determining discrimination.

Teach us to enrich our souls, our opulence, and our understanding, by broadening the circle of our patriotic love, including in it all earth's inhabitants, irrespective of caste, class, creed or color.

O Cosmic President, bless us that we may obey Thy laws of life; and respect, with kindness, the freedom of all Thy free-born children-citizens: not only the good, and the error-intoxicated men, but also the mammals, birds and beasts, frail flowers, mute grasses and jungle weeds, crushed low under the tread of our cruel, unheeding feet.

**32
Prayer-demand:
Make me anything: a Christian or a Hindu—anything to realize Thee.**

Let me be Christian, Jew, Hindu, Buddhist, Mohammedan, or Sufi: I care not what my religion, my race, my creed, or my color be, if only I can win my way to Thee! But let me be none of these, if it enmesh me in labyrinthine ways of religious formalities. Let me travel the royal road of realization which leads to Thee. I care not what bypaths of religion I follow, if at last I can travel by the one highway of common realization, which straightway leads to Thee.

Send the sunshine of Thy wisdom to guide me in the daylight of my dawning powers; and the moon of Thy mercy, if I travel in the dark night of sorrow.

**33
Demand to travel on the one Highway of Realization.**

Our One Father, we are traveling by many true paths unto Thy one abode of Light. *Show us the one highway of common realization, where all bypaths of theological beliefs meet.* Make us feel that the diverse religions are branches of Thy one tree of truth. Bless us, that we may enjoy the intuition-tested, ripe, luscious fruits of self-knowledge, hanging from all the branches of manifold scriptural teachings. In Thy one temple of silence, we are singing unto Thee a chorus of many-voiced religions. Teach us to chant in harmony our love's many expressions unto Thee, that our melody of souls may rouse Thee to break Thy vows of silence and lift us upon Thy lap of universal understanding and immortality.

MISCELLANEOUS DEMANDS

(In this group you will find demands for prosperity, efficiency, wisdom, dispelling of fear and anger, and many other conditions which occur in daily life.)

**34
Make me Thy Butterfly of Eternity.**

I burnt my past. I ignored the foreboding seeds of sprouting destiny. I waded through the strewn ashes of past and future fears.

I am the eternal present. I tore to shreds the cocoon of ignorance with the sharpness of my will.

I am Thy flitting butterfly of eternity, sweeping through immeasurable time. The beauty of my nature-wings I spread everywhere, to entertain everything. Suns and stardust are spread on my wings. Behold my beauty! Cut all the silken threads of thy shrouding folly: follow me in my flight to myself!

**35
I will not offer unto Thee mind-made, hothouse Songs.**

I will sing a song untouched by the voice of any. I will offer unto Thee my virgin song.

I will sing to Thee a song which lies singing in my heart, unheard by any. I nurtured my song-child, and I bring it out unto Thee for its training.

I will not offer unto Thee an intellectual, premeditated and disciplined song; I will offer unto Thee the wild songs of my heart. I will not offer unto Thee civilized, emotion-born music or mind-made song-flowers; but I will offer unto Thee the wild blossoms which grow on the high tracts of my soul.

36
Prayers on the Beads of Love.

I am saying my prayers on the beads of my love, strung with devotion. I hold to no names—God, Spirit, Brahma, Christ, Shankara, Krishna, Buddha, or Mohammed, for they are all Thine. Sometimes I use all of these names, for I know Thou lovest to take many names.

In Thy cosmic plays on the stage of centuries, and in Thy myriad appearances, Thou hast taken unto Thyself many names, but I know Thou hast one changeless name—Perennial Joy.

I played with Thee many times. I sang Thy songs. On Thine ocean-bosom of all life, Thou didst nurture me as a tiny drop of life. I remember Thy warm touches of centuries, whenever I returned home to Thee after the chill of separation. Again, in this day of time, I play with Thee and I sing Thy songs.

37
Hover over the Minaret of my Expectations, O Mighty Spirit.

Into the temple of peace, come Thou, O God of joy! Into the shrine of devotion, come Thou O Bliss-God! Make the sanctuary of my goodness sacred by Thy presence.

O mighty Allah, hover over Thy lone waiting minaret of my expectations. O Allah, the mosque of my mind exudes the frankincense of stillness.

Come! We are waiting to hear the tread of Thy footsteps. The temple *vihara* of my self-development is waiting for Thy coming.

Into the invisible church of my prayer, built of strong, white blocks of devotion, come Thou daily to receive the humble offering of my heart, renewed by love.

38
The Bee of my Mind loves to drink from the Blue Lotus of Thy Feet.

O Divine Mother, in Thy lotus feet of blue light, the bee of my mind is engrossed. It is drinking the honey of Thy motherly love. This royal bee of Thine will drink no other honey but that which is graced by Thy perfume.

O Divine Mother, flying over all the gardens of my fancy, denying myself the honey of all pleasures, at last I found the ambrosia hidden in Thy lotus-heart.

I have been Thy busy bee, soaring through the fields of incarnations, inhaling the breath of experiences; now I will roam no more, for Thy fragrance has quenched the perfume-thirst of my soul.

39
May I serve the cocktail of God-Intoxicated Eyes in the home of the rich.

In Thy temples, when many come to pray, I take God-intoxication from their eyes. I blend them together into a cocktail of devotion. I serve that to my thirsty thoughts; they drink and drink, and forget their fresh wounds and worries.

In the home of the materially rich and spiritually poor, I love to serve this magic cocktail in vessels of my heart's good-will and sincerity.

I pray that they who drink this wine may become so intoxicated that they will forget the pain of ignorance forevermore.

40
May I seize Thee at Eternity's end?

O Thou Thief of Hearts, the rays of joy spreading in the firmament of my inner silence heralded the promise of Thine approach.

Many nights in twinkling garments, many dawns donning green veils of glittering, dewy pearls, many twilights dancing in cadence with cow-bells, many years decked with spring-blossoms, summer-zephyrs, diamond-icicles, and the shining garment of fluttering rains blushing with joyous expectancy, waited for Thee in the bower of memory.

But the wolf of time stole upon Thy devotees, and they are no more. I am left alone—all alone—and love for fickle festivities has flown. Yet will I travel with the ever-roaming hours in search of Thy path. I mind not waiting even a thousand millenniums, for I know I shall seize Thee, O Thief of Hearts, sometime, at eternity's end!

41
Wake me, that I may know the terrors of mundane delusion to be but Dreams.

Wrapped in the blanket of hope, I slept long. I dreamt that I was sitting on a throne. My face held a bouquet of smiles. My smiles withered, and the petals of merriment dropped, one by one. Then suddenly, I beheld myself in rags, sitting on the hard stones of poverty. I cried, and my teardrops fell on the unheeding, unrelenting stones of my circumstances.

The world passed me by in mocking silence. I cried for Thy help. Thou didst wake me at last, through the force of my gathered cries. I laughed to find myself neither rich nor poor. So do Thou wake me from this dream of smiling opulence and crying poverty.

Deliver me, O Maker of dream-worlds, from the ugly nightmares of death!

Wake in me immortality: Wake in me unshaken calmness, that I may know that the fierce terrors of mundane delusion are but dreams.

42
I Demand to return Home.

Impediments, beware! Flee my path! I am homeward bound. Through the corridors of time, falling in the pitfalls of error, lifted by Thine unseen hand, I walked. Discouraging darkness, barbed fences of habit, stone embankments of indolence, mountains of indifference, oceans of unfaithfulness, sirens of sense, may stand in my path to prevent my march to Thy place; but a million kingdoms and sextillions of years of untrammelled worldly happiness will not tempt me to forsake Thee.

43
Make me a lion of Thy all-conquering Wisdom.

A lion-cub of the Divine Mother, I was somehow thrown into life in the sheep-fold of human frailties. Living long with the sheep of fear, failure and disease, I bleated with weakness. I forgot my roars which had frightened away all wicked, pestering sorrows.

O Lion of Realization, Thou didst drag me away from the sheep-fold unto the waters of meditation. And Thou didst say: "Open thine eyes and roar!" But I kept my eyes tightly closed and bleated with fear. The roar of Thy wisdom reverberated through me, and Thy hard shakings of spiritual urge made me open my eyes. Lo! there in the crystal pool of peace, Thou didst show me my face to be *like Thine!*

Now, I know I am the Lion of cosmic power. I will no more bleat in fear of weakness and suffering: I will roar with the vibrant power of the Almighty! Bounding in the forest of experiences, I will seize the little creatures of vexing worries, the timid fears, and wild hyenas of disbelief, and devour them ruthlessly.

O Lion of Immortality, roar through me Thine all-conquering power of wisdom!

44
I am Thy Bird of Paradise wishing to fly in Thy Astral Airplane.

Thine astral airplane of earthly parting came to take my soul away. I wondered through what strange skies I was to soar, and to what lands I was to travel.

I asked the mystic Pilot of Cosmic Law whither I was going. The Silent One answered, soundlessly:

"I am the Pilot of Life, mistakenly called the terrible Death by ignorant earth-folk. I am thy brother, uplifter, redeemer, friend—unloader of thy gross burden of body-troubles. I come to fetch thee away from the valley of thy broken dreams to the highland of light, where poisonous vapors of sorrow can never climb.

"I have mercilessly broken thy cage of flesh-attachment, that thy soul-bird may be free. I have broken thy chains of disease and mental fears. Thy long imprisonment behind the bars of bones made thee unwillingly become used to the cage. Thou didst want thy freedom always. Now, why art thou fear-filled, when thou hast won thy long-craved freedom?

"O bird of paradise! hop into My plane of omnipresence! Fold thy long-fluttering wings and restfully ride with me, anywhere, everywhere, in thine ethereal home!"

45 Come into the Garden of my Dreams.

In the garden of my dreams grew many dream-blossoms. The rarest flowers of my fancy all bloomed there. Unopened buds of earthly hopes audaciously spread their petals of fulfillment, warmed by the light of my dreams. In the dim glow, I spied the specters of beloved forgotten faces, sprites of dear, dead feelings, long buried beneath the soil of mind, which all rose in their shining robes. I beheld the resurrection of all experiences, at the trumpet-call of my dream-angels.

O King of my dreams and of countless dream-worlds, in the garden of Thy dream-galaxies let me be a tiny star, or let me twinkle by Thy side as Thy loved dream-star in the chamber of Thy cosmic dreams. Or, if I be not held by the string of Thy love as a tiny star-bead of life in the garland of Thy dreams, then give me the humblest place in the heart of Thy dreams.

In the chamber of Thy heart, I shall behold the making of the noblest dreams of life. O Master-Weaver of Dreams, teach me to make a many-hued carpet of dreams, for all lovers of Thy pattern of dreams to walk over, as they travel to the temple of eternal dreams. And I will join the worshipping angels of living visions that I may offer on Thine altar a bouquet of my new-born dreams of Thee.

46
Let me feel that Thou and I art One.

When the sparks of cosmic creation flew from Thy bosom of flame, I sang in the chorus of singing lights which heralded the coming of the worlds. I am a spark of Thy cosmic fire. Thou sun of life, as Thou didst peep into the mortal cups of mind, filled with molten liquid of vital sparks, Thou wert caught within the golden smallness of human feelings.

In each fragile, oscillating mirror of flesh, I see the restless dance of Thine omnipresent power. In the quivering lake of life, I behold Thine almighty life.

Christlike, teach me by the command of concentration to stop the storms of restless desires raging over the limpid lake of my mind. In the still lake of my soul, I love to behold Thine unruffled face of stillness. Break the boundaries of the little wave of my life, that Thy vastness may spread over me.

Make me feel that my heart is throbbing in Thy breast, and that Thou art walking through my feet, breathing through my breath, wielding my arms of activity, and weaving thoughts in my brain. Thy sleeping sighs wake when my sighs cry. Through Thy playfulness, the bubbles of Thy visions of creation float in the chamber of my delusive sleep.

It is Thy meteoric will which courses through the skies of my will. Make me feel that it is Thou who hast become I. O, make me Thyself, that I may behold the little bubble of me, floating in Thee!

47
Rock me in the Cradle of all Space.

Rocked in the cradle of the blue-colored past, bright-colored present, and grey-colored, dim future, I, Thy child of eternity, am restless.

I strained the feet of my power ineffectually, but at last I managed to jump from the cradle of duality's delusion. Thou didst catch me in Thine infinite arms and rock me in all space.

I am Thy babe of eternity, safe in the cradle of Thine omnipresent bosom.

48
May the Niagara of my Joys inundate all hearts.

May the Niagara Falls of the joys from my heart gush unceasingly over those whom I meet. May its flooding power sweep away the heavy logs of others' difficulties. Let all wash their melancholia with the moonbeams of my bliss.

I will be the tornado of laughter, marring the superstructures of sorrow, spread over miles and miles of mentalities. I will churn up and blow away all the troubles of hearts.

In the lightning-flashes of my mirth, I will swiftly bring to view the panorama of Thy beauty, hidden beneath the nocturnal darkness of unseeing minds.

Bless me, that by a single shaft of my light I may put to flight the gathering gloom of ages, nurtured in the dark corners of human minds. Through Thy grace, a little light of sudden wisdom will dispel the accumulated error of a million years.

49
Make me the Lark of Life, looking only for Thy Rain.

I am the lark of life, flitting in the skies of Thy cosmic presence, thirstily looking for the raindrops of Thy manifestations. Filter through the cruel clouds of silence Thy showering omnipresence.

I will be attentive to every raindrop of Thy perception which shall touch my parched and craving lips. I will drink Thee within, and I will embrace the feet of Thy raindrops of realization, gently falling on my frail body without.

This age-long thirst of mine will only cease when Thy touch shall cool my craving soul within and my zeal-warmed body without. The storm of despondency and hopelessness has passed. Thy raindrops of peace have moistened each dry particle of my being, and I will flit everywhere, singing Thy song of contentment.

Make me Thy lark, looking for no other drink but the waters of Thy solace, flowing through the heavens of Thy being everywhere.

50
Make me a Smile-Millionaire.

O Silent Laughter—smile Thou through my soul. Let my soul smile through my heart. And let my heart smile through my eyes.

O Prince of Smiles! Be enthroned beneath the canopy of my countenance, and I will protect Thy tender Self in the castle of my sincerity, that no rebel hypocrisy may lurk to destroy Thee.

Make Thou me a smile-millionaire, that I may scatter Thy rich smiles in sad hearts freely, everywhere!

51
Save us from the net of Matter-Attachment.

The fisherman of change has cast a net of cosmic delusion over us. We are swimming in the waters of false assurances of human safety, and all the while the net of death is closing in upon us. At every haul of the dragnet of delusion, many are caught—few escape. I dived into the deep-sea-spaces of silent communion, and fled from the net of time.

O Measureless Mercy, save me and my brothers, from this net of matter-attachment.

52
O King of all our ambitions, open the doors of Noble Aspirations in the Mansion of our Souls.

Open the petalled bars of our heart-buds, and let our imprisoned fragrance of love rush out to meet Thee. With the wind of cosmic perception, our fragrance will float to Thy temple of infinity.

O King of all our ambitions, throw open all Thy windows of red clouds, of charm-clad human dreams. Open Thou all the doors of noble aspirations in the mansions of our souls.

We want our fragrance to blow by Thine unseen feet, hiding behind all nature's windows.

53
Save me from shipwreck on the Ocean of my Dreams.

I was shipwrecked on the ocean of my dreams. My happy vessel of comfort was entirely shattered. I struggled and swam over those dreary waters of sad, blue dreams. A little raft of hope, sent by the winds of Thy mercy, came floating by me! I grasped it—I held on! Little by little, I moved on, and at last I touched the golden isle of pleasant silence. Nymphs of Thy blessings, gathered there, to meet and take me to Thy presence of eternal safety.

54
Tune us, that we may hear Thy Voice.

Volumes of Thy savior voice plunge through the microphone of loving hearts. The voice of Thy wisdom is roaming through the ether of minds, searching for ecstasy-tuned hearts.

Thy sermons of warning sadly pass, unheard by the souls deafened with the static of their sense-pleasures.

O Divine Broadcaster, tune our souls, smothered beneath the static of indifference; tune us with the fine touches of Thy perceptions, and thus grant us the privilege of hearing Thy magic song of ecstatic awakening!

55
I want to build a Rainbow-Bridge of Self-Realization.

The gulf of ages lay between Thee and me, and widened as the waters of my oblivion of Thee grew through the centuries.

I stand by this rocky shore of matter, looking for Thy smooth shores of peace, beyond. My inner architects are building for me a bridge of my constant remembrance of Thee. The girders of my strength of self-control are all being riveted together.

My dreams of Thee are gathering together to make a rainbow-bridge of Self-realization, by which I will soon reach Unto Thee.

56
Make me Silent, that I may eloquently converse with Thee.

I wandered through forests of incessant searchings, and arrived at the mystery door of Thy presence. On the doors of silence I knocked loudly with my persistent blows of faith, and the doors of space opened. There, on the altar of glorious visions, I beheld Thee, resting.

I stood, with restless eyes, waiting for Thee to speak. I heard not Thy creation-making voice. At last the spell of stillness stole upon me, and in whispers taught me the language of angels. With the lisping voice of new-born freedom, I tried to speak, and the lights of Thy temple assumed sudden brilliancy and wrote letters of light.

In my little chamber of quietness, I am always resting: I never speak but with the voice of my silence. Through my silence, eloquently converse with me.

57
Teach me to use every dig of criticism to bring myself near the Fountain of Goodness in me.

Teach me to wear every scar of trials as the medal of my chastisement, given by the sacred hands of Thy just law. Let every teardrop of sorrow, caused to flow in me through the actions of others, wash away some hidden taint of my mind.

Let every stroke of the pickaxe of my sharp experiences dig deeper and deeper into the soil of my life. Let every hurtful dig of circumstance into the soil of comfort, bring me nearer to the bubbling fountain of Thy solace, in me. Let every wound of life utter a cry for Thy love. Let all trials be antidotes for bitterness, and bring healing to my soul. Let every ugly unkindness of others urge me to be more beautifully kind. Let the blinding darkness stimulate me to rush for Thy light. Let harsh words scold me into using sweet words always. Let every bruise from the stones of evil thrown at me, intensify my fortitude and blessings of goodness.

Just as a jasmine vine fails not to shed its flowers on the hands administering axe-blows at its roots, so do Thou teach me not to deny the showering blossoms of forgiveness and help over those who cut me with their wickedness.

58
Teach me to fish for Thee in the deep waters of my Soul.

I went to catch Thee in the deep waters of super-consciousness. Little fishes of inspiration nibbled at my bait of meditation. The float of my concentration wavered, but every time I pulled, I missed Thee.

I spread my meditation-bait with love's spices: the little fishes tugged at it, and I watched the float of my mind with attentive zeal. Lo! my mind's float vanished beneath Thy bliss-waves.

O Colossal Denizen of my consciousness, I pulled at Thee, and with a bound Thou didst leap to the shores of my heart. Teach me to fish for Thee in the deep waters of my soul.

59
Make me remember that Virtuous Ways are more charming than vicious ways.

Teach me, O Spirit, to discern all laws of virtue not with dread, but with love. Teach me to remember that virtue may be difficult to follow at the start, but that when I obey its laws, it will adorn me finally with the laurel of Thy happiness. Teach me to remember that evil promises a little pleasure in the beginning but always brings great sorrow in the end.

Teach me to love virtuous laws, which exist for my interest and my good, and to shun vicious actions, which react against my interest. Implant in me that habit by which I may always perceive virtuous ways to be more charming than vicious ways.

Help me to remember that virtue, though bitter of taste in the beginning, eventually becomes nectar; and evil is that which tastes sweet in the beginning, but always acts as poison in the end.

60
I will broadcast my Voice with the Chorus of Thy Songs.

With the soft touches of my soul-antenna, I tuned the radio of my inner intuition. At first, I caught the voices of those near Thee—a symphony of soul-harmony, the sweet strains of my singing heart's orchestra of feelings, the chorus of my age-long cravings for Thee—all caught on the radio of my soul. I kept tuning my perception, waiting to catch Thy voice, O Guardian Angel of all souls.

With infinite patience I kept tuning, and, as I almost slept, Thy song gushed through my heart. I will broadcast my life's voice with the chorus of Thy songs.

61
Teach me to store honey of quality from all Soul-Flowers in the honeycomb of my Heart.

In the summer days of life, teach me to gather the honey from flowers of quality, which grow in the garden of human souls.

In the honeycomb of my heart. I will store perfumed forgiveness, myrrh-scented devotion, the rare essence of lotus-souls—fragrant honey of a million soul-flowers.

And when the snowflakes of wintry experiences and earthly

separation dance around me, I shall hide in the honeycomb of my heart, where I often found Thee stealing the honey of my stored devotion.

Where Thou camest—in that spot made hallow by the dust of Thy feet—I will lie. In the depth of Thy footprints may I find my nook of safety.

62
Teach me to give Sweet Forgiveness, though crushed by Criticism.

Teach me to behave like the orange which, though crushed and bitten, fails not to impart its sweetness. Battered by unkindness, bitten by carping criticism, or hewed with hard words and cruel behavior, teach me yet to pour the unceasing sweetness of my love.

Teach me to be like the soap-flakes which, when beaten and rubbed, give out the cleansing foam. Tried and hard-beaten by ingratitude, teach me, nevertheless, to offer the snow-white mental driving foam of my wisdom's help.

63
Spiritualize our Thoughts and Ambitions

O Infinite Alchemist, spiritualize our weakness into strength, our wrong thoughts into right thoughts. Grow Thou a flower of Thine understanding out of every seed of activity. With Thy magic wand of foresight, teach us to transmute our ugly demons of selfish ambitions into fairies of all-serving, noble aspirations. Train Thou each stallion of desire to race for Thine abode. Transform our dark ignorance into golden wisdom. Transmute all base ores of disqualifications into liquid streams of spiritual gold, steadily rushing for Thy shore.

64
Teach us not to follow the Will-o'-the-Wisp of False Happiness.

Through the night of errors, we pursued the will-o'-the-wisp of false happiness. Gloom heaped upon gloom, and our feet on the path of progress slipped into many ruts and marshes of disillusionment. These deceiving fog-born fires of passions lure many people to their doom. Thousands drown in the marshes of sense satiety.

O Divine Hand, blow out this false torch-light of destruction which misleads Thy blood-relations, headed for Thy home. Burn Thy beacon of holy light instead, that Thine eager children-pilgrims may safely reach Thy home.

65
May the showers of Thy love flood through the walls of Color, Class and Race-Prejudice.

The kingdom of my mind lies clogged with the dirt of delusion. Pour the showers of Thy power into my city of spiritual carelessness. Send Thy streams of mercy to inundate the cruelty of ignorance within myself. Let the downpour of Thy love wash away the embankments of race, color and class prejudice. Bathe the untidy children of my thoughts with the waters of Thy wisdom.

Strew and cover the dark path of life with carpets of Thy love's roses. Inhaling Thy fragrance, treading on the cushion of blossoms, I will hasten my footsteps to Thy palace of roses.

66
Burn Thou my frailties in the furnace of trials.

In the furnace of trials, the ore of my life is smelting. The fire of experience melts everything in me. But O, Divine Artisan, burn away all the dross of weakness in me; bring out the steel of endurance, and harden me into the strength of calmness. Shape Thou sharp weapons of self-control and tenacity out of the tempered metal of my balanced mentality. With the weapons of mind-equilibrium, teach me to fight my enemies of distraction.

67
The Caravan of my Prayers is moving toward Thee.

The caravan of my prayers is moving toward Thee. In the kind eyes of all men, I notice sparks of Thy mercy. The trees of dark lives flicker with a myriad of glow-worms of Thy shining life. The caravan of my prayers has been slowly working its way through the furious sand-storms of despondency. Yet, at last, the glimpse of the oasis of Thy silent assurance has roused my drooping efforts. I will dip my thirsty lips of faith, and drink deep from Thy well of bliss.

68
Save us from the bait of Modern Comforts.

We were swimming happily in the waters of peace; then the bait of fame, friends and name attracted us. Some nibbled at the bait and some fled at its sight. But alas, some swallowed the hook of worldly lure and the sinker of sense-pleasure deception, and they were pulled out to the shores of satiety. They fluttered with sadness, choked with indifference, and finally panted and died without Thy breath.

69
May I reap the greatest Harvest in the short season of Earthly Life.

My allotted plot of consciousness was small. I let it lie barren, producing no crops of life-sustaining culture. And now the bleak winter of dead opportunities is approaching with its shroud of unproductivity.

My lot is small and my season is short, yet I want a mighty harvest. So, forging through the kingdoms within, I conquered many states of new acquirements, and now the territory of my consciousness is large.

But, Father Divine, I have billions of my hungry thought-families and their little ones to feed. So Thou must know that I need a big harvest of Thy whispers in the short season of earth-life.

The waters of craving fell many times, and yet I kept my soil of culture untilled. Now, I am using the motor-plow of my incessant, scientific search for Thee.

May Thine unseen hand, O Divine Sower, throw the living seeds of Thy thoughts into the cultivated furrows of my mind.

In the short season of earthly life, I want to reap the largest harvest of Thy cosmic contact.

70
Make me the Eagle of Progress.

Make me the eagle of progress, soaring far above little lanes of narrowness and bigotry. Call me higher and higher, that I may fly above all clouds of earth-vibrations.

With the sharp talons of my soul, I will tear all birds of miseries which prey upon man. I will keep the skies of human mind free from all hawks of ignorance which attack the dove of peace.

I want to fly with balanced wings of right-living, in the fine regions of Thy perception. Above the tornadoes of worry-vibrations, I want to fly higher and higher, and climb to those unimagined heights where Thou dost dwell.

Make me Thy tame eagle of progress.

71
Flood me with Thy Omnipresent Love.

O Fountain of love, make us feel that our hearts and our love for our dear ones are all flooded by Thine omnipresent love. O Great Source of the rivers of our desires, teach us not to run ourselves dry or lose ourselves in the sands of short-lived sense-satisfactions.

We demand from Thee that the rivers of our cravings pass through all lowlands of humbleness, self-sacrifice and consideration for others; and at last, reinforced by Thee, we demand, O Thou Fountain of Love, that they merge in the ocean of fulfillment in Thee.

Bless us, that the rivulets of all our sympathy, affection and love, lose not themselves in the drought of dreary selfishness.

Let the little, lonely, separately-moving streamlets of our love, coming from Thee, at last merge in the vastness of Thy presence.

72
O Divine Sculptor, Chisel my Life.

Every sound that I make, let it have the vibration of Thy voice. Every thought that I think, let it be saturated with the consciousness of Thy presence.

Let every feeling that I have glow with Thy love. Let every act of my will be impregnated with Thy divine vitality. Let every thought, every expression, every ambition, be ornamented by Thee.

O Divine Sculptor, chisel Thou my life according to Thy design!

**73
Keep the Needle of my Attention ever pointing toward Thee.**

Whether soaring with the steel eagles of the air, whirling in steam-stallion-pulled chariots, rolling on rubber wheels, or roaming in the soul-breaking home of all noises, the needle of my attention, magnetized by Thee, will ever and ever turn toward Thee.

Beaten by winds of chance, drenched in the rain of misery, wallowing in the mud of entangling activity, my life may wander in gloom-hidden tracks, yet my mind will ever be looking toward Thee.

My mind-raft, driven by storms of want, was drifting toward rocks of insatiable desire.

O North Star of our wisdom-skies, the twinkle of Thy light called me back to Thine eternal shores of contentment.

The dove of my love, whether winging through whirlwinds of destiny, coursing through bursting shells of impediments, or flying across dense smoke-screens of colossal bewilderments, must ever be attracted toward Thee.

74
Be Thou my General in my invasion of Ignorance.

I bled for Thy name and for Thy name's sake I will ever bleed. With gory limbs, broken body, wounded honor, and wearing the thorn-crown of derision—yet, like a mighty warrior, I will fight undismayed through the thickest skirmish of trials.

With the sword of peace, I will smite the soldiers of persecution. My armies of Thy disciplined love, blowing trumpets of Thy name, are marching in triumph to seize the kingdom of dark souls.

I may receive blows on my lifted hands, and persecution's wounds may be given me instead of love, but I am content to realize that Thou knowest Thy soldier's craving to spread Thy name. I will wear my tribulations, not as scars, but as roses of courage and inspiration, to fight ignorance and conquer its darkness with Thy golden message of light.

O! Be Thou the General in my invasion of the continents of ignorance!

75
Make me see that I am just acting in Thy super-Sense vitaphone Cosmic Pictures.

Beholding the elusive sound-pictures, I am sure this daily-changing drama of turbulent and dancing lives is nothing but a vast dream-vitaphone presentation.

World-tragedies, comedies, paradoxes of life, dreams of birth and death, news of changing facts, are nothing but talking pictures—to keep all our senses and thoughts deluded and entertained.

O Divine Operator, through Thy cosmic-vibratory current, Thou art showing us a new, infinite series of all-talking and all-sensing cosmic motion pictures, every day, just to keep us amused and entertained.

O Magic Operator, Thy cosmic pictures not only can we see and hear, but we can touch, and feel them. Thy visible, true-to-touch, noisy, pseudo-living sound-shadows are daily shown on the screen of our consciousness.

Through Thy grace, I was chosen to play both tragic and comic parts in Thy special super-talkies. It is well that I act my part of sorrow or joy. But, Father, give me a few days of respite, now and then, from my task, that I may retire to the balcony of my introspection, among my thought-audiences, and behold, with a laughing heart, my own tragedies or comedies being enacted.

Teach me to look upon the tragedy-pictures of my own life with a thrilling, interested attitude, so that, at the end of each terribly sad picture, I may exclaim: "Ah, that was a good picture, full of thrills and life. I am pleased to have seen it, for I have learned much from it."

76
Teach me to abhor flies of Sarcasm, which sit on the Wounds of Others.

The bee of silence has made its way to the garden of my heart, where murmuring thought-trees hold out in tender branch-hands their fragrant bouquets—lilies of discrimination, butter-cups of recipient prayers, chrysanthemums of soul-rays, and violet-dreams of love's offerings unto Thee.

There, in my heart's patch of many flowers, fanned by the sweet odors of my love's breeze, where the dew of Thy sweetness hides in the core of flowering qualities, my naughty mind-bee hovers, reveling riotously over Thy treasures of honey-sweetness.

O, teach me to abhor the flies of cruel sarcasm, which love to sit on the wounds of others, and thus swell their troubles.

Let me be Thine eager bee, "robbing" only the honeyed qualities from the heart-hives of others.

77
Demand for Seeing the One Fire beneath all Soul-Flames.

O Eternal Fire, Thou art shooting little flames of souls through the pores of each human consciousness drilled in the plate of the great burner of Thine universal consciousness. Thou dost appear many, limited, small, divided, when Thou dost shoot through the pores of living organisms as souls. But Thou art the one eternal flame, under the pores of all human minds.

78
Demand for Prosperity.

Thou art my Father, I am Thy child. Thou art the Spirit; I am made in Thine image. Thou art the Father who owns the universe. Good or naughty, I am Thy child, and, as such, have the right of possession over all things; but I have been truant and wandered away from Thy home of cosmic plenty. Help me to learn, first, to identify my consciousness with Thine universal consciousness. Rescue my consciousness, shipwrecked on the tiny island of the body. Expand me, and make me feel that I am again Thine image. And when, by Thy grace, I shall find that, like Thee, I am everywhere, then I shall have dominion over all things, as Thou hast.

79
Teach me to feel that all Men are my Brothers.

O, our One Father, teach me to feel that all men are my brothers. Teach me to love all brother-nations as much as the nation in which I am temporarily placed by Thy grace. Teach me, above all, to love those who love me not. Teach me to see Thy presence in my erring brothers. Teach me to heal ignorance-stricken brothers as eagerly as I yearn to be healed myself.

O Mother Divine, teach me to rejoice not in the segregation or punishment of erring brothers when it becomes unavoidably necessary to punish them in order to protect the weaker ones from their tyranny. Teach me to heal the misguided with Thy kindliness, and my better example.

Teach me to feel that even he who does me mortal injury is my brother, made in Thine image; he is only temporarily in ignorance. Destroy in me the vengeful spirit, the "tit-for-tat" spirit. Teach me to heal my criminal brothers, instead of punishing them. Teach me not to increase their ignorance by my wrong ways and revengefulness. Teach me to make them better by my forgiveness, self-control, determination, wisdom, better example, and prayer, and by Thy love.

80
Demand to be freed from self-created Evil Habits and Temptations.

Teach me, O Spirit, to distinguish between the soul's lasting happiness and the temporary pleasures of the senses: touch, taste, smell, sight and hearing. Strengthen my will-power; teach me not to be enslaved by bad habits; teach me to be guided by good habits, formed through good company and meditation; teach me, above all, to be guided by wisdom; teach me to stay away from evil, by right judgment and discrimination; teach me to adopt willingly the good, being guided by my free choice, and not compelled to evil by hardened habits.

**81
Demand for Balance.**

O Spirit, teach me to pray and pray, with deep concentration. O Spirit, balance my meditation with devotion, and purify my devotion with all-surrendering love unto Thee.

**82
Demand for fervor in Divine Love.**

O Spirit, teach me to love Thee as whole-heartedly as the miser loves money. Make me attached to Thee as the drunkard is addicted to wine. Teach me to cling to Thee as erring ones do to their bad habits. Teach me to be as attentive to Thee as a mother is to her child. Teach me to perform my duties diligently and with my attention riveted on Thee. Teach me to love Thee as the worldly man loves possessions. With the first love of true lovers, teach me to love Thee.

**83
Demand that the love of God may never fade, through tests and trials.**

O Spirit, I care not if all sufferings come to me or all things are taken from me; I pray only that my love for Thee may never fade through my own negligence. May my love for Thee forever burn on the altar of my memory.

84
Special universal daily demand for Divine guidance.

O Father, Mother, Friend, Beloved God, I will reason, I will will, I will act: but lead Thou my reason, will and activity to the right thing that I should do.

85
Be the Captain of my boat of daily activity.

O Divine Father, be Thou the Captain of the boat of my daily efforts and bring it to the shore of fulfillment.

86
Be the Pole-Star of my shipwrecked thoughts.

O Heavenly Father, be Thou the Pole-Star of my shipwrecked thoughts, and guide them to eternal bliss.

87
Worship of God as sacred Joy found in Meditation.

O Father, *from joy* I come; *for joy* I live; in joy dost Thou melt me! *Thou art sacred perennial joy;* Thou art the joy I seek; Thou art the lasting joy of the soul. Teach me to worship Thee through the joy born of meditation and good action, and not through pleasure born of the misguided senses.

88 Demand for the enjoyment of everything with the joy of God.

O Spirit, teach me to enjoy Thee in spirit, that I may enjoy the world and my earthly duties with Thy joy. O Spirit, help me to train my senses so that they may enjoy all good things. Teach me to enjoy earthly pleasures with Thy joy. Save me from negation.

89 Demand for Calmness in Activity.

Father, teach me to be calmly active and actively calm. Let me become the prince of peace, sitting on the throne of poise, directing the kingdom of activity.

90 Demand to love God as all Saints love Him.

O Heavenly Father, fill my heart daily with the love and prayer of a new saint who found Thee in bygone ages. Fill my heart with the love of all Thy saints who have ever loved and found Thee.

91 Demand that God's Light drive dark Ignorance away.

O, Divine Friend, if the darkness of my ignorance be as old as the world, still make me realize that with the dawn of Thy light, the darkness will vanish as though it had never been.

92 **Demand for Healing of any bodily disease.**	O Heavenly Father, Thou art in my affected bodily part. It is well—for Thou art there. O Heavenly Father, Thou art perfect. I am made in Thine image. I am perfect.
93 **Demand for Healing others.**	O Spirit, Thou art in me—I am well. O Spirit, Thou art in (him/her.) (He/She) is well.
94 **Demand for freeing the mind from Mental Bacteria.**	O Father, Thou art in my mind—I am Thou. O Father, Thou art strength: Thou art in me—I am strength.
95 **Demand for Wisdom.**	O Spirit, Thou art I—I am Thou. Thou art wisdom—I am wisdom Thou art bliss—I am bliss.
96 **Demand for Bliss.**	O Heavenly Spirit, may Thy fountain of bliss burst through all my thoughts, will, and feelings.

97
Demand that my bubble of life become the Sea of Life.

O Father, I am the wave of consciousness on the bosom of Thy cosmic consciousness. I am the bubble: make me the sea.

98
Demand that God respond.

Thou, O Father, hast come into my temple today. With Thine approach, all the lights of my servant-senses awakened, and all the doors of my heart opened. Through Thy blessing, the darkness of ages is no more. It has vanished at the sight of Thy signal. The loud-beating drums of my craving herald Thy presence. The incense of devotion from the bowl of my soul is rising to Thine altar. Bless me! Respond to me!

99
Demand that God reveal Himself.

O Father, with the bursting language of my craving for Thee, I pray Thee to reveal Thyself. With my soul-grown prayers, I invoke Thee: Come! Appear unto me as Thou art!

100
Demand to the Holy Trinity.

O heavenly Trinity—*Om, Tat, Sat*—: God the transcendental Father, God the immanent Christ Consciousness, and God the Holy Creative Vibratory Force! Grant me wisdom to know the truth! And through my self-effort and knowledge of the law, let me climb the precious ladder of realization—to stand at last on the shining summit of attainment, face to face with the *One Spirit Divine!*

**101
Demand that Cosmic Sound lead from ignorance to Wisdom.**

O Cosmic Sound of *Om*, guide me, be with me, lead me from darkness to light, from ignorance to wisdom, from disease to health, from poverty to prosperity, from misery to eternal joy.

**102
Demand for Thy Light.**

I am here before Thee, O Father, throwing again and again the shafts of my prayer to pierce the bulwarks of Thy dark silence. Shell after shell of my yearning for Thee shall break down the ramparts of my ignorance and my delusion. I invoke Thee to cast about me the searchlight of true wisdom, that I may find Thee in the broken castle of my ignorance.

**103
Demand* for the opening of the Spiritual Eye, to find God in everything.**

My eyes are enthralled, O Father, with the beauty of the flowers, the passing scenes of life, and the sailing, silent clouds. Open that eye in me which sees nothing but Thee. With that gaze—above, beneath, around, within or without may I behold Thee. Teach me to see in all things nothing but Thee. Open in me that eye which beholds in all beauty only Thy reigning beauty!

---

* This demand is to be repeated mentally with deep concentration, until the prayer-thought becomes fixed in the super-consciousness by faith and conviction.

**104
Let all rest in the Shade of my Peace.**

The breeze of Thy love wafts through me, O Father, and the tree of my life gently trembles its leaves in response to Thy coming. The leaves of my soul are just awakening. Their rustling murmur, floating through the ether, calls the weary ones to rest in the shade of my peace, which comes from Thee.

**105
Demand for realizing the expansion of consciousness in the Cosmic Sound.**

Manifest Thyself to me, O Father, as the light of reason, as the blaze of wisdom, as the breeze of amity and harmony. Manifest Thyself through the song of atoms and electrons, and the vibration of their music. Teach me to hear Thy voice—Thy *cosmic voice* which commanded all vibration to spring forth, which commanded each melody to sing its own song. I want to hear Thy cosmic voice, undrowned by creation's multitudinous songs. The magic wand of meditation touches all sounds, and melts them into the One cosmic sound of *Aum*—coursing down the earth, down the sky, and down the stars. Appear to me as *Aum, Aum,* the cosmic song of all sounds. All tissues of my body, all cords of my nerves, now sing Thy cosmic song of *Aum*!

**106
Demand for an Immediate Need to be supplied.**

Father Divine, this is my prayer: I care not what I may permanently possess, but give to me *the power to acquire at will* whatever I may daily need.

107
Demand for removal of the Veil of Illusion.

Veils are around me, Father—they hide Thee from me. I love the gorgeous veils of daisies and roses, the clouds of burning gold. How long wilt Thou remain hidden behind the dark, star-decked screen of night? I love Thy veils because they hint at Thy presence, even though they hide Thee. Yet I want to see Thee as Thou art—without any outward veil.

108
Demand for seeing God in Everything.

O Father, may I behold Thee: above, beneath, behind, around—wherever I turn my gaze! Train the children of my senses to wander not away from Thy home. Turn my eyes within, to gaze upon Thine ever-changing beauty; train my ears to listen to Thine unheard song. I will catch the breath of Thy scented presence. Orient-wise, I will worship Thee, placing on Thine altar the candles of my five senses. So will I contact Thee in the first pale shaft of dawn, in the bright light of noon, in the hidden glow of twilight, in the silver moonlight—keeping alight before Thee, always, the mystic taper of my love.

109
Demand to be kept Awake and Ready.

O Father, if Thou wakest me, how can I ever sleep again? If sleep should steal over me, wilt Thou wake me again? The terrors of the dreamland of life are forgotten now. My sorrow Thou hast changed into tears of joy. My joys are blazing into bliss. My body-temple is filled with light. The rays of Thy light will keep the eyes of my wisdom from drooping. I thank Thee, my Father, for keeping me always awake and ready!

**110
Master Mariner, come and take charge of my Boat.**

O Father, my little raft of meditation is floating toward Thy shore, buffeting the furious storms of distraction. The sea of my mind is rough, yet I am heading toward Thy shore. Master Mariner, come, take charge of my boat!

**111
Demand to find God at any time and anywhere.**

Teach me, O Father, to find Thee within, that I may find Thee without. Teach me to find Thee without, that I may find Thee within. Teach me to find Thee within and without—in the silence within, and the noises without. Noise or silence, I care not, if Thou wilt teach me to find Thee at any time and anywhere.

**112
Demand for Union with the Almighty.**

O Father, behold me through the pores of the sky, and through the twinkle of the stars. Watch me through the sun and moon. Caress me through the breeze. Love me through my love. Throb in me through my heart. Breathe Thine immortality through this mortal frame of mine. Speak through my voice. Help others through my hands. Use my mind to inspire others. Breathe through my breath, for within this fragile viol Thou alone canst sing Thy complete, eternal song.

113
I want to feel Thee just behind the Voice of my Prayer.

O Father, Thou art just behind my vision, with which I see Thy beauty without. Thou art just behind my listening power, with which I hear Thy voice in creation. Thou art just behind my touch, with which I feel Thy world. In the sweetness of flowers, and in the zest of sustaining food, lies hidden the essence of Thy being—Thine eternal sweetness. Thou art just behind the voice of my prayer. Thou art just behind the mind, with which I pray. Thou art just behind my glistening feelings. Thou art just behind my thoughts. Thou art just behind my cravings for Thee. Thou art just behind my meditations. Thou art just behind the veil of nature's splendors. Thou art just behind the screen of my love. *Reveal Thyself as Thou art*, behind these mystic screens.

114
Demand for the Realization of God's Presence.

O Divine Father, Thou art just behind my prayer—but why dost Thou seem so far away? Thou dost tremble through my feelings, and Thy presence pushes through the veil of my thoughts, yet Thou seemest so far away. Come, Father, take away the veil! Come, Father, come! Listen to the voice of my prayer. I want to know Thee. I want to talk to Thee. I want to hear Thee speak to me. I want to pray to Thee, and know that Thou dost hear my prayer. Show me the way that leads to Thee.

115
Prayer between Sleeping and Waking.

O Father, when I am on the borderland between wakefulness and sleep, Thou dost come and play with me—Thy servant. I float in the ocean of Thy love. I dance on the boisterous waves of emotion. I play hide and seek with Thee. Thy greatness makes me, Thy servant, sit on Thy throne.

116
Prayer-Demand for Devotion.

O Father, let me hold my heart in my folded hands. Teach me to saturate my prayers with Thy love. Give me the simple, sincere devotion of a child, toward Thee. Teach me to realize Thy nearness behind the voice of my prayer. Teach me to realize Thy breath in my own breathing. Teach me to feel Thee in my emotion. Teach me to know that Thy wisdom is in my understanding. Teach me to feel Thine all-pervading life in my life. Flood my senses with Thy light.

117
Prayer-Demand for Illumination.

O Spirit, beloved Father, Oversoul of the Universe, Spirit of Spirits, Friend of Friends, teach me the mystery of my existence! Teach me to worship Thee in breathlessness, in deathlessness. In the fire of devotion, burn my ignorance away. In the stillness of my soul—come, Spirit, come! Possess me and teach me to feel Thine immortal presence in and around me. Come, Spirit, come! Come, Spirit, come!

118
Prayer before Meditation.

O Father, my little prayers are all aroused in reverence, waiting for Thee. My little joys are dancing in tune with the temple-bells of harmony. The muffled drum of my craving beats deep for Thee. My passion, my ignorance, tremblingly wait to be sacrificed before Thine altar. I shall say my prayers with mystic beads, made of my crystal teardrops and polished with my love for Thee. I shall cleanse the altar of my heart with my repentance. Come! I pray for Thy presence!

119
Hidden in the ashes of burnt sadness, I found Thy Golden Presence.

Father Divine, banish me not in silence. I stand lonely without Thee. Let me not become imprisoned in my work, so as to forget Thee. I will go within, to bring Thee without. Where Thou hast placed me, Thou must come. Hidden in the ashes of my burnt sadness, I shall find Thy golden presence.

120
Receive the orphans and the stricken, who have come to Thy door.

The orphans and the stricken have heard of Thy healing power. They have come to Thy door. Wilt Thou turn them away empty-handed? Those whose hearts are breaking with sadness and despair: may Thine invisible hand dry their scalding teardrops. Those who are lost in delusion: to whom shall they turn but to Thee? Lift Thine unseen veil of silence and appear in all Thy divine compassion. With the advent of the dawn of Thy presence, their dark troubles will take wing.

121
Come to me as Kindness.
(Inspired by Ram Prasad's Song)

Will that day dawn on me, O Divine Mother, when the utterance of Thy name will cause a flood of tears which will inundate the drought of my heart, and burst the dark gates of my ignorance? Then, in the lake of my gathered tears will grow the lotus of luminous wisdom, and the darkness of my mind will be dispelled. O formless, all-pervading Mother Divine, come to me in the form of tangible kindness, and take me away from the shores of sadness.

122
Satisfy my Soul-Hunger.

O All-Pervading Spirit, the breeze of Thine inspiration has removed the clouds from my heart. The firmament of my mind is clear, and with a purified soul, I behold Thee alone—everywhere. The sunshine of Thy joy rapidly spreads to the farthest reaches of my being. After my hunger of ages, I feed upon Thy light. By Thy grace and by my constant wakefulness, may such joy be mine, forever and forever.

123
O Divine Hart, I will hunt for Thee in the forest of my Soul.

O Divine Hart, I ran after Thee, equipped with spears of selfish desires. Thou didst fly! I raced after Thee in the plane of loud prayer. It crashed to the earth of my restlessness, and the noise frightened Thee away from me! Stealthily I crept upon Thee with the dart of my concentration. But my hand shook with unsteadiness, and Thou didst bound from me, and Thy feet echoed—"Without devotion thou art a poor, poor marksman!" With firmness of devotion, as I held the dart of meditation, I heard Thy divine steps resound again—"I am beyond thy mental dart; I am beyond!" At last in despair, I entered the cave of celestial love and, lo! Thou, the Divine Hart, camest willingly within.

124
Make me the Drops of Sympathy in tearful eyes.

May my spark commingle with Thy great spark and twinkle through all eyes. Bless me, that I may swim in the sea of souls. Make me slide with Thee on the avalanche of noble desires. Make me feel Thee in the budding hopes of rosy minds, and the silence of saints. Make me the drops of sympathy in tearful eyes. Thou and I will dance with the waves of feelings, and cheer all hearts with Thy divine delight. Thou and I will be the throb of life in all souls.

125
From peak to peak and heart to heart, I will Fly, singing Thy name.

Bless me, my Father, so that I may fly with Thee from peak to peak, or lie on the grass and sing Thy song to the birds. Bless me, that I may wade through human hearts to bring them the song of Thy glory. Bless me, that I may whirl around the starry rim and blaze Thy name. With the nebulae, I will spread Thy holy name. Bless me, that with the humming atoms I may time my song with Thine.

126
Teach me to Dream Peace with the poppypetals.

Teach me to descend as rain drops on thirsty soul-flowers, and shower Thy nectar-name. Teach me to dream with the poppy petals their golden dreams of Thy waking light of peace. O Divine Breath, blow with me as the little breath of men and the vast breath of all things living.

127
Whether dead or living, I am held in Thine Immortal Arms.

Mother Divine, the brave may laugh while passing amidst flying bullets, though death lurk in every one. But I laugh because, whether I float on the surface of the present life, or sink beneath the waves of death, I rest on Thy protecting, omnipresent eternal life—I am held in Thine immortal arms.

128
I beheld Thee hiding behind the Flowers.

I looked at a flower and prayed. Suddenly, O Father, I beheld Thee, hiding there. The perfume of Thy presence, it exhaled. The blush of Thy purity colored its petals. The gold of Thy wisdom shone in its heart. Thine all-embracing, upholding power filled the delicate calyx. The mystery of life and Thine immortality lay in the pollen—on the breast of the bee tasting Thy sweetness. O teach me Thy wonders of creation, which even the tiniest roadside weed bears on its bosom!

129 Thou art slowly rising on the horizon of my Mind.

O Father, I pray that my storm-tossed soul may find the silver lining of Thy presence behind the clouds of my indifference, and the moon of Thy hope may gleam in my heart. Thou art slowly rising on the horizon of my mind; mists of ignorance are clearing with the coming of the moonbeams of Thy love. O Father of light, my shipwrecked soul rejoicingly beholds Thy shores of bliss.

130 Demand to see the love of God in all human love.

With the love of all human loves, I have come to love Thee, Thou God of all loves. Thou art the protecting father. Thou art the little child, lisping love to his parents. Thou art the mother, showering infinite kindnesses. Thou dost flow in the all-surrendering love of the lover to the beloved. Thou art the love of friends. Purify me with the reverence of a servant to his master. Teach me to love Thee with all pure loves, for Thou art the fountain of love, heavenly and earthly. Bathe me in the spray of all loves.

131 Open my Inner Eye.

Open my inner eye, O Fountain of Light, that I may behold Thee in the dance of myriad hued atoms. Burst open the doors of space, that I may see Thee behind the mists of the illusion of matter. Thou dost hide behind the walls of Thy brilliant cosmic rays. Open the portals, that I may see Thee everywhere.

**132
Cure my jaundiced Vision of Duality.**

I have long been suffering from the jaundiced vision of duality. Everywhere, pale matter distorts Thy living presence. Wilt Thou heal my sight, that I may behold, with the eyes of wisdom, *Thy presence only*, everywhere?

**133
Demand for Quickening Activity.**

Let the waves of Thy power dance on the river of my activity. As Thou art intelligently busy in making atoms, flowers, universes: so teach me to be cheerfully busy always. Thou art ever busy and yet eternally smiling through joyous hearts. Bless me, that I may wear Thine unfading smile, while working in the factory of life.

**134
Bless me, that I may perceive Thee through the windows of all activities.**

Bless me, that I may perceive Thee through the windows of all joyous activities. Mayest Thou look at me and cheer me always, while I am engaged in my duties. Let my every activity—waking, sleeping, dreaming—be sprayed with Thy presence.

135
Teach me to perform every Work just to please Thee.

Father, teach me to perform every work just to please Thee. Let me feel that Thou art the electricity of my life, which moves the machinery of my bones, nerves and muscles. In every heart-throb, every breath, every outburst of vital activity, teach me to feel Thy power.

PRAYERS OF DEVOTION

136
I bring for Thee the Myrrh of Devotion.

With folded hands, bowed head, and heart laden with the myrrh of reverence, I come to Thee. Thou art my parents; I am Thy child. Thou art the Master; I am ready to obey the silent command of Thy voice. I conjured the fragrant devotion of all hearts and mixed it with my tears. Now I am ready to wash Thy feet in the silence. A river of my ardent crystal tears of craving will rush to meet Thee. Wilt Thou see that my boisterous flood of devotion is not lost in the desert of disappointment? Wilt Thou see that my mad flood of devotion follows the right course, which leads to Thee?

137
Intoxicate me with the Wine of Thy Love.

Intoxicate me with devotion's wine: I will drink of Thee until death. My earthly desires shall die, and I will live in Thee for ever. A thrilling fountain-spray runs throughout each cell of my body and through each opening of my love for Thee. Saturated with devotion, I will enter the heaven of Thy presence. Blindly groping, the urge of my devotion suddenly flings open the soul's secret door, and O, what bliss I feel at the sight of Thy light!

**138
Open my
Soul's Secret
Door.**

I am crying in the wilderness of my loneliness. With eyes closed, I long have knocked at the doors of darkness, that they might open and reveal Thy light. With the million thirsty cravings of my heart, I long for Thee. Wilt Thou come?

**139
I want to
hear Thy
song in the
silence of my
Soul.**

Thy gentle voice saying, "Come home," I often heard; but it was drowned in the noise of the wild cravings of many lives. Then I forsook the jostling crowds of desires. In the solitude of my mind, my devotion is bursting to hear Thy voice. Take away the dreams of earthly sounds, which yet lurk in my mind: I want to hear Thy quiet voice, ever singing in the silence of my soul.

**140
Nothing can
steal my Love
for Thee.**

No loud or whispered words of prayer shall steal my love for Thee. With the soul's unspoken language I will express my urge for Thee. Thy voice is silence, and through my silence, Thou must speak to me and tell me Thou didst love me always, but that I knew it not.

141
I will be the naughty baby of the Divine Mother.

In the hall of life, decorated with mountains, cataracts, and wild scenery, I have played long. When tired of play, each time I cried for Thee, Thou didst drop to me, through the window of my desire, new dolls of fame, friends, prosperity—to quiet me. Now, this time, Divine Mother, I will play the naughty baby. I will sob unceasingly. No more toys of earthly pleasures shall stop my cries. O Divine Mother, Thou wouldst best come soon, or I will wake all creation with my cries. All Thy sleeping children will wake and join me in a chorus of wails. Forsake the busy-ness of the housework of Thy creation! I demand attention. I demand Thee, and not playthings!

142
Make me clean again, Divine Mother.

Dressed with Thy luster, clean and holy, Thou didst send me to play. I played in darkness, with ignorance, and lost myself in the mire of suffering. I went out clean, but I came back to Thee all besmirched with the mud of delusion. O Divine Mother, wash me with Thy wisdom and make me clean again.

143
I loved all things, that I might learn to crave Thee only.

I may lose everything and be roaming in darkness, but O Divine Mother, see that the tiny taper of my remembrance for Thee be not extinguished by the gusts of disbelief. I loved all things, only to find that I craved Thee alone. Come! Be with me always!

144
Make me feel Thee through the Touch of the Breeze.

Father, make me feel Thee through the touch of the breeze and the sunshine upon my body. Enter into me through the fragrance of flowers. Make me feel Thee ever through my innermost thoughts. Forget me not, though I forget Thee. Remember me, though I remember Thee not. Be with me always, always, always!

145
Make me Win the Battle of Life.

O King of Kings—train, Thou, in the camp of discipline, the nobilities of self-control and calmness in me. Be Thou their Divine General, like Krishna of yore, against the invading hordes of darkness, passion and greed. Protect, Thou, the celestial kingdom of my mind against the entry of the tenacious evil warriors. Let Thy banner of peace forever wave over the living soil of my soul.

146
Demand to eject enemies of Bad Habits.

Fierce foes, obstinate unhallowed habits of restlessness, often entrench themselves in the territory of my heart. Let me defeat my enemies, who are bent on robbing me of my wealth of peace. Lead Thou my battling power to the kingdom of fulfillment.

147
Demand not to be enslaved by the ego or by passivity.

I want to use my own will; but lead it, O Father, for use in the golden paradise of all fulfillment. For I would be infinitude's happy child, knowing that Thou hast not limited me behind the prison bars of fruitless desire and withered hope.

I would break the shameful cords of lethargy, and step forth in fearless freedom, to blaze my way through forests of limitations and delusions.

O! My little, vain ego may strut in pride, saying : "Behold my glory! Worship *me!*" But I will look beyond its shadowy form and see the unimaginable beauty of Another Form. The silence-tuned ears of my soul shall ignore the tiny, boasting masquerader, impersonating Thee, and listen in rapture to the wind-winged, fragrant music of Thine own matchless voice, whispering across the ages: "I am He!"

148
I offer Thee a Garland of Devotion.

Let the flowers of my devotion blossom in the garden of my heart, with the dawn of Thy coming. Let me weave a garland of them, and place it at Thy feet!

149
Demand to set fire to the Forest of Darkness.

I built a fire of devotion in the dark forest of delusion, but the fire only smouldered. Then, Thou didst come and set fire to a few frailties. Thy fire quickly spread over the bushes of my prickly desires, over my tall vanities, and through the thick underbrush of my arrogances. The whole forest of my darkness is blazing, and Thy light I behold, everywhere. I thank Thee, Father, for Thy help. Help me thus always—I want to create a path of light for all!

150
Save me from Wrong Beliefs.

I am lost, Father, in the wastelands of wrong beliefs; I cannot find my home. Always I have kept the doors of my soul open, expecting Thee, yet I have not found Thee. Rise on my darkness, and be the Pole-Star of my groping mind. Lead me to Thyself, who art my home!

151
Lead my body-chariot on the Right Path.
(Inspired by the Hindu Scriptures)

Teach me, Thou, to conquer myself by myself. Bless me, that my discrimination may be the charioteer of the steeds of my five senses, holding properly the reins of my mind. Let my soul, in the little chariot of the body, on the wheels of discipline, drive triumphantly over the speedway of many earth-lives, until on the last lap of the last race it shall find itself safe in the limitless royal chariot of the King of Kings!

152
Teach me not to be deceived by the Senses.

O Divine Teacher, train me to recognize the difference between my soul's lasting happiness and the passing pleasures of the senses. Keep my eyes open, that the senses deceive me not by wearing stolen royal trappings and the mirage-cloak of sacred happiness, and so disguised, enter the mansion of my life.

Discipline my unwise, wayward senses, that they may spiritualize their pleasures, and ever look beyond the illusion of glittering, visible form: to find divine pleasure hidden behind simplicity's white robe.

153
Teach me, that my Senses may contact nothing but the Good.
(Inspired by the Hindu Scriptures)

Bless me, that I may behold nothing but that which is good. Teach me, that I may touch nothing but purity. Train me, that I may listen to Thy voice only in all good speech and in the beauty of songs. Direct me to inhale only the breath of purity-exuding perfumes from the flowers of the Spirit. Invite me to indulge in the wholesome taste of soul-nourishing food. Teach me to touch that which reminds me of Thy touch.

154
Keep me away from Evil.

Bless me, that I shall hear no evil, see no evil, speak no evil, dream no evil, think no evil, and feel no evil.

155
Demand for the opening of the Spiritual Eye, the Eastern Star of Wisdom

Bless me, Father, that I may behold the Eastern star of wisdom. May it gleam before my human eyes, alike in daylight and in gloom. My eyes were long blinded by the tinsel-glitter of material things. Always seeing such things outwardly, I saw not the Spirit within their bosom. I looked at the mustard-seed of matter but spied not the oil of Spirit hidden within it. The third eye of my wisdom is now being opened. Keep it, Thou, always open. Let that *single eye* of realization lead me to behold, through all the veils of matter, the infinite presence of Christ, everywhere. Bless me, that the sacred, wise thoughts in me, following this star of knowledge, meet the Christ in everything.

156
Demand for the rising of the Aurora of Intuition.

Infinite Spirit, Thy presence is hidden equally behind the warm rays of the sun and the cool moonbeams. These lights, which reveal only dame nature's gorgeous robe of matter, and not Thee, are but darkness to me. Thus, Thine all-revealing great light hides behind the darkness of matter-revealing lights. Take this darkness away! When I sit with eyes closed, surrounded by my own darkness, cause to blaze upon me in splendor the aurora of intuition, that in its light I may watch Thee with worshipping eyes.

157
Keep my Spiritual Eye open forever.

O Spiritual Eye, once opened, always remain open before me, that I may avoid the pitfalls in the path of life and take the highway which leads to Thy palace of peace. Show me the solution of all my problems.

158
With every stroke of my Prayer, I am moving nearer to Thee.

Father, I am Swimming in the sea of my craving for Thee, beaten by the winds of severe trials. As I float on the crest of the waves of pleasure and pain, or sink down into the depths of indifference, still am I looking for Thy shoreless shore. With every stroke of my powerful prayer I am moving nearer to Thee. I shall never give up, for I know that Thou lookest for my coming.

159
Demand to be fed with the Cosmic Rays.

I started to enter the temple of silence. I switched off the dazzling, diverting lights in the bulbs of eyes, ears, taste, smell, touch; I told the blood-cleansing breath to make no noise. I told the heart that it should enslave my myriad cells with physical blood no longer, for I heard Thy footsteps, O Divine Mother, as Thou didst come, bearing with Thee a cupful of life-sustaining spiritual rays.

Feed me with them, O Divine Mother, evermore! The heart, the cells, the mind, the thoughts, will no longer waste with decay, for they are immortalized with Thine everlasting life.

160 Demand for the Cure of the Anger Habit.

O Spirit, Father, save me from attacks of the fever of wrath, which burn my brain, shock my nerves, and poison my blood.

O Father, when I am angry, place before me my mirror of introspection, wherein I shall behold my face made horrid and ugly by my wrath. Father, I do not like to be seen with a disfigured face, so do not let me make my appearance before others with a wrath-wrecked countenance.

Father, teach me to dissolve this anger, which makes me and others so unhappy and miserable. Bless me, that I may never soil by selfish vexation the love of those whom I love and who love me.

Bless me, so that I shall not feed my anger by allowing myself to become still more angry. Teach me to cure anger-wounds by the salve of self-respect and the balsam of kindness. Command the lake of my kindness ever to remain undisturbed by the waves of misery-making anger-storms.

Make me know, O Father, that even my worst enemy is still my brother and that Thou lovest him, even as Thou lovest me.

**161
Demand to
be able to
Conquer
Fear.**

Infinite Spirit, teach me to comprehend the utter uselessness of being afraid. Help me to remember that death, if it must come, does not come twice; and that when it does occur, through the mercifulness of nature, I shall not know of it nor care. Thus, I need not tremble at the thought of death.

Teach me not to paralyze my nerves by the dread of any imagined accident, and thus invite it to happen in reality.

Bless me, that I do not through fear anaesthetize my unlimited power, as Thy child, to overcome the tests and trials of life. Make me know that whether I am awake or asleep, alert or dreaming, *Thine all-protecting presence encircles me.*

Make me feel that, though I may be in a strong, man-made castle and clad in armor, I am vulnerable to disease, earthquake and accident if I am without Thee, but that, though I walk where bullets fly or bacteria abound, I am protected behind the battlements of everlasting safety if Thou art with me.

**162
Demand for
Control of
the Unruly
Senses.**

O Spirit, let not my insatiable sense-cravings be fed with wrong actions. Teach me to discipline them, that they may want only my true happiness. If my senses become unruly, teach me to govern them with the rod of non-cooperation with their desires, and to feed them only with wholesome activity.

As electricity can either illumine or destroy a building, so human power can glorify or devastate a life. Let me, then, learn to govern wisely the finite forces Thou hast entrusted to me, so that each possession with two-fold potency may be used for good only.

Let the greedy flames of my many desires destroy even their own dross in the white heat of Thy wisdom.

Let me, O Spirit, co-operate with Thy will, harmoniously playing my little note, doing my little deed, singing my little song—until all of my unruly senses conform joyously to the harmony of Thy plan.

Let sense-craving be transmuted into soul-craving. And, O Spirit, let me feel the rod of Thy discipline if ever I stray senseward, from the path of Thy desire!

163
Make me feel that everything is Joy.

I am the sea foam of happiness, spumed out of the sea of joy. The ocean of my life bounds with the billows of joy. And the endless ripples of my laughter and eddies of life, after spreading through all hearts, will retire to sleep on the bosom of infinite joy. I am a ripple of joy, seeking to dance with all billows of joy. I am a ripple of joy, struggling to be the ocean of joy. Make me the lighthouse of joy, guiding storm-tossed vessels of life to safety, to the shores of joy. Let every vine of activity bear clusters of joy. Let me drink the divine wine extracted from the vineyard of all life's little joys.

164
Slip Thy dewdrop in Thy Pool, not to lose itself, but to enlarge itself.

Teach me to be like Thy love-enchanted dewdrop, sliding over the lotus-leaf of seductive sense-lures to Thy glistening waters of wisdom. I am Thine immortal dewdrop, playing o'er the leaf of present-past-future.

I oiled the track of my mind with wise restraint, so that the thirsty pores of temptation might not drink my strength.

I am Thy prodigal dewdrop quivering on the hollow, trembling leaf of life and death, which floats in Thy shoreless sea. I am Thy truant dewdrop, homeward bound at last.

After this dance of rhythm, after the rising footsteps of birth, and the falling footsteps of the symphony of death, I will slide into Thy sea.

I do not want to lose myself—only Thy tiny dewdrop craves, by Thy contact, to be a larger dewdrop of eternity.

I will be a rainbow-hued, omnipresent dewdrop, imbibed by all God-thirsty lips.

165
The fire of my ambition and all my rainbow-dreams, are for Thee.

The fire of ambition has been waxing strong, fed by the fuel of my rainbow-dreams. As often as old dreams faded, fresh die-hard hopes burst into new, thirsty flames, that swallowed up many a sturdy tree of my fresh powers.

My garden was green with life. Now, gray ghosts of half-dead vitalities glide amid dark doubts, to frighten my timid footsteps marching toward Thee.

Come Thou to my aid, Divine Friend, and usher me ever forward with Thee.

166
We buy everything but Thee. Pray give me Thyself.

O God, let me not whine with complaint and say: "Thou hast kept me yoked to the heavy demands of flesh-needs, hunger and earthly comforts." I blame no business man for being busy. Hast Thou not kept the bee busy? the rain, watering the life-yielding crops? and the dark water-wagons of the skies sprinkling life-liquid to thirsty greens?

The Master Potter of life molded earth's clay-ball, and is ever busy whirling it round its orbit , keeping it ray-strung to the sun and revolving in rhythm around it.

The Cosmic Potter forms the fragile vessels of flesh by the trillions, from His wheel of life. The amoeba, the whippoorwill, and the gigantic, fiery-eyed planets, growling in the forest of space—all are leashed to do some of His work.

Even the fickle fire of the sky has to help in the spraying of showers.

O Lord of all Life, Thou art the busiest of all Thy workers. Thou art ever alert, noting the fall of a sparrow, attending the slightest scratch of flesh and coursing the path of meteors.

Thou art producing *everything* out of Thine unseen creation-factory. Thou art the Maker and Displayer of Thy nature-products, and Thou art the Divine Salesman, selling health, mental electricity, and nuggets of wisdom to us.

And Thou dost make us pay for everything! We pay in effort for hygienic living and for acquiring right food with which to buy health. We pay coins of culture to Thee to receive the current of power which lights our cozy mental cottage. And we pay nuggets of devotion, perchance, to hold Thee.

We can buy all other things by paying something for them; but I am sure Thou art not for sale, though Thou art well aware that some people try to buy Thee.

O Priceless One, Thou canst not be bought; there is no par value on Thee.

Yet Thou dost freely *give* Thyself when we know that we are Thy children: heirs of Thy all-containing kingdom and of Thyself.

167
Teach us to consider no work more important than Thy Work.

O Spirit, teach us to consider no work greater than Thy spiritual work, as no work is possible without borrowing from Thee the power to perform it.

Teach us to feel that no duty is more important than our duty to Thee, since no duty is possible without Thee; and teach us to love Thee above everything, as we cannot live or love anything or anybody without Thy Life, Thy love.

168
Bury the seeds of my Devotion in Thy heart-soil.

In the dawn of awakening, I beheld the gathered dewdrops of repentance resting on Thy many-petalled lotus-feet. In those dear dewdrops, my soul cleansed itself. The drought of despondency is dispelled by the shower of Thy blessings.

The petals of past, present and future—of dawn, noon and night—all opened out, revealing the tenderness of Thine ever-expressing life.

Bury Thou, unceasingly, the seeds of Thy blessings in the prayer-plowed soil of my heart, and let them grow into plants bearing many fruits of realization.

169
I want to know that Thou wilt be Mine.

I care not if I have to shatter all desires, or jostle through a host of sextillion lives, or undergo the throes of birth or pangs of death, or of all pains—if I can but find Thee. And I mind not if I leave a mangled heap of my fleshly form, in my struggles to reach Thee.

In exchange for all my happiness, I want Thy happiness. All elusive joys I disown for Thee. Thy joy alone is mine, alone is mine.

Tell me clearly Thou wilt surely be mine! Then, I can patiently wait a hundred thousand years, as if they were but a day.

Tell me—*wilt Thou be mine?*

170
Teach me to drown in Thy Light and Live.
(Inspired by a Hindu song.)

I come to Thee with the song of my smiles. Whatever treasures lie in the secret safe of my soul, I have brought eagerly to Thee. I have brought all the honey from the hive of my heart. Whatsoever is mine, that also is Thine.

The sun of my fickle hopes and happiness has burned me with dissatisfaction; and now my desires will forever quench their thirst, drinking of Thee.

The taper of my happiness will merge with Thy blaze of bliss. The aroma of Thy scented flame and its murmuring joyous waves come floating to me. In Thine enchanting light I will swim forever. Teach me to drown in Thy divine light and *live,* rather than live in a mirage-paradise of earthliness and die.

171
I want to pour the scent of gratefulness at Thy feet.

The doomsday clouds of inevitable happenings thundered; the showers of quick-flickering joys and hard-beating trials shot out to drench and drown the soil of my courage; a million difficulties sprang forth with knives of destruction, ready to stab me.

When cannons of uncertainties are booming, and shells of suffering are falling fast around me, then must Thou make me feel that I am protected in the impregnable trench of Thine immortal arms.

When the light of fortune dawns on the dark tree of hard struggles, it is easy for its answering flowers of gratitude to open out and welcome the light of Thy grace.

During the dark nights of misfortune, I want the flowers of my appreciation to exhale the scent of gratefulness at Thy feet of sacred silence.

172
My Soul-Submarine is searching for Thee.

The searching submarine of my soul fled from the dark vapors of earthly ambitions and dived into the unplumbed regions of cosmic consciousness.

Swimming like a whale, the submarine of my mind moved in Thy deepest astral sea in search of Thee. The long-strained searchlight eyes of my soul-submarine suddenly wore the mystic flaming radiance of Thy blessings, and I beheld Thy presence everywhere.

173
Bless me, that I may know that I am Dreaming, while I think that I am Awake.

As we rest, and wake a little, to slumber again—so from beneath the cover of fleeting dreams of birth and death we rise for a while and fall asleep again, and dream another earthly dream of struggle.

On the sleigh of incarnations, we slide from dream to dream. Dreaming, on a chariot of astral fire, we roll from life to life. Dreaming, we pass through dreams, failures, victories. Dreaming, we sail over trying seas, eddies of laughter, whirlpools of indifference, waters of mighty events, deaths, births—dreams.

It was only in Thee that I awoke!

And then I knew that I had been dreaming, while I thought I was awake.

174
I locked my Sacred Aspirations in my Soul-Vault.

My finiteness has slumbered, cradled in the arms of Thine infinite perception. The noisy pleasures have quieted down at the sound of Thy softly-treading feet of peace.

I awoke and waited.

Whistling elations, soul-melodies, chant-buds, burst out to welcome Thy majesty, O King Silence, approaching my peace-decked throne.

Darkness-hidden, diamond-chips of broken dreams, dimly glittered in the flash of Thy visit.

I removed my sacred aspirations and all the priceless bonds between Thee and me, which lay so long locked in the vault of my memory, and cashed them into love's invaluable gold. With this, I would build Thee a secret, ever-enduring temple within my soul, wherein will rest Thy throne of peace.

175
Dance in me Thy dance of Infinity.

Thou lovest, O Mother Divine, to dance the dance of destruction.

Thou dost shatter fragile mortal flames in Thy war-dance of destruction, to show, smilingly, that our souls remain unbroken.

With Thy mercy Thou dost scale the hardened, mud-encrusted cover of delusions coated over us.

Since Thou lovest the dance of devastation, Mother, I have cremated all my desires, frailties, weaknesses and finiteness, forever and ever, and joined Thy dance of destruction of all evils.

O Mother, since now nothing more is left of my finiteness for Thee to destroy, dance in me Thy Dance of infinity and of love, instead.

176
We are Thy burned children, wailing for Thy help.

The fascinating fire of false red pleasures attracted Thy children to play with it.

Thy silent voice warned them of the scorching, burning power of these desecrating flames. But eagerly they rushed, and tried to seize the flames of temporal exhilarations. Some plunged greedy hands into the devouring blaze, and their fingers of ambition became badly scorched. And then, their wounds of dissatisfaction and satiety brought wails from them for Thee and Thy help.

O Patient Physician, Thou art ever-near with Thy never-failing unguent of forgiveness and love. O, teach us to heed Thy warning voice, that we may give to Thee our joyous song, instead of helpless wails, as we writhe in unnecessary pain.

We are Thy heedless children, and the playthings of the world allure us. Teach us to play only with the divine flames of Thy Spirit.

**177
I want to Merge in the Vastness of Thy Presence.**

O Fountain of love, make us feel that our hearts are all flooded by Thine omnipresent love. O Great Source of the rivers of all our desires, teach us not to run ourselves dry, nor lose ourselves in the sands of short-lived sense-satisfactions.

We demand from Thee that the rivers of our cravings pass through all lowlands of humbleness, self-sacrifice and consideration for others, and at last, reinforced by Thy torrential blessings, merge in the ocean of all fulfillment in Thee.

Bless us, that the rivulets of all our sympathy, affection and love, lose not themselves in the drought of dreary selfishness.

Let the little, lonely, separately moving streamlets of our love coming from Thee, merge at last in Thine ocean of all-fulfillment.

**178
Blow Thy music through my Shattered Reed.**

Thou Master Piper, blow Thy music through the broken reed of all religions, and bring forth Thy *one theme* of truth. Dress that divine theme with many golden robes of the richness of Thy Spirit.

And O, Master Piper, gather together, from the highways and byways of expression, all incomplete songs of hearts that seek attunement with Thee, and let them flow into the joy of completeness, through the love-played flute of life!

For those familiar shrill-soft notes of Thine, I listened every day in this silence-tuned radio-mind of mine. I tried to tune in for Thee, from so far, far away, and at first many noises of restlessness shot through my silence, but, after a few fine, careful touches of concentration, Thou didst fly on the wings of space—and suddenly I heard Thee singing a silent chorus of all earth's goodness and the nobility of all hearts.

179
Heal my Nerves and install in me a new set of Telephonic Nerves.

My soul-cottage by the little brook of life smiled when Thou camest. O Mystic Electrician, the many-tinted bulbs of my senses refuse to scintillate with Thy light. The nerve-wires are shaken and torn by the winds of a busy life. O Thou, who art the builder of nerves and the maker of the shining currents of life, resurrect the dead wires of wrecked nerves and breathe into them the unleashed current of Thy power, that all the unlighted bulbs of my senses may suddenly shine with Thy glory.

I am the bulb and Thou art the holy light gleaming within it. Thou art *the bulb and the light.* Make me realize this miracle.

Heal the shattered nerves and flood the disease-clouded bulb of flesh with the divine effulgence of Thy light.

180
Make us Transparent, that Thy Light may shine through us.

The sunbeams of Thy love shine with equal ardor on all the members of Thy cosmic family—the prophet, the hero, the moth, and me. It is our own fault if we make ourselves opaque through our own dullness. Teach us to wipe away the mist of error from the mirror of our right understanding.

The arms of our spiritual resistance are weak. O Master Cleaner, switch Thy power into our limbs, that we may cleanse away the dark vapors which settled on our transparency and dared to prevent the free entry of Thy light. Make us unmarred, bright mirrors, reflecting Thee.

181
Teach me to Conquer Discord by holding close my own Harmony.

I care not if the shell-fire of trials whistle around me. And I take no notice of salvo-shots launched in my honor. I mind not if machine-guns of mischief pour their shot at me; for when Thou art with me I am safe behind ramparts of liquid fire; but without Thee, I am unsafe even in the most impregnable fort of modern science. I seek not to rouse the wrath of others and awaken their fiery tempers, but I thank Thee for Thy rock-of-refuge in the hidden recess of my soul.

Bless me that I may heal the shrapnel wounds of inharmony in the flesh of circumstances.

Teach me to dethrone darkness by Thy triumphal coronation, O King Light.

Bless me, that I may be the salve of smiles to melancholy souls; the soothing shower to arid minds; the sentry of light, chasing away the thief of gloom; the nectar of peace to sorrow-parched hearts; the glow of kindness to dispel black cruelty.

Teach me to conquer discord by my octopus-grip on my own harmony. By sincerity, teach me to conquer insincerity. Bless me, that I may overcome the habit of idle criticism of others by censuring myself instead.

And teach me to give the nectar-opiate of Thy peace to groaning minds, that they may rest in Thee.

**182
Baptize the bubbles of my blood and flesh in the flood of Thy Grace.**

The cloud-born rains, the mountain springs, the blood of parents, the milk of mother-breasts, baptized me in the feel of flesh.

My imprisoned soul cried for freedom from behind the bars of fragile flesh and indulgent maternal care. Behind the steel-fenced garden of sweet senses, no more I loved to abide. Then the cloud of silence burst and Thy mercy heavily rained upon me and formed a flood of Thy grace. The rushing of Thy Spirit broke the boundaries of my soul, and I was baptized with Thine embankment-breaking, bounding waters of eternity.

The power of Thy flood of cosmic consciousness broke the enclosing fence of my senses, and the little bubbles of my flesh, blood, and being melted and were baptized in infinite omnipresence.

**183
Demanding Forgiveness.**

Teach me to behold myself in others. As I love to forgive myself my own faults and correct myself silently, so do Thou teach me to forgive others, and quietly suggest that they correct their faults, if they wish it so.

Through the kindly strength of tolerance, instead of the weak brutality of force, let me lead all stumbling and stubborn ones unto Thee.

Teach me to see that Thy light shines equally on good, diamond-bright souls and bad, coal-black beings. Guide Thou my understanding and powers, so that I may turn evil, dark minds into sparkling seers—that they may fully reflect Thine impartial wisdom rays.

Thou didst wipe away the soot of indifference which covered my soul, and it shines with Thy light. I know now that I am Thy child. Likewise, enable me to wash all souls with love, and to behold even the darkest souls as Thy children, as my very own—as my sleeping brothers. Thy light stays hidden even in the weakest gloom-shrouded soul and indefinitely waits to be revealed and appreciated through the power of self-effort-found-good-company. Likewise, soften me with such patience that I shall ever wait and stand ready to help all truth-forsaken souls when they wish to awake.

As even to the condemned murderer Thou dost give fresh chances to be better, in a new, unrecognizable body and in another environment on the tracts of a new incarnation, so teach us to shelter the world-forsaken wrong-doer in the haven of our forgiveness. O, Spirit, may our love's sunshine, received from Thee, dispel the chill in his error-frozen soul!

Thou art eagerly waiting to reveal Thyself whenever the world wants to emerge from the sea of wrong-doing. Thy silence before an error-steeped world proves Thy patience and ever-ready forgiveness. Teach us not to deny our sweetness of help to those who bitterly try us with cruel wounds; but, without any self-expectation whatsoever, teach us to help others to help themselves, so that we may still learn to forgive, even though they should turn against us when we cease to be able to help them.

Teach us to forgive others who offend us most, inwardly first, then outwardly. Bless us, that we may scatter the fragrance of forgiveness, and impart sweet speech for sour exclamations, love for hatred, kindness for anger, and good for injury. Awaken us, that we may feel that even the most night-black soul is only an error-dreaming immortal. With the divinity of our forgiveness, inspire us to awaken him to the consciousness of his celestial sonhood, potential purity, and immortality.

**184
Cutting
through the
Cocoon of
Ignorance.**
I hear Thy voice, O Divine Mother, saying: "You have long remained enclosed in the cocoon of wrong human habits. Come out, before the silk-man, Death, comes to destroy you! Cut the delusive, comfort-making, silken, charming cords of habits, which hold you in their exquisite chamber of death.

"Come out! Cease being a human worm of error, sleeping and dreaming weakness. Come out of the cocoon of delusion! Grow and spread your wings of eternal power and splendor, by spiritualizing your prayers and ambitions.

"Come out! Become the butterfly of eternity! Decorate your wings of realization with nature's infinite charms, and spread them over all space to entertain everything, everywhere.

"Fly through skies of infinity on wings of beauty, attracting all beauty-lovers toward the most beautiful Sun-and-star-dust will glimmer on your wings; driving away gloom from the hearts you will soar past, winging your joyous way as the *butterfly of eternity*."

185
I will hop from Eternity to Eternity.

My golden-gossamer astral body, shining with a spark of immortality, hopped from one blade of existence to another.

Thou hast clothed barren eternity with grass-leaves of man-colored cycles. I will hop to them all, one by one, and I will jump gaily from one pleasure-blade to another, until I rest on the safe hand of Thine assurance. With the living threads of Thy beauty my winsome wings were woven. I will escape from every audacious touch of blasphemous change trying to hold me, until I reach Thine empire of changelessness.

On slow camels of cosmic evolution's lives, and across deserts of deaths, this gossamer body of life has passed from planet to planet, to find at last Thy velvet-soft cushion of revelation.

186
I want to be Thy cleansed Bird of Paradise.

With golden plumes of unfoldment, with the softest down of tenderness, and wearing a costume of grace, color and beauty of form, I am Thy soul-bird of paradise.

My wings of insatiable desire for progress, beat their way through life's somber skies, continually seeking to approach the paradise of peace.

Despondency's darkness daubs the fragile feathers of my sunny mind.

O! Bathe Thy blackened bird of paradise with the cleansing sun-rays of insight, and the soft-singing waters of peace.

187
Bless Thy Humming Bird to drink of Thy honey.

Miles and miles of eternity I traversed, humming Thy name, seeking the garden of my dreams.

I am Thy tiny humming bird; yet I keep the wings of my activity ever working, for I must travel far to find Thy rarest orchid blooms, reveling in a color symphony on the very highest mountain crag of dreams.

I am the humming bird which hums Thy name, and dips its long beak of feeling deep into the heart of golden, blue, marigold, many-hued flower-qualities. May Thy grace save me from tasting any bitter honey of evil.

I am Thy tiny humming bird, buzzing with Thine unceasing power, drinking honey from love-drunk blossoms which grow in Thy hanging gardens of glory and in the humblest wayside plots of human sweetness.

188
Many Doors opened before Me.

Many doors opened of themselves before me because of Thy coming. O Lord, everything shone with life when Thou camest. The temple's marble floor, on which I stood, thrilled me because of Thee. Everywhere dumb matter spoke, spirit-resurrected by Thy touch. Everywhere throbbed the incense-breeze of stillness, bearing to me Thy perfume of bliss.

I behold Thy sanctuary, hidden beneath the broken rocks of silence.

On the altar-stone of sacredness plays Thy fountain of joy.

With uplifted palm-cups of craving, I catch and drink the vital waters of Thy solace, and I know that I need thirst no more.

189
Driving the Rebel-King, Ignorance

O mighty, mystic Judge of Life, I asked Thee in the chamber of soul-stillness: "What is sin?"

Thy dim whispers of silence grew into bright articulations of thought, and I knew the meaning of Thine answer: *The rebel-king of sin is Ignorance.* It is the pioneer originator of all organized evil, the main root of the tree of ill-health, the primal cause of all inefficiencies and soul-blindness.

King Ignorance, and his army of physical bacteria of disease, mental bacteria of incapacities, greed, false ambition, and lack of God-concentration, have been marching to devastate the harvest-fields of nourishing spirituality.

Thy harvest of many fulfillments was about to be reaped, when the cruel feet of error trampled it down. As I was about to weep in despair, I heard Thy voice saying: "The sun of My protection shines equally on thy ruby-days and on thy coal-black hours. So must thou have faith and smile, for the greatest of all sins against Spirit is *not to be happy.* Let the ripple of perpetual smiles play on thy face. Through the transparency of thy smiles, My light will come to thine aid. By being happy, thou dost please Me."

190
Cure Spiritual Deafness and make me listen to the chorus of Noble Qualities.

Can a blind man ever appreciate the beauty and glory of light? Can a deaf man appreciate the song of divine voices?

O Father, how can one, blinded by the brief pleasures of the senses, behold the health and beauty rays which flow from the sun of self-control?

Father, how can the materially rich, but

spiritually deaf, listen to the celestial, peace-giving chorus of noble qualities in the soul of the sacred?

Bless us, that we may behold in the light of good habits, that virtue is more attractive and comforting than vice, and that we may hear Thy guiding voice above all other sounds.

191
Teach me to spend for Others as I spend for Myself.

If, through Thy grace, I hold more wealth than others, teach me to share the surplus with those who have nothing. For it is Thou who art playing poor in one body and acting rich in another. Thou gavest the wealth to Thyself, while playing rich, to test whether Thou wouldst Thyself be broad enough to give Thy riches to Thyself, playing poor.

The fortunate one who cares not for the unfortunate, cannot feel Thine omnipresence. Those blinded by selfish opulence have to be poor again, if they see not Thee in the abode of the poor. The unfeeling rich must be poor again and learn to part with comforts, that they may feel the pinch and pangs of their own and others' wants.

Blessed are those who share Thy gifts, which were given to them that they might learn to give. But those who keep locked away Thine useful gifts, mildewing with idleness, while many of their brothers are wailing by the wayside for help, die in the poverty of an unexpanded soul.

To die rich, without giving anything, is to die poor. And to pass the portals of death as poor, because of giving to others, is really to be rich.

Teach us to consider and feel for others, who have already lost wealth or health, more than we would for our own loss of prosperity or of bodily strength. If we shiver even at the thought of poverty for ourselves, teach us to sympathize still more with those who are already under the wheels of want.

Teach us to spend for others' necessities as happily and freely as we spend for our own real needs. Teach us not to love Thy gifts and forget Thee, the Giver of all gifts.

Those who think more of Thy gifts than of Thee. separate themselves from Thee.

Those who offer Thy gifts to others freely, even as Thou didst give to them, find themselves as one in the many selves of all.

192
Teach me to spend for God's work as I spend for myself.

Give me holy health, but give my brothers more, that I may enjoy my greater health in the *greater myself.*

Give me power, but to my dear ones give it more abundantly, that I may wield the strength of all minds in my united mind.

Give me wisdom, that I may make my loved ones more wise, and that I may feel its rays spreading on the vast tract of merged brother-souls.

Teach me to behold through all eyes, work through all hands, and feel my heart-throbs in all. Teach me to feel, act, strive, earn, and especially to spend, for all—as I do for myself.

I want health, to be a model for others' health as well as for my own. I want to be efficient, to turn inefficiency away from earth's door. I want wisdom's freedom, that I may enjoy my liberty only in the universal freedom of all—in the spiritual emancipation of all!

193
Teach me to see Thine Omnipresent Spirit suffering in the sick.

Teach me to feel that, but for the right use of Thy grace and wisdom, I might have been lame, leprous or blind; and, no matter if I deserved to be lame or blind, I would earnestly crave to be healed.

So do Thou make me feel, whenever I see halt or sorrow-shattered men, that it is Thine Omnipresent Spirit suffering in those forms; and teach me to install in them the health and peace resting in my dwelling of flesh.

Teach me to sympathize with others' cries, wants and sufferings, that I may fight to free them, even as I would fight to free myself.

Craving, struggling, weeping, and smiling for all, may I at last find *Myself* in all.

194
In the Whisper-Sobs of my mind I heard Thy Magic Voice

I pulled down the stubborn veils of material music. And, o Song Infinite, I heard Thy voice. In the wail of the viols, in the humming of harps, and in the whisper-sobs of my mind, I heard Thy song. O magic song of my soul, hidden beneath the strings of my heart, at last I beheld Thy soft, gentle dawning, spreading over the dark firmament of mind. Magic Voice, Thou hast made me forsake the slumber of ages, and here I come to offer all my songs unto Thee, upon Thine altar of ever-solacing song.

195
I will be Thine always

I may go far, farther than the farthest star, but I will be Thine always! Devotees may come, devotees may go, but I will be Thine always.

I may bound over the billows of many lives, forlorn beneath the skies of loneliness, but I will be Thine always.

The world may leave Thee, while engrossed with Thy playthings, but I will be Thine always. Thou mayest take everything away that Thou gavest me, but I will be Thine always.

Death, disease, and trials may riddle and rend me, and yet, while the embers of memory shall flicker, look into my dying eyes and they will mutely say, "I will be Thine always."

My voice may become feeble, fail and forsake me, and yet, with the silent, bursting voice of my soul, I will whisper to Thee, "I am Thine always!"

196
I Baptize myself in the sacred waters of my Tern of Love for Thee.

Through long, winding ways of misgivings, crossing chimerical chasms of age-long separations, racing over endless tracts of lives, dogging the steps of many ambitions, following the trail of many desires, freeing myself from whirlpools of sadness and hilarity—at last I am at my journey's end. I look upon my past travails with joy; every rock of past agony has now opened up a spring of joyous tears. In the sacred waters of those tears of love for Thee, I daily baptize myself.

197
Mayest Thou reinforce our blended Prayers.

The streamlets of our prayers, rushing out together from our hearts, are joined in one mighty flow. These wide and deep-flooded rivers of our prayers are moving swiftly in search of Thine oceanic presence. Our flood is breaking through embankments of indifference, intoxicating human habits, and world-delusions. Our flood is rushing through sands of human oblivion, and is bounding through vast tracts of trials and life-experiences. Yet Thy shores seem far off, and our thirsty flood is impatiently, yet doggedly, seeking Thy shining vastness.

Pour, Thou, the unceasing raindrops of Thy mercy. Reinforce our flood of prayers, and race it triumphantly to Thine ever-waiting shores!

198
Rock me to sleep on Thy Bosom of Peace

Thou hast come into my temple at last. The doors of my senses are open wide. The bird of darkness has taken wing. I am tuning the harp-strings of my heart to sing an old song newly—the song of my age-old love. I will sing unto Thee a song newly-costumed with the fresh notes of my soul.

The waves of my song shall dance on Thine ocean of cosmic-rhythm and float me on billows of devotion to Thy shores.

O lullaby of song-waves, sing to me the song of my beloved mother eternity.

O fairy song of God's love, rock me in thy cradle of melody and bring me sleep on His bosom of peace.

199
I perched in the many trees of Lives and sang Thy songs.

I, the nightingale of heaven, perched in the trees of many lives, and sang Thy songs.

My songs reverberated through the green-clogged veins of soul-leaves fluttering with Thy life. I am the nightingale, which sang Thy songs through the garden of centuries, rousing sleeping souls unto Thee.

I travel, giving concerts of Thy songs in the bowers of hearts, and I will come again and again to lure all the stray song-birds, to teach them Thy songs, and to fly with them to Thy skies of cosmic freedom.

200
Endless throngs of Intoxications visit me.

I attuned my life with Thine, and now my life is an unbroken inspiration. Thy fountain of bliss intoxicates me night and day in my wakeful states, dreams, or hours of deep sleep. O, what has become of me? Intoxication on intoxication! Endless, indescribable throngs of divine intoxications ceaselessly come to me!

O my aged nectar, wine of centuries, I found Thee at last, and I will taste of Thy sweetness, forever, forever, forever.

201
Teach me to fish for all Goodness in the net of Searchlights.

A long time ago I had a mental flashlight: I played with it. Tiptoe I would quickly work it, and it would shoot a searchlight through the dark. In its gleam I would behold, trapped, many, many little golden creative-idea-minnows.

I baited them to catch bigger denizens of my consciousness. But it was dark, and the circumference of my pulling net of light was small, so many a good one slipped away.

Now, I carry a bundle of my nets of searchlights. I bought them from everyone with the precious coins of gold-spun dreams and silver songs. And with these countless dragnets of woven light, all joined together, I will sweep Thy wisdom's ocean. Watch! I will haul all Thy spawn of unborn goodness, schools of bright minnow-feelings, golden deeds—and Thyself!

202
I shall ne'er turn my Gaze away from Thee. Make me see that Health and Sickness both are Dreams.

I take a sacred vow! Never will I throw my love's gaze below the horizon of my constant thought for Thee. Never will I take down the vision of my lifted eyes and place it on aught but Thee! Never will I turn my mind to do anything which reminds me not of Thee! I will abhor nightmares of ignorant acts. I will love dreams of noble achievements. I will love all dreams of goodness, for they are Thy dreams.

I may dream many dreams, but I am ever awake thinking of Thee. In the sacred fire of constant remembrance burning on my soul's altar, I will ever behold Thy face with my ever-watchful eyes of love.

Through Thy grace, I know that health and sickness, life and death, are but dreams. When I finish my dream-story of good dreams, and awaken behind the world-painted screen of delusion, I will behold Thee as the only Reality.

203
In the Bursts of Blue Brine I shall bound with Thee.

In the bursts of blue brine my Spirit bounds in joy on the calm shores. Banished are the discouraging vapors of lowlands and the dry aloofness of proud hills. The salty fragrance dives into my bloodstream and overflows the reservoir of my strength.

Oh! what vitalic volumes of life flow in me through the ocean breeze! Oh, smooth shore by the blue, thou art the heaven of health next to paradise. By the blue brine I will drink health from Thee. As Thou didst knit the deep blue brine with the pale blue sky, so dost Thou weave the vastness of Thy Spirit with our pale faith, trying to spread everywhere.

204
Save us from Religious Bigotry.

Our One Father, we are traveling by many true paths unto Thy one abode of Light.

Make us feel that the diverse religions are branches of Thine one tree of truth. Bless us, that we may enjoy the intuition-tested, ripe, luscious fruits of self-knowledge, hanging from all the branches of manifold scriptural teachings.

In Thine one temple of silence, we are singing unto Thee a chorus of many-voiced religions. Teach us to chant in harmony our love's many expressions unto Thee to break Thy vow of silence and lift us on Thy lap of universal understanding and immortality, that we may hear Thy song's refrain in all our tender chants to Thee.

205
Prayer-demand to reach the One Highway of Realization.

O Beacon of Light and Flower of Fragrance, awaken our senses!

Even as the "*Hound of Heaven*", let us scent the right bypath which leads quickly to the *One highway of realization and straight to Thee*.

O Thou Unfailing Beacon of Light, point Thy Finger of illumination across the darkness of our ignorance—that we may find the *right way*, without being sidetracked and without unnecessary delay.

No matter which bypath of formal worship we may follow, guide us at last to the highway of common intuition, which leads to Thee.

Above narrow lanes of bigotry and unyielding walls of prejudices, let our souls travel safely in Thy plane of upliftment. And let us meet, at last, for universal worship, in Thy temple of free skies (that cannot be walled in by man-made, man-interpreted, man-prescribed beliefs and limitations), where we may chant to Thine omnipresence all the sacred hymns of our hearts!

Teach us the scientific technique of salvation, and the spiritual technique of realization, the light-born child of mother-science.

Even as in this age of physical flight, we may guide our steel-bird planes safely through fog and night-darkness, by following the electric finger of light sent from tower to tower, in man-directed course from city to city, state to state, and country to country.

O! Thou Beacon of Light! Send Thy guiding ray of sweet-scented brightness of knowledge across the darkness of our ignorance; so that we may safely and quickly find our spiritual way from landing-place to landing-place, incarnation to incarnation.

And O! Flower of Fragrance! Send Thy breath of love to cheer us always, as we climb the spheres of realization, on our way to Thee: that we may dream of Thy skiey garden, and speed our souls' journey, in our unquenchable thirst for Thee.

**206
Flowers and
Skies, heralds
of Thee.**

Flowers and skies, and beautiful blossoming scenery in the gardens of heaven—they are but suggestions of divinity.

I enjoy them—I revel in them!

But after they remind me of Him these glorious messengers vanish, and the beauty of my own beloved infinity enthralls me.

**207
Divine
Mother,
come Thyself
into the
waiting
Temple of
our Love.**

Divine Mother, be Thou the only flame in our hearts, burning away all darkness within us.

Divine Mother, be Thou the fragrance ever exuding from the vase of our hearts and permeating the nooks of devoted souls whom we love.

In the tears of our love for Thee, wash away all our love for material possessions. In the tears of communion with Thee, wash away all sorrow forevermore.

Divine Mother, unite our little hearts into a greater heart for Thine omnipresence to rest in, forever and forever. Teach us to behold ourselves as perfect in the mirror of Thy divinity. Let the flame of our love for Thee soar triumphantly above the little hissing flames of earthly desires.

O Divine Mother, may the shooting star of our love for Thee race gloriously through the dark skies of forgetfulness, even as the thunders of boisterous daily activities burst within us.

Divine Mother, temples, organizations, money, a million distractions, have come in Thy divine role to delude us. 'Tis time that Thou dost come *Thyself* into the waiting Temple of our love.

O! Be Thou the pole-star of our wandering activity in the dark night of ignorance, leading us safely to our haven in Thee.

208
O Divine Mother, I am thine, for Thou art eternally Mine.

Divers-colored gorgeous garlands of my devotion will encircle Thy lotus feet of omnipresent love.

I beheld the dance of the feet of Thine activity in the twinkle of the starlets. I beheld the dance of Thy light in the bluebells and the larkspurs. Thy footsteps echoed over bounding billows of aurora lights. I beheld Thy fantastic dance of life in the halls of evolution. But, Divine Mother, the calm grace of Thy bliss-face has remained ever-veiled behind the clouds of appearances and the chimerical veils of my flickering thoughts.

I have waited long to behold Thy face. My impatience has burned with a million tongues of flame, with the flame of my burning craving for Thee.

I burnt the sky. I ignited the stars. I melted the binding atoms of planets. In my melting light, searching for Thee, the heavenly lamps and lights lost their balance in space and plunged headlong. The space shadows, mind shadows, ignorance shadows, all shifted before the strong burst of my life's light.

My powerful light consumed everything; and, as the many arms of my luminous love sought to embrace and hold Thee, the heart of my loving light was broken—for voidness laughed at me from everywhere.

My light wept dewdrops of trickling stars, until all space was filled with the beam of my light. The crying flame called aloud for Thee, everywhere, and in its echo in Thine omnipresent Space, I heard Thy voice, saying without sound: "The light of thy love, which swallowed up everything in one light, is *Myself!* Thou hast sought thyself as Me, and hast kept Me afar from thee. Finding thyself by *Myself*, seek Me no more as apart from thee and as beyond the boundaries of thy heart. *I am thou and thou art I!"*

The earth may be shattered to dust and thrown into cosmic space—pictures of universes may come and go on the screen of time—but I will ever be Thine, O Divine Mother, for Thou art eternally mine.

209
Thou didst reveal Thy silver rays of Speaking Silence.

Divine Mother, I heard Thy voice in the speaking fragrance of the rose. I heard Thy voice in the lisping whispers of my devotion. I heard Thy voice beneath the din of my noisiest thoughts. It was Thy love which spoke through the voice of friendship. I touched Thy tenderness in the softness of the lily.

O Divine Mother, break the dawn and show Thy face of light! Break the sun and show Thy face of power! Break the night and show Thy mooned face! Break my thoughts and show Thy face of wisdom! Break my feelings and show Thy face of love! Break my pride and show Thy face of humbleness! Break my wisdom and show Thy face of perfection!

As I called to Thee in the wilderness of my loneliness, Thou didst burst through the dawn to greet me with Thy joy. Thou didst emerge from the molten door of the sun to pour Thy power into the pores of my life. Thou didst tear away the night of my ignorance to reveal Thy silver rays of speaking silence!

210
In the Temple of United Hearts.

It behooves not Thy lily-tender feet to dance on the hardhearted soil of souls. On the petals of sympathy for others may Thy tenderness dance forever.

Divine Mother, may I feel in my heart Thy heart-throbs; in my happiness, Thy joy; in my activity, Thy power of direction; in my soul, Thy Spirit.

Divine Mother, I lay all the flowers of my love at Thy feet of eternity.

Divine Mother, open wide the bud of my devotion and release Thy fragrance, that it may spread from my soul to the souls of others, ever-whispering of Thee.

I pray that I may behold my love in others, and in the light of that greater love, may I behold Thine unveiled face of peace.

May I behold myself in others, and may I ever perceive Thee enthroned in our united hearts.

In the heart of my whispers, I feel the stir of Thy whispers. In the light of my burning love for Thee, I behold Thy sacred face of silence at last.

O Divine Mother, unite our hearts as one heart, that on the sacred altar of united hearts, we may find Thine omnipresence enthroned forever.

211
I pour my Love at Thy roseate Feet of Immortality.

Blossoms of light I plucked from the heart of the dawn as offerings unto Thee. The lamps of my wakefulness and of dawn, I have lighted in the temple of my morning silence.

I beheld Thy bliss-face come out of the shadow of ignorance, which had kept Thee hidden in my temple for aeons. And seeing Thy face of joy in the mirror of my inner eye, I know that my life's face was made after Thine own blessed image.

In the mirror of Thy love, I have beheld the countenance of my love bearing Thy likeness.

I will blame the fates no more. Beloved Divine Mother, it was my self-made darkness which hid the glory of our love. Now, in the translucent mirror of Thy bliss, I see myself and know myself as perfect joy. And in my unwavering mirror of happiness, I behold Thee—the ever-sacred, only, perfect bliss.

I pour my love at Thy roseate feet of immortality! I pour my heart from the over-flowing chalice of my soul! I pour the intoxicating musk of my reverence at Thy ever-moving feet of progress in everything.

212
All futurity danced in me the Infinite Rhythm.

I disconnected the rays of my mind from the little territory of the senses and switched them on in the land of the infinite. The aurora of my attention spread in all directions, embracing infinity.

When thus I delved into the infinite, thought was no longer veiled behind flesh and appearances, but I stood in the land unveiled, and found streams of rushing, glistening thoughts, felt rippling thoughts of millenniums—of born and unborn civilizations.

All futurity danced in me the infinite rhythm!

213
With the Torch of our Devotion, blaze our dark indifference.

Divine Mother, let all the slaps of our trials wring from us only the one cry for Thy love. Transmute our trial-born wails into unceasing cries for Thee.

O Divine Mother, teach the voice of our pain to sing only Thy soothing songs of joy. Melt our pride in the furnace of Thy purifying flames, and transmute it into the pure gold of humbleness.

Divine Mother, shatter the small hamlet of our selfishness, in which lie huddled all the urchins of ignorance, and build Thy temple of omnipresence for Thy votaries of devotion, reverence, soul-love, to find sanctuary there and to worship Thee with songs of heart-whispers.

In the golden temple of Thy whispers, they will offer to Thee their ever-fragrant frankincense of unceasing soul-chants.

O Divine Mother, we lay at Thy feet all the new-grown, fresh-cut flowers of our eager devotion.

Divine Mother, place Thine omnipresence on the little altar of our united hearts.

Divine Mother, be Thou the only love of our souls.

Divine Mother, ignite our earthliness with the flame of infinity. With the torch of our devotion, blaze our dark indifference, our restlessness and our ignorance.

Inflame our minds with Thy thoughts! Inflame our hearts with Thy love! Inflame our souls with Thy joy!

214
The Rocket of my Love.

I drew my life from my body, and the breath which tied me to the flesh vanished. My burning rocket of life flew through the star in the all-seeing eye of light.

Then the rocket of my bursting feelings spread to countless hearts in atoms, and at last the unchallenged rocket of my love sank like a vast plummet into the deep spaces of the Spirit and into the inmost heart of Thine omnipresent silence!

215
My lost Music sprang from the Heart of everything.

I heard the sweet, enchanted music of my life faintly in the dim bower of my dreams. Atiptoe, I listened, and the music faded ever more and more and became softer and sweeter still, until I could hear it no longer with my earthly ears.

Patiently I waited, striving to think of any music similar to the divine melody of this new music. But no, in my rich storehouse of memory I could find no likeness of the music that had come and gone like the dim ghost of a dream.

Had I really heard that music, or had I only dreamt its harmony? Was it the exquisite, real *music of all my dreams, of all my aspirations*—or was it but the harmonious whisper of a passing dream?

I waited. Deeply I went within. Behind the portals of all senses I fled wildly, madly, to listen once more to the lost music of my dreams.

At last, I saw shining waves of my dreams and all the dear wavelets of my cravings of earthly incarnations dancing therein. I heard many strains of heavenly melodies, but they were not like those I had once heard and lost.

Of a sudden, methought I dreamt and heard again the lost music of my soul.

I beheld every dream at once—and craved for no one music of one dream. 'Twas then that my lost music sprang from the heart of everything—from the living heart of all my dreams.

No ear hath heard,
No thought hath held,
No love hath felt,
No dream hath dreamt,
No tongue hath told,
Can ever tell,
Of that—my beloved music.
But behind the curtains of everything –
I *felt* the lost-and-found
Beloved music of my soul!

216
A million Salutations at Thy petaled feet, O Lotus of Light

A million salutations at Thy petaled feet, O Lotus of Light! I pour my heart at Thy feet. I pour all my soul at Thy feet. I pour all the fragrant musk of my love at Thy feet of omnipresence.

O precious, Blessed One, ever pipe the song of Thy bliss in the dark bower of my heart. I am all Thine own! I shall be Thine forever! I will laugh at all dangers, for always I hold Thy protecting love in the golden chalice of my constant remembrance of Thee.

I throw all my passions and earthly pleasures on Thy sacrificial fire, as the offerings and oblations of my devotion to Thee. In Thy blessed light I shall burn all shadows and fears of my imagination. In Thy blessed light I shall remain awake forever, watching Thy precious, omnipresent face with ever vigilant eyes, through all the aeons of eternity.

May Thy love shine forever on the shrine of my devotion, and may I be able to awaken Thy love in all hearts.

O! Make my soul Thy temple! Make my heart Thine altar! Make my love Thy home!

217
The imprisoned Bird of Omnipresence was released.

Through the door of meditation, the imprisoned bird of omnipresence was released. It flew and spread its wings over infinite spaces. Its wings of joy cast the shadow of peace on every unhappiness-scorched being.

Then, again, the bird of heaven remembered its little cage of past memories of habits, and it folded its wings and lodged itself behind the bars of earthliness.

O bird of eternity, break thy little torturing cage of dreams and fly to thy nest in everything!

218 A Prayer

(Received after a great test of God)

In disease or health, in failure or joy, in poverty or prosperity, in disaster or security, in death or life, I stand immutably, unalterably, unchangeably loyal, devoted and loving unto Thee, my Heavenly Father, forever, forever and forever.

PRAYER-DEMANDS FOR THE USE OF CHILDREN

219
Thou art Love because my Mother loves me.

Dear God, I know Thou art Love, because my mother and my father love me; Thou art my Father and my Mother. My friends love me, for Thou art in their hearts: Thou art my best Friend. Thou art my Teacher; even as Thou lovest me, teach me to love Thee.

220
Teach me to give Smiles to all.

Father Divine, teach me to give smiles to all at all times. Teach me not to laugh at others. Teach me not to hurt others even by a smile. Bless me, that I may make others happy, just as I wish to be happy myself.

221
Come to me as Peace in sleep and as Joy when I am awake.

Dear Heavenly Father, while I sleep, Thou dost come to me as peace. When I awake, Thou dost come to me as joy. When I love my friends. Thou dost come to me as love. When I run, Thou dost run with me. When I think, Thou dost think with me. When I will, Thou dost will with me. Teach me to think, play, behave, and will rightly, for Thou art near me. I love to be guided by Thee, for Thou art my greatest Well-wisher.

222
Thou art so plainly Present everywhere; I bow to Thee.

When I dance with the waves, dear Heavenly Father, I am dancing with Thee. Every day I see Thee painting the sky with bright colors. I watch Thee clothe the bare soil with green grass. Thou art in the sunshine. O, Thou art so plainly present everywhere! I bow to Thee.

223
My parents and friends Love me, dear Father, because Thou dost Love me.

My parents love me, dear Heavenly Father, because Thou dost love me. My friends love me because Thou dost love me. I love my country because Thou dost love it. I bow to Thee.

224
Thou art the Cause of everything—I bow to Thee.

Dear Heavenly Father, the moonlight comes to release me from darkness. The sun comes to give me light. The seasons come to yield me food. Thou dost cause them to do this. I bow to Thee.

225
I bow to Thee in the sunshine, breeze, dawn, and hearts of Loving Friends.

Dear Heavenly Father, when I am thirsty and drink the cool water, it is Thou who dost give its life to me. When I bathe and am refreshed, I feel Thy cleansing, refreshing power in the water made by Thee. When the sunshine falls upon my face, I feel Thy loving, warm touch. I bow to Thee in the sunshine, in the breeze, in the dawn, in the noon, in the evening light, and in the hearts of loving friends.

226
Teach me to find Happiness in the Joy of others.

O Mother Divine, teach me to love others and to serve others. Teach me to be true to my word, even as I want others to be true to me. Teach me to love others as I wish them to love me. Teach me, O Mother, to make others happy—to make others smile. Teach me, O Mother, to find my happiness in the joy of others.

227
Teach me to feel Thee as Silence when I close my eyes.

Father, teach me to understand that which I hear. Help me to practice in my daily life all the good which I learn. Teach me to watch Thee working in nature. Teach me to feel Thee as silence, when I close my eyes. I bow to Thee—*Aum!* Amen!

CHANTS

Make me the Sea.

(From a Bengali Song)

So may it be, my Lord –
Thou and I, never apart;
Wave of the sea,
Dissolve in the sea!
I am the bubble;
Make me the sea!

O God Beautiful.

(From Nanak's* Song.)

O God Beautiful; O God Beautiful;
At Thy feet, O I do bow.
In the forest Thou art green;
In the mountain Thou art high;
In the river Thou art restless;
In the ocean Thou art grave.
O God Beautiful; O God Beautiful!
At Thy feet, I do bow!
To the serviceful Thou art service;
To the lover Thou art love;
To the sorrowful Thou art sympathy;
To the yogi Thou art bliss.

---

*see glossary

I am Om, I am Om.

I am *Om*, I am *Om*,
Om, Om, I am *Om*,
Omnipresent, I am *Om*,
All-blessed, I am *Om*,
Omniscient, I am *Om*!
Om, Om, come to me,
Come to me, O come to me;
O my Guru, come to me,
Come to me, O come to me;
O my Jesus, come to me,
Come to me, O come to me,
Swami Shankara, come to me,
Come to me, O come to me;
O my Allah, come to me,
Come to me, O come to me;
O my Moses come to me,
Come to me, O come to me;
O my Nanak, come to me,
Come to me, O come to me;
O my Krishna, come to me,
Come to me, O come to me;
Om, Om, come to me,
Come to me, O come to me;
O my Father, come to me,
Come to me, O come to me;
I am *Om*, I am *Om*,
Om, Om, Om! Om Tat Sat, Om!

The Door of my Heart is Open for Thee.

The door of my heart,
Open I keep for Thee:
Wilt Thou come, wilt Thou come?
If but for once, come to me!
Will my days fly away without seeing Thee, my Lord?
Night and day, night and day,
I look for Thee night and day.

Lotus-Feet of Divine Mother.

Engrossed is the bee of my mind
On the blue lotus feet of my Divine Mother.
Divine Mother, my Divine Mother,
Divine Mother, O my Divine Mother!

I am He; I am He!

(Swami Shankara chant.)

Mind, nor intellect, nor ego, feeling;
Sky nor earth nor metals am I,
I am He, I am He, Blessed Spirit, I am He!

No birth, no death, no caste have I,
Father, mother, have I none,
I am He, I am He, Blessed Spirit, I am He!

Beyond the flights of fancy, formless am I,
Permeating the limbs of all life,
I am He, I am He, Blessed Spirit, I am He!

Bondage I do not fear; for freedom I do not care;

For I am free, ever free; I am free, ever free,
I am He, I am He, Blessed Spirit, I am He

POEMS

MY INDIA

Not where the musk of happiness blows,
Not in the land where darkness and fears never tread,
Not in the homes of perpetual smiles,
Not in Heaven or the land of prosperity
Would I be born—
If I have to put on a mortal garb again.
A thousand famines may prowl
And tear my flesh,
Yet would I love to be again
In my Hindustan.
A million thieves of disease
May try to steal the fleeting health of flesh,
Or the clouds of fate
May shower scalding drops of searing sorrow—
Yet would I there
In India love to reappear!
Is this, my love, a blind sentiment
Which beholds not the pathways of reason?
Ah, no! I love India
Because there I first learned to love God and all things beautiful.
Some teach to seize the fickle dewdrop—Life—
Sliding down the lotus leaf of time.
Some build stubborn hopes
Around the gilded, brittle body-bubble.
But India taught me to love
The soul of deathless beauty in the dewdrop or the bubble,
Not their fragile frames.
Her sages taught me to find my Self
Buried beneath the ash heaps
Of incarnations and ignorance.
Through many a land

Of power, plenty and science,
My soul, garbed as an Oriental
Or an Occidental, traveled far and wide,
Seeking Itself:
At last in India to find Itself.
If mortal fires raze all her homes and golden paddy fields,
Yet to sleep on her ashes and dream immortality,
O, India, I will be there!
The guns of science and matter
Have boomed on her shores,
Yet she is unconquered.
Her soul is free evermore!
Her soldier-saints each day
Rout with realization's ray
The bandits of hate, prejudice, patriotic selfishness,
And burn the walls of separation dark
Which lie 'tween children of the One, One Father.
The Western brothers by matter's might have conquered my land;
Blow, blow aloud, her conch-shells all!
India now invades with love, to conquer their souls.
Better than Heaven or Arcadia,
I love thee, O my India,
And thy love I will give
To every brother-nation that lives.
God made the earth, and man made his confining countries,
And their fancy-frozen boundaries.
But with the new-found love I behold—
The borderland of my India expanding into the world.
Hail, mother of religions, lotus, scenic beauty, and sages!
Thy wide doors are open,
Welcoming God's true sons through all the ages,
Where Ganges, woods, Himalayan caves and men dream God.
I am hallowed; my body touched that sod!

THE LOST TWO BLACK EYES
(Written after my mother's death.)

Whence came
The black-eyed light
Flickering in my life a moment?
Whither did it flit away?
The twilight of many incarnations
Has burned in those eyes;
Many lights of love dreams
Have met in the bower of yonder eyes.

Today, only the Godless altar—
The lifeless eyes—
Remains before me.
Thou Secret Queen,
From what unknown region
Did'st thou in silence come
To bewitch the fortress of those eyes?

The bitter speech
And sadness-driven
Boat of my life
Many a time found safety
In the harbor of those two eyes.
Now the cruel death-quake
Forever has marred
The dream-harboring eyes.
Losing the harbor of those eyes,
In search I sailed my boat
In the sea of the sky.
Threefold-sorrow storm-driven
Life boat of mine
Has become motherless.
That is why in the unknown region,
In the sea of the sky,
My mind's boat sails on

Directionless
Seeking those two lost eyes.
In the star-eyed lights
All starry eyes
Twinkled black eyes,
But they were not
Those I had lost.

Merely affection-saturated,
Many black eyes
Called—offering to nurse
My motherless sorrow—
This orphan life of mine.
But none matched
The love-call glance
Of those lost two dark eyes.
The love of those two black eyes
Had forever set from the region
Of all black eyes I beheld.
Seeking those two eyes
In birth and death,
In life and dreams
And in all the lands of the unknown,
At last I found the all-pervading
Divine Mother's
Countless black eyes
In space and heart,
In earth-cores, in stars,
Within and without,
Hungrily staring at me
From everywhere.

Seeking and seeking my dead mother,
I found the Deathless Mother.
The lost love of the earthly mother
I found in my Cosmic Mother.
Seeking and searching,

In Her countless black eyes
I found those lost two black eyes.

I asked Mother Divine—
"With ruthless heart,
Why did'st Thou tear away
The diamond of my mother's love
From the ring of my heart?"
The cloud-voice
Of Mother Divine spoke,
Bursting in my firmament within.
"Many times have I fed thee
The blood of My milk
From the breasts of many mothers.
Your black-eyed mother
Whom you lost awhile
Was none else but I, only I.
When I saw
Thy wisdom and cosmic love
Had lost their way
In the dark jungle of those two eyes,
Then I set fire
To the alluring darkness
Of those two black eyes.

"I stole those
Imprisoning two black eyes
That thou might'st be free
To find those eyes
In My eyes,
And in the soulful eyes
Of all black-eyed mothers,
And that thou might'st behold
In all black eyes,
Only the shadows
Of My eyes.
"I broke the dream-made,

Little finite,
Thy mother-form of Mine,
That thou might'st behold Me,
Thy Divine Mother,
In every form of a soulful woman
And in My Infinite Cosmic Form."

I AM HERE

Alone I roamed by the ocean's shore,
And watched
    The wrestling waves in brawling roar—
Alive with Thine own restless life.
Thine angry mood in ripply quiver—
Until Thy wrathful vastness made me shiver
And turn away from nature's heated strife.
And then
    A kindly, spreading, sentinel tree
Waved friendly arms to comfort me—
Consoling me with gentler look sublime,
Its swaying leaves in tender lullaby-rhyme,
Singing a message that I knew was Thine.
Above
    I saw the gaugeless, mystic sky;
And, childlike, in the valley dim I sought to pry
At Thee, and to play with Thee.
But in vain I sought Thy body, hiding there,
Cloud-robed, foam-sprayed, leaf-garlanded—
Too rare for mortal eyes to see, or ears to hear.
And yet,
    I knew that Thou wert always near,
As if to play at hide-and-seek with me,
Receding when I almost touched Thee,
Groping to find Thee through the maddening fold
Of ignorant darkness—old as time is old.

At last,
    I ceased my search in dim despair,
My search for Thee! O Thou Royal Sly Eluder!
    . . . everywhere,
Yet seeming nowhere . . . lost in unplumbed space,
Where none may clasp Thee or behold Thy face!
In haste,
    I ceased my fruitless search and hied *away* from Thee!
Still, still no answer from the wrathful sea,
And only whispers from the friendly tree;
Just silence from the limitless blue sky—
Silence from valley low and mountain high!
Like a hurt child, *within the depths of me*
I hid and sulked-no longer seeking Thee.
When, lo!
    Unheralded, some Unseen Hand
Suddenly snatched away the all-black band
That had so blinded me with fold on fold.
No longer weary, filled with strength untold,
I stood, and watched again
A laughing sea, instead of wrathful roars,
A gay, glad world, with mystically opened doors.
With only mists of dreams between,
Someone beside me stood unseen—
And whispered to me, cool and clear:
    "Hello, playmate! I am here!"

SAMADHI*

Vanished the veils of light and shade,
Lifted every vapor of sorrow,
Sailed away all dawns of fleeting joy,
Gone the dim sensory mirage.
Love, hate, health) disease, life, death,
Perished these false shadows on the screen of duality.
Waves of laughter, scyllas of sarcasm, melancholic whirlpools,
Melting in the vast sea of bliss.
The storm of *maya* stilled
By magic wand of intuition deep.
The universe, forgotten dream, subconsciously lurks,
Ready to invade my newly wakened memory divine.
I live without the cosmic shadow,
But it is not, bereft of me;
As the sea exists without the waves,
But they breathe not without the sea.
Dreams, wakings, states of deep *turiya* sleep,
Present, past, future, no more for me,
But ever-present, all-flowing I, I, everywhere.
Planets, stars, stardust, earth,
Volcanic bursts of doomsday cataclysms,
Creation's molding furnace,
Glaciers of silent x-rays, burning electron floods,
Thoughts of all men, past, present, to come,

---

* Samadhi means oneness of human consciousness with cosmic con-sciousness. The human consciousness is subjected to relativity and dual experience. In meditation, there are: The meditator, the act of meditation, and God (as the object of meditation) . Samadhi is the final result of deep, continuous, right meditation, in which the above mentioned three factors of meditation become one. Just as the wave melt' in the Sea, so the human soul becomes the Spirit.

Every blade of grass, myself, mankind,
Each particle of universal dust,
Anger, greed, good, bad, salvation, lust,
I swallowed, transmuted all
Into a vast ocean of blood of my own one Being!
Smoldering joy, oft-puffed by meditation
Blinding my tearful eyes,
Burst into immortal flames of bliss,
Consumed my tears, my frame, my all.
Thou art I, I am Thou,
Knowing, Knower, Known, as One!
Tranquilled, unbroken thrill, eternally living, ever new peace!
Enjoyable beyond imagination of expectancy, *samadhi* bliss!
Not a mental chloroform
Or unconscious state without wilful return,
Samadhi but extends my conscious realm
Beyond the limits of the mortal frame
To farthest boundary of eternity
Where I, the Cosmic Sea,
Watch the little ego floating in me.
The sparrow, each grain of sand, fall not without my sight.
All space like an iceberg floats within my mental sea.
Colossal Container, I, of all things made.
By deeper, longer, thirsty, guru-given meditation
Comes this celestial *samadhi*
Mobile murmurs of atoms are heard,
The dark earth, mountains, vales, lo! molten liquid!
Flowing seas change into vapors of nebulae!
Aum blows upon the vapors, opening wondrously their veils,
Oceans stand revealed, shining electrons,
Till, at last sound of the cosmic drum,
Vanish the grosser lights into eternal rays
Of all-pervading bliss.
From joy I came, for joy I live, in sacred joy I melt.
Ocean of mind, I drink all creation's waves.
Four veils of solid, liquid, vapor, light,
Lift aright.

Myself, in everything, enters the Great Myself.
Gone forever, fitful, flickering shadows of mortal memory.
Spotless is my mental sky, below, ahead, and high above.
Eternity and I, one united ray.
A tiny bubble of laughter, I
Am become the Sea of Mirth Itself.

Through Oneness in *samadhi*, the dualities of human experience disappear. Everything is perceived to change into Spirit. In this state, the man in *samadhi* can perceive the spiritual ocean, with its waves of creation; or see the same spiritual ocean, transcendentally calm, existing without the waves of creation.

In the first state of *samadhi*, the yogi (one who unites his soul with Spirit by right meditation) is so absorbed in Spirit that he is oblivious of the material and created universe. A somewhat similar experience on a lower plane is experienced when one is so absorbed in books or thoughts that he is unaware of what is happening around him. This state is not unconscious, for unconsciousness implies lack of awareness, both inwardly and outwardly. Such unconsciousness is easily brought about by the use of drugs, anesthetics and other outward means. The full spiritual consciousness of *samadhi*, however, can be attained only through the regular, continuous, right discipline of meditation, and has nothing in common with unconsciousness.

The first state of *samadhi*, in which the yogi finds everything withdrawn and absorbed into Spirit, is called *sabikalpa samadhi*. The higher and greater state of *samadhi* is *nirbikalpa*, in which the yogi, after realizing the Spirit alone—without creation—perceives it also, simultaneously, both as above creation, and as manifested in all creation. Here his consciousness becomes the cosmic consciousness. The domain of his consciousness now extends from his body to include the whole universe. He becomes the Ocean of Spirit, and watches the bubble of his body floating in it. His consciousness perceives all motion and change of life, from the circling of the stars to the fall of a sparrow and the whirling of the smallest electron.

The yogi who has entered into these two states of *samadhi* finds that solids melt into liquids, liquids into gaseous states, these into energy, and energy into cosmic consciousness. He lifts the four veils of solids, liquids, gases and energy, and finds the Spirit, face to face. He sees the objective universe and subjective universe meet in Spirit. His expanded material self mixes with the greater spiritual Self and knows their unity. The spiritual Self, being the first cause, and capable of existing without material manifestation, is therefore greater than the material self.

Thus, the negative conception of God is removed. The yogi, instead of finding cessation of life and joy, becomes the fountain-head of eternal bliss and life. The tiny bubble of laughter becomes the sea of mirth itself. By knowing God, one does not *lose anything*, but *gains everything*.

OM

Whence, whence this soundless roar doth come,
When drowseth matter's dreary drum?
On shores of bliss, *Om*, booming, breaks!
All earth, all heaven, all body shakes!
Cords bound to flesh are broken all,
Vibrations burst, meteors fall!
The hustling heart, the boasting breath,
No more shall cause the yogi's death;
All nature lies in darkness soft,
Dimness of starlight seen aloft;
Subconscious dreams have gone to bed...
'Tis then that one doth hear *Om's* tread;
The bumble-bee now hums along—

Hark! Baby *Om* doth sing His song!
From Krishna's flute the call is sweet:
'Tis time the Watery God to meet!
Now, the God of Fire is singing!
Om! Om! Om! His harp is ringing.
God of Prana now is sounding—
Wondrous, breathing-bells resounding!
O! Upward climb the living tree;
Hark to the cosmic symphony.
From *Om*, the soundless roar! From *Om*
The call for light o'er dark to roam.
From *Om* the music of the spheres!
From *Om* the mist of nature's tears!
All things of earth and heaven declare,
Om! Om! Resounding everywhere!

GOD! GOD! GOD!

From the depths of slumber,
As I ascend the spiral stairways of wakefulness,
I will whisper:
God! God! God!

Thou art the food, and when I break my fast
Of nightly separation from Thee,
I will taste Thee, and mentally say:
God! God! God!

No matter where I go, the spotlight of my mind
Will ever keep turning on Thee;
And in the battle din of activity, my silent war-cry will be:
God! God! God!

When boisterous storms of trials shriek,
And when worries howl at me,

I will drown their noises, loudly chanting:
God! God! God!

When my mind weaves dreams
With threads of memories,
Then on that magic cloth will I emboss:
God! God! God!

Every night, in time of deepest sleep,
My peace dreams and calls, Joy! Joy! Joy!
And my joy comes singing evermore:
God! God! God!

In waking, eating, working, dreaming, sleeping,
Serving, meditating, chanting, divinely loving,
My soul will constantly hum, unheard by any:
God! God! God!

ALL BOW TO THEE

Thou art the One Infinite of the monist;
Thou art God and Nature of the dualist;
Thou art the finite many of the polytheist;
Thou art everything, O God, of the pantheist.
Thou art the God of monists, dualists, polytheists and pantheists.
Thou art both the Infinite Ocean and all its waves of finite creation,
Because Thou art everything—
The souls of monism, dualism, polytheism, pantheism;
All bow to Thee!

GOD'S BOATMAN

I want to ply my boat, many times,
Across the gulf-after-death,
And return to earth's shores
From my home in heaven.
I want to load my boat
With those waiting, thirsty ones
Who are left behind:
And carry them by the opal pool
Of iridescent joy—
Where my Father distributes
His all-desire-quenching liquid peace.
Oh! I will come again and again!
Crossing a million crags of suffering,
With bleeding feet, I will come-
If need be, a trillion times—
As long as I know
One stray brother is left behind.
I want Thee, O God,
That I may give Thee to all!
I want salvation,
That I may give it to all!
Free me, then, O God
From the bondage of the body—
That I may show others
How they can free themselves!
I want Thine everlasting happiness,
Only that I may share it with others—
That I may show all my brothers
The way to happiness,
Forever and forever, in Thee.

FLIGHT!

I closed my eyes and saw the skies
Of dim opalescent infinity spread round me.
The grey chariot of the dawn of awakening,
Displaying searchlight eyes,
Came and took me away.
I zoomed through space—
Boring through the ether of mystery.
I passed through age-hidden spiral nebulae.
Willy-nilly, I went on and on,
Left, right, north, south, above and below.
I found no landing.
I went through many tailspins of distractions,
But I spun through limitlessness.
I whirled through an eternal furnace of lights.
At last, bit by bit, my plane melted
In that transmuting flame;
And then, bit by bit, my body melted
In that purifying fire.
Bit by bit my thoughts melted—
My feelings became pure liquid light.

MY DEVOTION

O Thou Mother of all conscious things,
Be Thou consciously receptive to my prayers.
Through Thee I know all that I know;
And Thou knowest all I know,
So Thou knowest my prayers.
And knowing and feeling Thee constantly thus,
I know Thou art I, I am Thou.
My little wavelet has vanished in Thee.
I know Thou alone existed;
And Thou alone dost exist now and ever shall.

Thou art impersonal, invisible,
Unseen, formless, omnipresent,
But forever I want to worship Thee
As both personal and impersonal.
By my devotion
I beheld Thee
Sometimes as Krishna,
Sometimes as Christ,
Personal, visible and imprisoned
In the little space
Hidden within the temple of my love.
O Invisible, just as Thou didst freeze
Thine unseen Infinitude
Into the sea of cosmic finitude,
So do Thou appear unto me,
Visible and living—
That I may serve Thee.
I want to see Thee as the ocean of life
With and without the ripples of finite creation.
O Creator of all things,
I want to worship Thee both as personal and impersonal.

AFTER THIS

After the prison-petals of earth-life fade,
And the soul-scent slips
Into the mighty cosmic wind of Spirit,
No more would I love a flower-cage life—
If I must return—
Unless to mingle the dewdrop tears of other prison'd souls with mine,
And show them the way that I, at last, my freedom won.
O! I would not mind dwelling
In roses and daffodils, for a time,
If that is of my own free will;

But *forever* to stay behind the bars of beauty
Of violet-sun-gold-rays, I care not.
No more will I be compelled to live
Even in a golden, heavenly cage.
From flower to flower will I fly!
I will wear the blackness of the night,
Shimmering with busy stars—
I will be the twinkle of their lights,
And I will be the waking of the dawn—
And burst forth with the warming rays of friendship!
I will be the shepherd of stray souls,
Or the humblest lamb in all His fold.
I will be the most famous man,
Or the least-known one of a cycle!
I will be the tiniest cosmic spark,
Or roll as the mighty vapors of life,
Dashing my power-fed soul
Against the rocks of worldly strife!
I will be the clouds, donning rainbow-garlands.
I will puff bubbles of planets with my breath,
And float them on the waves of space!
I will be the babble of the brook,
And the voice of the nightingale!
As emotion-waves, I will surge in the sea of souls!
Holding to the log of laughter,
I will float to the shores of bliss!
I will sing through the voices of all;
I will preach through all temples and prayers;
I will love with the love of God!
I will think with the thoughts of all;
The hearts of all will be my heart;
The souls of all will be my soul,
And the smiles of all—my smile!

SHADOWS

Beds of flowers, or vales of tears;
Dewdrops on buds of roses—
Or miser-souls, as dry as desert-sands;
The little, running joys of childhood,
Or the stampede of wild passions;
The ebbing and rising of laughter,
Or the haunting melancholy of sorrow;
The will-o'-the-wisp of our desire,
Leading only from mire to mire;
The octopus-grip of self-complacency,
And time-beaten habits;
The first cry of the new-born babe—
And the last groan of death;
The bursting joy of health
Or the ravages of cruel disease—
These, all, are but shadows
Seen by us on the cosmic mental-screen.
Shadows, and nothing but shadows!
Yet shadows have, O, so many shades!
For there are dark shadows,
And there are light shadows—
So even shadows may entertain!

WHEREVER WE GO

Whether in Himalayan caves or crowded subway;
Whether in jungle of modern life or Hindustan;
Wherever we go, teach us to discover Thee
In all Thy secret nooks—east, west, north, south
    —everywhere.

THY DIVINE GYPSY

I will be a gypsy—
Roam, roam and roam.
I will sing a song that none has sung!
I will sing to the sky,
I will sing to the winds,
I'll sing to my red clouds!
I'll roam, roam and roam—
King of the lands through which I roam.

By day, the shady trees will be my tent.
At night, the stars shall be
My candles, twinkling in the firmament;
And I will call the moon to be my lamp
And light my silver, skiey camp.
I will be a gypsy—
Roam, roam and roam.

I will eat the food which chance may bring;
I will drink from crystal sparkling spring;
I will doff my cap and off will go.
Like a wayward brook of long ago,
I will roll o'er the green
And scatter the joy of all my heart
To birds, leaves, winds, hills—then depart
To stranger and stranger lands, from East to West.
Oh! I will be a gypsy—
Roam, roam and roam!

But always, when I lay me down to rest,
I'll sing to Thee my gypsy prayer,
And find Thee, always, everywhere.

LISTEN TO MY SOUL-SONG

Come... Listen to my soul-song!
The darkness burst,
And Thy descending shafts of light
Pierced the hearts of gloom
To listen to my soul-song!

Behind the screen of my eyes,
Though hidden Thou art,
Thou dost remain unseen
To listen to my soul-song.

Burst the veils! Burst the blue!
Burst all lights!
And come to me as Thou art,
To listen to my soul-song.

Burst my senses and my mind!
Burst my heart and feeling!
Burst my silence and my soul
To listen to my soul-song.

Burst the heart! Burst the sky!
Burst the soul!
And come, listen to my soul-song,
Come, listen to my soul-song!

In the breeze I feel Thy touch;
In the sun, Thy warm love;
In the colorful scenery, Thy beauty-face;
In the waves, I see Thee dancing—
Dancing, ever anon!
Thou art dancing o'er my thoughts
To listen to my soul-song.

Listen to my soul-song!
Break the heart, break the sky, break the soul!
Come, listen to my soul-song!
Hovering o'er the clouds,
Lingering o'er the lea—
Thou hast come
To listen to my soul-song.

Beneath the gloom of my dim devotion,
Hidden Thou dost remain—
To listen to my soul-song.

FOUNTAIN OF SMILES

Behold not the sarcastic smiles
Born from the dark womb of hate.
Welcome not the bandit smiles
Which rob thy trueness.
Wear not serpent smiles
Which hide their venom
Behind the sting of laughter.
Banish the volcanic smiles
Of subterranean wrath.
Bedim not the mirror of soul—
Thy face—with shades of pitying smiles.
Let no witless, noisy, muscle-contorting laughs,
Like rowdies, echo the emptiness of thy soul.

A fountain of joy
Must gush out of the soil of thy mind
And spread sprays of fine smiles
Running in all directions,
Spreading their vital veins
Through laugh-thirsty hearts.
Let the lake of thy smiles break its embankment

And spread to territories of infinitude.
Let thy smiles
Rush through lonely stars
To brighten their twinkles.
The flood of thy laughter
Will inundate the drought of dry minds,
Sweeping away the barriers of cold formalities.

Spread thy smile like the dawn
To vanish the gloom of minds.
Paint thy golden smiles on every dark spot,
Brightening cloudy days.
Command thy smiles to resurrect life
Into the walking dead.
Smile for the dead,
For their grim peace bespeaks their victory o'er pain.
Let thy smiles
Pulverize the rocks of sorrow to atoms.
Let thy smiles meander
Through desert-souls and oasis-hearts alike.
Let the deluge of thy fearless smiles
Sweep through all minds and every place,
Drowning, washing away
All barriers for miles and miles.

When God laughs through the soul,
And the soul smiles through the heart,
And the heart smiles through the eyes,
Then the prince of smiles
Is enthroned beneath the canopy of thy celestial brow.
Protect thy prince of smiles in the castle of sincerity.
Let no rebel hypocrisy lurk to destroy it.
Spread the gospel of smile,
Purify all homes with thy healthful smiles,
Let loose the wild fire of thy smile
And blaze the thickets of melancholia.
Open the long-bottled-up musk of smile,

Scattering its perfume in all directions.
Intoxicate all with the wine of thy smiles.
Take the rich smiles from every joyous soul,
And from the mine of all true mirth.
North, south, east, west, wherever thou goest,
Thou smile-millionaire,
Scatter thy golden smiles—
Freely, freely, everywhere.

IN THE LAND OF DREAMS

Each night, as my Spirit roams
In spheres of slumber vast,
I become a hermit and renounce
My title, body-form, possessions, creeds—
Breaking the self-erected prison walls
of flesh and earthly limitations;
I am an all-pervading Son of God,
No longer caged in brittle, dingy clod,
Nor tied by tangible cords of birth,
Or man-made smallness, social standing,
And duty-shadows of earth.

There in sleepland's ether eternal,
I have no country, no homeland dear;
Nor am I Hindu or Christian seer;
Nor Occidental nor Oriental,
Race-bound behind the bars of inheritance.
In dreamland's limitless acres,
My Spirit revels in freedom—
Its only religion freedom—
Gypsying gaily there,
Pilfering joy from everywhere.
There, no lordling god o'ershadows me,
For there is none but Myself to rule myself.

Behold, the slave-man hath become the God!
The sleeping mortal, the awakened, deathless Lord!
An unseen, unheard God am I,
Drinking, breathing gladness;
Gliding in winged glory
Through the endless land!
Free from haunting fears
Or possible crash and shattered skull
No solids there to give me hurt,
No liquids to drown me deep;
No vile, dank vapors to choke me,
No fire my unseen form to burn.

Free from e'en the memory
Of a fragile body-dream,
O'er all space am I spread.
All things am I!
How, then, could aught
Dare injure me?
The heart of the big Myself
Would break
If it should strike
The little myself.
Unknown to others, but known to Myself,
I wake and walk and dream,
Eat and drink and glide in Joy.
I Myself am the Joy which I so sought—
And I am that Joy which everyone seeks.
So little, ah, so little was I
When I dreamt in my sleepy-wakefulness.
Boundless big am I when I am awake
In my sleepless-wakefulness!

FRIENDSHIP

Is friendship the weaving of the red strings of two hearts?
Is it the blending of two minds into a spacious one-mind?
Is it the spouting of love founts together—
To strengthen the rush of love on droughty souls?
Is it the one rose grown 'twixt twin mind-branchlets
Of one compassionate stem?
Is it the one thinking in two bodies?
Or, is it like two strong stallions,
Disparate in color and mien,
Pulling the chariot of life together
To the single goal with one mind sight?
Is friendship founded on equalities or inequalities?
Is it built on diverse stones of differences?
Is friendship the unthinkingly agreeing,
The hand in hand, blind walking of two souls,
Foolishly rejoicing in their united folly,
Falling at last into pits of disillusionment?

Friendship is noble, fruitful, holy—
When two separate souls march in difference
Yet in harmony, agreeing and disagreeing,
Glowingly improving diversely,
With one common longing to find solace in true pleasure.
When ne'er the lover seeks
Self-comfort at cost of the one beloved,
Then, in that garden of selflessness
Fragrant friendship perfectly flowers.
For friendship is a hybrid, born of two souls,
The blended fragrance of two unlike flowers
Blown together in love's caressing breeze.
Friendship is born from the very core
Of secret, inexplicable likings.
Friendship is the fountain of true feelings.
Friendship grows in both likeness and difference.
Friendship sleeps or dies in familiarity,

And decays in lusts of narrow-eyed selves.
Friendship grows tall and sturdy
In the soil of oneness in body, mind, and soul.
Demands, deceptions, sordid sense of possession,
Courtesy's lack, narrow self-love, suspicion,
These are cankers which eat at the heart of friendship.
Ah, friendship! Flowering, heaven-born plant!
Nurtured art thou in the soil of measureless love,
In the seeking of soul-progress together
By two who would smooth the way each for the other.
And thou art watered by attentions of affection
And the tender dews of inner and outer sweetness
Of the inmost, selfless heart's devotion.
Ah, friendship! Where thy soul-born flowers fall—
There, on that sacred shrine of fragrance,
The Friend of all friends craves to come and remain!

TO THE AURORA BOREALIS

From the heart of the northern horizon
A dim, palpitating fountain of flame
Spread flickeringly
Through the dark, stray clouds and the milky way,
And across the space overhead
Softly glowing liquid fleecy lights
Rose, quivered, and flooded the southern land.
Aurora lit the sky,
Played with shadows within the deeps of the limpid lake—
Fluttered scintillating transparent lights o'er the stars
And the sky o'erhead, shone on the rippleless lake beneath—
Then floated like dream waves of light
In my mental sea.
Still thoughts, like stars, would flutter
Through the dim mental clouds;
My wisdom's aurora light would rise from medulla's horizon

And spread, tremblingly, lighting
The dark vapors of mind.
Thou lone matchless imitator of all these—
O Aurora! Spreader of light and joy
O'er cloudy hearts—
Thou reminder of bursting, glowing light in my forehead!
Some invisible lamps on the left or extreme right
Would throw sudden iridescent red or blue sky kissing searchlights—
Then the ends of those lights would send out ethereal mystic flames,
Which joyfully bounded and vanished in the eternal ray.
Ever-burning radium, thou Aurora—
My fountain of strange colors—
Flooded my mental sky,
Illumining the opaque darkness
Behind which the Light of all lights hides.
It was a vision of ever-changing, rolling, molten light—
Trying to coax the stars, trees, water, earth, and all matter
To melt their grossness
And become the Cosmic Light.
Aurora, there is hope,
For I shall liquefy in my *samadhi's* fire
All grossness of my mortal being and all creation's dust.
Matter shall change to light;
The darkness will burst into atoms of leaping fire;
The little soul will breathe with the eternal breath—
And with each birth of my breath new solar systems will be born,
And with the escape of each eternity's breath of mine
Many a universe shall cease to breathe;
The feeling of the body will fly
To feel the universe.
No more shall I clasp but a little clod,
But in my bosom I shall bear the burden
Of the twinkling atomic vapors of nebulae,
All shining stars, planets, and manifold living things.

For I am the life—
And my big body is the universe.
I am smaller than all little things made—
I can hide behind a speck of electron;
And I am bigger than the biggest thing that breathes.
I am the life which shattered its littleness
Into the bigness of all big things.
I am most subtle—the subtlest of forces is thick enough to hide me—
Yet everything speaks of me.
I wake with the dawn,
I exercise my vital muscular rays in the sun;
I sleep in the night—
oft peeping through the twinkling lights.
I smile in the moon,
I heave in the ocean,
I paint, and wipe away the pictures on the canvas of the sky.
I make the dewdrop and conjure the flowers with my invisible wand;
I whistle in the canaries and sing in the nightingales;
I melt and sigh in human breasts;
I whisper through conscience and roar in the thunder;
I work in the noisy wheels of factories,
And I play hide and seek with the sky, stars, clouds and waters—
As the mystic light of the aurora.

THOU AND I ARE ONE

Thy cosmic life and I are one.
Thou art the Ocean, and I am the wave;
    We are one.
Thou art the Flame, and I am the spark;
    We are one.
Thou art the Flower, and I am the fragrance.

We are one.
Thou art the Father, and I am Thy child;
    We are one.

Thou art the Beloved, and I am the lover;
    We are one.
Thou art the Lover, and I am the beloved;
    We are one.
Thou art the Song, and I am the music;
    We are one.
Thou art the Spirit, and I am all nature;
    We are one.

Thou art my Friend, I am Thy friend;
    We are one.
Thou art the Master, and I am Thy servant;
    We are one.
Thou art my Mother, I am Thy son;
    We are one.
Thou art my Master, I am Thy disciple;
    We are one.
Thou art the Ocean, and I am the drop;
    We are one.

Thou art all Laughter, I am a smile;
    We are one.
Thou art the Light, and I am the atom;
    We are one.
Thou art Consciousness, I am the thought;
    We are one.
Thou art Eternal Power, and I am strength;
    We are one.

Thy peace and I are one.
Thy joy and I are one.
Thy wisdom and I are one.
Thy love and I are one.

That is why Thou and I are one.
Thou and I were one, and Thou and I will be
    one ever more.

I WAS MADE FOR THEE

I was made for Thee alone. I was made for dropping flowers of devotion gently at Thy feet on the altar of the morning.

My hands were made to serve Thee willingly, to remain folded in adoration, waiting for Thy coming; and, when Thou comest, to bathe Thy feet with my tears.

My voice was made to sing Thy glory.

My feet were made to seek Thy temples everywhere.

My eyes were made a chalice to hold Thy burning love and the wisdom falling from Thy nature's hands.

My ears were made to catch the music of Thy footsteps echoing through the halls of space, and to hear Thy divine melodies flowing through all heart-tracts of devotion.

My lips were made to breathe forth Thy praises and Thine intoxicating inspirations.

My love was made to throw incandescent search-light flames to find Thee hidden in the forest of my desires.

My heart was made to respond to Thy call alone.

My soul was made to be the channel through which Thy love might flow uninterruptedly into all thirsty souls.

THY HOME-COMING

Thy mansion of the heavens is lit by perennial aurora displays of mystic light.

The stellar system swings across the endless dark highways of eternity which lead to Thy mystic home.

The comet-peacocks spread their plumes of rays, and dance in wild delight in Thy garden of many moons.

I sit on a little patch of the milky way and watch the glory of Thy kingdom spread endlessly everywhere.

The festivities of the heavens are dazzling with the fireworks of meteors and meteorites.

Shooting stars are hurled across the blue vaults by Thine unseen band of obedient devoted forces.

Everybody, everything, every atom, rejoices during Thy coronation as the uncrowned King of Universes.

Every day the trees drop flowers in Thine honor, and the skiey vase sends wisps of fire-mist incense to Thee.

Candlesticks of heavenly powers hold the burning stars to light Thy temple.

Meteorites skip, glow, swoon, and fall to earth, mad with Thy joy.

The planetary dance glides in stately rhythm awaiting Thy home-coming.

Because Thou hast been away, Thy mansion of matter has been dark.

Now darkness is being dispelled and Thy gloom-drenched chamber of eternity is becoming radiant at the news of Thy return.

Heavenly lights have opened their gates. Bonfires of nebulous mists are heralding Thine approach.

The speedy sentinels of sun and moon patiently are waiting for Thy home-coming.

And I am running wild, dancing in my little body on my little earth, or skimming over the Milky Way, coaxing everything, every atom of space, every speck of consciousness, to open its gates and let Thy light shine through completely and drive darkness evermore from the lonesome wilderness of matter.

DREAMS OF GOD
(An Inspirational Revelation of what God is.)

The Spirit was invisible, existing alone in the home of all space. He piped to Himself the ever-new, ever-entertaining song of perfect beatific bliss. As He sang through His voice of eternity to Himself, He wondered if aught but Himself were listening and enjoying His song. To His astonishment, He felt that He was also the cosmic song and He was the singing. Even as thus He thought, lo, He became two: Spirit and nature, positive and negative, man and woman, the peacock and the peahen, stamen and pistil of the flowers, the male gem and the female gem.

All these He became in thought only, as yet. All these dualities He only dreamt within Himself, as yet. Then He loved His dream of dualities, and He thought: *My dream is Reality! My imagination is Truth!*

So this vast cosmic dream became the cosmic soul of nature!

Then the Creator began to clothe His subtle dream with grosser dream-decorations and to condense His beautiful dream; and He asked the cosmic dream to awake into consciousness, to come to life and shine like a piercing star of cosmic vitality in the dark skies of consciousness. He said: "My shadows of imagination and My dreams must have life; being a part of Me, they must be living, even as I am living."

So the dream-thoughts began to take luminous forms, until all things were created as light. Star, man, herb, flower and bee—all shone as living stars in the limitless firmament of His dream. Being endowed with motion, they danced and dazzled. Behold, the Spirit had become God—the Father Protector of creation.

Now, although so many dazzling things were suddenly within Him and about Him, He saw that they suffered from sameness; so He dimmed the light of His power and focused all His rays in space and began to condense His astral cosmos. Lo! All things began to change their vibrations, becoming different in color and form and density. His astral cosmos became frozen, and the earth took a brown, solid form, and the lunar men became fleshly forms of definite, condensed dreams, and the nightingale dreamed its feathery plumes, and the trees wore flowers. He caused all things to dream with intensity, to dream definitely and continuously; He caused them to dream astral and gross dreams, even as He dreamt them into being. Thus the gross cosmos came.

The idea cosmos was born out of the Creator's desire to be twain. The idea cosmos froze into the astral cosmos, and the astral cosmos froze into the gross cosmos.

As in a dream one can create a complete idea universe, or can see a cosmos made of lights, and can see, touch or hear a gross cosmos: so God created in His one dream other dreams and the relative experiences of an idea cosmos, of an astral cosmos, and of a gross cosmos. As in a dream, one can think and feel, or can see electric lights or experiment with the atomic or astral composition of the universe, or see or taste or touch a piece of ice, or move across the hot sands of the desert of Sahara, or can see people, born or as yet unborn: so God, the Creator, began to dream of nebulae, of born and unborn planets of an astral, electrical cosmos, of thermal laws and laws of gravitation, and of thought, feeling, will, flesh and sensations.

This cosmic dream is like our human dreams. Our human dreams are miniature and relatively changing dreams, created after the pattern of the relatively unchanging (only changing in cycles) huge cosmic dreams. While the human being dreams that he is dying from an accident, it is hard for him to realize that the experience is a dream, but upon awakening it is easy for him to forget the ugliness and the pain and mental suffering endured during the fleeting life of the dream. It is only when the dream breaks and is known to have been a dream that one can laugh, realizing the unreality of that dream suffering.

The mental picture of an automobile accident, when condensed and focused, becomes a dream reality. The accident in a dream is relatively more real and painful than a like accident in a mental picture. If a little condensed imagination can cause pain, then the condensed imagination of a cosmic dream with all its trials must necessarily create a greater complexity of pain and suffering. And it is only when we are fully awake in cosmic consciousness in God, and not in our human consciousness, that we can realize that all the trials and the joys of the universe are but God's dream.

It is then that we can laugh at the trials and pleasures of life, and laugh equally at birth and death. When one dreams about a wall and knocks his dream-perceived head on the wall and it hurts, he must realize that even dreams have power to hurt. As long as God makes a man imagine or dream his body, it is subject to the joy and grief dreams of life and death, of pleasure and pain, of heat and cold, for all of these accompany the consciousness of the body.

The Invisible Dimensionless became visible with dimension— not in reality, but in a cosmic dream. For, according to the laws of cause and effect, the effect must be similar in essence to the cause. So this universe body made up of bodies that appear so divided, separate, relatively contradictory, full of wars between solids and liquids, gases and energy—is in essence invisible and dimensionless. For the universe and the body-cells of its being are the frozen thought of God. Science shows us that all matter is frozen light. And light is the frozen dream of God's intelligence. The universe, as an effect, could not be different from the Spirit as its cause.

When the Invisible, the One, became the many, He condescended to give freedom of choice and power of independent self-evolution to all His creations. So He gave to everything His own power—"to be able to do whatever one may want to do." Thus, all things went farther and farther away from Him by believing in the cosmic delusion and painstakingly working for it. Yet, all things, by the right use of self-evolving reason, can move ever nearer and nearer to Him until the many again become the One. But the cosmic creation, or nature— being conscious, and having received unlimited independence— wants mostly to move farther away from the Divine Father, or God, thus creating self-imposed suffering from self-made or man-made laws of evil.

Man stands in a position of independence, able to reinforce the misguided or wrong reason in him and so move away from God, or to reinforce God's emancipating wisdom and help God bring him back to the divine Oneness of infinity, as in the beginning. But God is powerless to help man unless he will voluntarily accept God's ever-willing help. God can help only those who help themselves. After having once given unlimited personal freedom to man, God cannot become an autocrat and prevent His independent creation from doing evil, for God would contradict Himself should He take away the freedom of man after having once given it to him.

THE COSMIC DREAM-IDOL

The Spirit, the Silent One, who remained hidden behind dream space as an Invisible, tore away the veil of eternity and appeared as a Visible Cosmic Dream-Idol of Finitude. In the boundless temple of space, in the shrine of cosmic dreams, the Idol of Finitude rests or moves slowly or dances with His millions of feet of motion and life. Every day—when with closed eyes I seek to grasp infinity, until my brain aches from the strain—I open my spiritual eyes and fly my mind-architect far away into the region of eternity, and there build for myself a measureless temple of space, a sanctuary of silence; and there I place my Cosmic Dream-Idol of Finitude, my Idol with starry eyes, blue skiey body, bejeweled with moons, decorated with garlands of the milky way, blossoms of light, and wearing on His head a golden crown of jeweled rays.

I behold Him in the cosmic temple, His ever-busy hands working through the electrical forces and through the millions of hands of all living creatures. I behold this, my Great Idol, walking through fifteen hundred million pairs of feet. I hear His footsteps in the floating feet of the gossamer and in the fast flying footsteps of the hunted deer. In the throbbing of all hearts, I hear the throb of His one heart. I feel His one thought and one feeling and one will through all the thoughts, feelings and wills of all mortals. It is the Cosmic Idol's one brain which is the brain of all brains.

Every day, during sunset hour, with open eyes I fly my mind's gaze into infinite space and its temple of golden rays, and in it I behold this vast Idol of Finitude.

Every day, India-wise, with the rod of my fancy, I beat the drums of the Atlantic, Pacific, and Indian Seas, and they roar to honor my Idol of Souls. I play the harp strings of electronic rays and they all sing. I blow the conch shell of cosmic vibration through the opening in all atoms. I join the chorus of soul desires of all creatures, and they chant in one language of heart their craving for the Idol of Finitude.

O! I have lighted the candles of all human inspirations and aspirations, of all devotions, of all hearts, of the love of all saints. The incense sticks of my love slowly and ceaselessly send wisps of fragrance in spirals of eternity to His infinite temple. And in the temple choir, even the moth and the glow-worm fold their wings in devotion, and tiny-eyed lights fold their palms of rays together, along with mine, to worship Him. The temples, mosques, *viharas* all sing in choruses of harmony only, offering unto my Idol of Finitude the different songs of multitudinous teachings.

When I lost my earthly mother, I sought her two black eyes in the stars—until they twinkled black eyes everywhere. But they were not those eyes that I had lost. There were many black eyes that sought to mother me, but they were not those eyes that I loved. I pulled the Divine Mother's veil of silence within me very hard, and I asked Her: "Why art Thou so cruel? Why didst Thou take away my beloved earthly mother? Why dost Thou deny her to my heart's gaze?"

She replied, "Little child, it was I who became your mother. Many times have I nurtured you. Some times it was as a mother nightingale, sometime as a deer in the forest. I have suckled you through many breasts. The last mother whom you loved so dearly was I. Now I have broken that little form, because your love was becoming too locked up and clogged within a limited boundary, which I broke, that your released love might flood through all mothers and feel My one vast love in all hearts. I shattered the little form of your mother, that you might seek Me, your same Mother, in the form of infinitude, and in the form of the infinite Cosmic Idol of finitude."

In the chain of universes, I beheld the luminous spine of my cosmic Idol. Around it was built His vast blue body of eternity. Tiny sands, crystal drops of blue brine and my tears, the tissue of stones, flowers, and my flesh, air, earth, clouds, space, time, and life: all these I had viewed as existing apart and engaged in perpetual strife. Now, with the vision of my Cosmic Idol, I suddenly found all these diverse created things were but His living cells, and in them I saw the flow of His one ever-living blood of life. There was no death possible. for in this blood I saw the continual birth of His new cells of life.

My Cosmic Idol, made after our pattern, indulges in many moods, even as do we. I beheld His smile on the lips of the lotus, His rays of smiles in the light of all faces; I caught Him sadly gazing with the moon at the folly and pride of delusion-intoxicated, truth-forgetful civilizations. I saw Him angry with the storm, uprooting trees, and then shedding repentant tears of rain on the earth's lap. I saw His somber face in the cloudlets and in the mists of the earth. I felt Him sorrowing in discouraged hearts and coaxing them to smile with the joy of His omnipresent beauty.

I realized that He was the fountain of joy, percolating through the joys of all human hearts and all the pores in the soil of omnipresence. I beheld Him as the ocean of immortality, heaving with the sighs of change.

I gazed in ecstasy at His skill as He showed me His cosmic motion pictures on the screens of human consciousness. I spied the glimmering fountains of creation, of time, of space, of immortality, of duality, of life, of love, of all forms of consciousness, and of ever-new bliss—playing over the limitless gardens of His unfading memory.

My Cosmic Idol broke His vow of silence, and came out of His invisible home to lure us with the assumed laughter and cries of His nature-moods, to make us forget our dream-sorrows and divert our truant footsteps homeward to His bosom of eternal joy.

The many called to the One through the lisping prayers of conscience, theology and intuition—and my Idol of Finitude responded. He was invisible; He became visible. He was one and He became many. He found that the many children of phenomena, especially His human children, became entangled in their self-woven nets of delusion, and were unable to release themselves by their misused reason from the pits of illusion, dug by themselves. So He took pity and became the Father to protect the little helpless child; and then again He stabbed His heart and let the blood of His most precious heart's love flow earthward; and He clothed the blood clot of His love with a divine form, and it became the Mother—divine love became mother love.

The Divine Mother's love in the human mother became the unconditional lover of the baby, so that, even if the baby should later become a criminal, forsaken by all the world—still he could go to this miniature incarnated Divine Mother, the earthly mother, and find ready forgiveness, tender sympathy and wise assistance to find a way out of the error.

He became the baby, to keep the cold, reasoning fatherly love balanced and expanded by the unconditional love of the mother. He gave the motherly divine love to soften the stern, calculating love of the father. He became the baby so that He might keep the protecting and surrendering love together, unified to express the divine, unconditional love in the baby. By becoming the helpless child, He united the parents in a greater unselfish love, felt for the baby. He unified the father and mother in body, mind, and all-surrendering love, to express unconditionally His divine love in their souls.

He became the lover in order to give love, to teach and express unconditional, unselfish love; and He became the beloved to receive love and to appreciate unselfish love and to rouse unconditional love in the lover. He became the teacher to warn Himself with love, thus warning Himself as the erroneous many.

But when the many heeded not the voice of their One Cosmic Lover, they hurt themselves. And as often as they hurt themselves, He admonished visibly, vocally, tangibly, through the father, and shed soul-softening, protesting and loving tears through the mother's or the beloved's eyes.

He was not satisfied to become only the protecting parents, so He appeared as immortal life, to destroy death. He became the minister of wisdom in each temple of conscience to give secret, silent sermons to erring souls.

He was not contented to render help through the family instincts, so He appeared as the unlimited number of friends, to offer continuously fresh added help to all individuals. He throbbed as health to eject sickness. He smiled in the minds of men and women to destroy the intruder, sorrow.

He became the light to shut out darkness in which many of His children stumble. He became the golden sun to give vitality, and he spread the silver rays of the moon as salve to soothe the fever-parched body of man. He sang as the nightingale in the halls of nature, that His children might be induced to sing the spontaneous songs of the heart to Him. He peeped through the beauty-window of the blue bell to give His children a glimpse of His beauty, that they might run after Him.

He spread Himself as fragrance to lure the mind to seek His undying fragrance hidden within the ignorance-corked bottles of the human senses. He visited as determination in the hearts of the weak that they might awaken the all-freeing, all-accomplishing cosmic will sleeping in their souls. He became love in all hearts, so that through the doors of their little loves they might escape forever and find protection in His omnipresent land of love.

He sowed the soul-seeds on the soil of larger love, and they grew into petals, all joined together on the stem of family love. Now, when the petals of souls exuded the fragrance of one family-love, they began to fall away through separation or death. The divine love and the fragrance of family love were harvested on the petals of souls. Blown by the wind of omnipresent love, the progeny pollen of these souls migrated and fell on the wider soil of social, patriotic and international love; and then they became bigger and brighter flowers, emanating volumes of sweeter fragrance of social, patriotic and international love.

At last, from these were born larger living seeds. These better and more vital soul-seeds no longer were satisfied to grow on soil with boundaries; so God planted them in the garden of infinitude; and there they all bloomed as His immortelle of infinite love, the one flower from all flowers, forever knitted in the heart of His omnipresence—ever-fragrant, with ever-new, everlasting joy.

CONQUERING FEAR OF DEATH
The Dying Youth's Divine Reply

In his laughter he had often heard the echo of God's merriment. This laughing youth of many charms lay dying in a hut, yet the blast of illness was unable to wither his smiles. The doleful doctors came and said to him, "But a day, but a day, we give you to live."

The dear ones of his family cried aloud, "Leave us not, poor youth of our hearts, our souls are bursting for thee, for thy plight."

The smiles of the youth grew brighter and he joyously and pityingly spoke in a voice of song, "Ah, just a day, yea, but a day between me and my long-lost Beloved. Yea, the hours of the day are slow to die. When they have expired, my Beloved will open the prison gates of my life and embrace me in Her infinite arms, the balloon of life will break, and the imprisoned breath of life will cross the mortal shore and reach my immaculate kingdom of dainty dreams, where no nightmares of illness will dare to cross the threshold of my peace.

"I am the billow of the sea; in the sea I will be free. I am dust of light; I will swim in the stars. I am a drop of ambrosia; I will be a sea of nectar. I am the river of the moon; I will melt in iridescence. My nightmare of desires has ceased, my dreams of grief are broken, the light of laughter has awakened. The lamp of many lives, flickering over my earthliness, is extinguished forever. My light has plunged into the divine light and is playing over the splendors of eternity. The shadows of fanciful fears have slipped away, and the infinite light has spread over the dark nooks of my soul.

"I am making preparations with laughter and songs. I have clothed all my thoughts with new robes. I have asked my reverent feelings to sing a celestial chorus, and I have roused all the inhabitants living in the villa of inspiration to observe this gala day for me—the day of my entry into the infinite kingdom as a son of the King of Peace. I have asked the sentries of my will and determination to banish all sad inhabitants from my kingdom and kill the Satan of fear, pain, sorrow and attachment, at sight. My celebration of entering the bliss kingdom must be attended only with laughter and songs—no timidity or dark sorrow will be allowed to join my festivity. All the subjects of my mortal kingdom are roused today to continuous unleashed watchful merriment. They are all waiting to welcome the entry of the divine messenger, delightful death, when he will come to open the latch of finitude and let them out into the free kingdom of infinity.

"All the inmates of my consciousness are rejoicing to leave this mortal prison, where they have been lashed with worries, thrown into the dungeons of uncertain, unsafe living, and constantly pounded by accidents, failure, disease and unhappiness. My inmates are glad to dump the broken cage of brittle bones and throw the cage of flesh into the fire of infinity, letting the bird of paradise out to soar in the skies of blissful omnipresence. The inmates of my life are quiveringly, joyously waiting for the slow hours to pass by, in order to welcome Savior Death to come of his own sweet accord and let them into his kingdom at his sovereign command.

"Oh, dear ones," the youth continued, "rejoice in my joy on the eve of my freedom from the mortal prison—long before you. For me no breaking of bones, no accidents, no fear of failure or financial loss will ever exist; no thought of unpaid bills will ever keep sawing through my mind, no greed for possessions will ever be gnawing at my soul. No discourtesies, nor naggings, nor quarrels, nor pain, nor disease will ever dare make a noise when all the doors of my senses are closed, for I will be out roaming with my Beloved on the tracts of cosmic freedom. Pray do not wish me to be back in your prison, just to join you helplessly in your chorus of wails. But if it is needed I will gladly come a million times, wearing the robes of immortality, to take you out of your mortal prison to my home of blessed freedom.

"I am free! I will soon be out! But it will be sad to look at you through your prison bars of mortal life, locked up in your misery-making mundane prison.

"'Tis now less than a day, as the doctors say. I shall be gone on my infinite way. No music is sweeter than the song I shall sing every moment, 'Now less than a day. Less than a day, 'til my Beloved comes in the dazzling chariot of Death to take me away, to take me away to the kingdom of deathlessness, to the palace of bliss-dreams, far, far, away.

"You weep for me dark tears, weeping for your loss in me, but I weep for you joyous tears, because I am going before you, for your welfare's sake, to light candles of wisdom all the way, and will wait to welcome you there, where I shall be with my Only Beloved and yours."

GLOSSARY

ALLAH: Moslem name for God
ALLAH-HO-AKBAR: God is most Great!
AUM OR OM: The basis of all sounds; universal symbol-word for God. "Amin" is used by the Moslems, "Amen" by the Christians and "Aum" by the Hindus (see Cosmic Sound).
BABAJI: The Master of my Master's Master, is a deathless avatar, living secretly in the Himalayas. His powers are Christlike.
BHAGAVAD GITA: Hindu Bible; the sacred sayings of Sri Krishna (compiled millenniums ago by the Sage Vyasa).
BODHI TREE: A banyan tree in India, under which Buddha found illumination.
BRAHMA: The all-pervading Spirit as immanent in creation.
BUDDHA: One of the avatars of India: called Buddha, "the enlightened one"; born in the 6th century B.C. at Kapilavastu in northeastern India.
BUDDHIST: A follower of Buddha.
CHRIST CONSCIOUSNESS: Consciousness of Spirit as immanent in every unit of vibratory creation.
COSMIC CONSCIOUSNESS: Consciousness of Spirit transcending finite creation.
COSMIC SOUND: Om or Aum, the all-pervading sound emanating from Cosmic Vibration- the voice of all creation, or of God. It can be heard through practicing the Self-Realization method of meditation.
GURU: The spiritual preceptor who introduces the disciple to God. The term Guru differs from teacher, as a person can have only one Guru but may have many teachers.
HINDU: A member of one of the Aryan races in India, of the Caucasian race. Also, an adherent of Hinduism, or one of the various religious systems based on the Vedas.
HOLY VIBRATION: Aum or Om; God as intelligent vibration.
INTUITION: The "sixth sense"; true inner apprehension or knowledge derived immediately and spontaneously, not through the fallible medium of senses or reason.
KALI DIVINE: Mythological Hindu Goddess, represented as a woman with four hands. One hand symbolizes nature's creative powers; the second hand represents the cosmic preservative functions; the third hand is an emblem of the purifying forces of dissolution.

Kali's fourth hand is outstretched in a gesture of blessing and salvation. Through these means, she calls all creation back to Her soul.

KORAN: Sacred sayings of Mohammed: the Moslem Bible.

KRISHNA: The Divine Cowherd. He was a king as well as a prophet, and is considered in India as an incarnation of God. He lived in the world and performed the engrossing duties of a ruler, but he was not of the world. He played the flute, and in his early life was a cowherd. Allegorically Krishna represents the soul playing the flute of meditation to lead all the misled thoughts back to the fold of omniscience.

KRIYA YOGA: An ancient science developed in India for the use of all God-seekers. Its technique is referred to and praised by Krishna in the Bhagavad Gita, and by Patanjali in the Yoga Sutras.

LAHIRI MAHASAYA: My Master's Master; the one who revived the highest part of Yoga calling it Kriya Yoga. He was Christlike, and had miraculous powers; he was also a family man with business responsibilities. His life-teachings of Yoga-to be calmly active and actively calm-coincide with the needs of the spiritually aspiring business man of the West. I have given him the title of "Yogavatar", or "Incarnation of Yoga."

MOHAMMED: Great prophet of God, who, by his divine martial spirit, led his spiritual army to the Kingdom of God. The founder of Islam.

MOHAMMEDAN: Follower of Mohammed.

MOSES: Great prophet of God, who saw Him as Light burning the bushes of ignorance.

NAMAZ: The chief prayer of the Moslems.

NANAK: Great leader and saint of the Sikhs in India.

OM_TAT-SAT: Holy Ghost, Son and Father:or Cosmic Vibration: Christ Consciousness in creation; and Cosmic Consciousness in the blissful nirguna ("without qualities") void beyond creation.

PARAMHANSA; A religious title, signifying one who is master of himself. It can only be bestowed on a disciple by his guru. *Paramhansa* literally means "supreme swan". The swan is referred to in Hindu scriptures as a symbol of discrimination.

PRANA: Specific life force in the human body and in all living creatures.

RAM PRASAD: One of India's greatest devotional saints.

SAT-SANGA: Fellowship with man by appreciation: fellowship with God by meditation.
SAMADHI: See footnote, page 191
SHIVA: Represents The Infinite transcendental Spirit existing in relation to his consort, Kali, the finite creator of nature. Often spelled Siva.
SRI YUKTESWAR: My great Master and guru, (1855-1936). To him I owe all my spiritual inspiration. He had miraculous powers. I have given him the title of "Jnanavatar" or "Incarnation of Wisdom."
SUFI: An adherent of a Mohammedan system of mysticism.
SWAMI: A member of the monastic Swami Order, reorganized by Swami Shankara in the 8th century. A Swami can receive his title only by being ordained as such by another swami; he renounces the world and considers himself as belonging to the entire human family. There are ten subdivisions of the Swami Order, such as Giri, Puri, Bharat, Tirtha, and others.
SWAMI SHANKARA: Reorganizer of the Swami Order; his date usually given as 8th century. He was the greatest commentator on Vedanta philosophy, and a practical Yogi. He expounded God, not as a negative abstraction, but as positive, eternal, ever-conscious, omnipresent, ever-new bliss. He performed many Christlike miracles.
SYMBOL OF LOTUS: The lotus outline on the title page symbolizes the single spiritual eye of meditation, the pranic star door through which we must enter to find cosmic consciousness-taught by the Self-Realization method of meditation. "Therefore, if thine eye be single, thy whole body shall be full of light.......Take heed, therefore that the light which is in thee be not darkness." –Luke 11:34-35
TURIYA: The state beyond deep, dreamless sleep, in which the superconscious is active.
VEDAS: The four ancient scriptural texts of the Hindus.
VIHARA: A Buddhist temple.
YOGA: Communion with God through the practice of scientific meditation.
YOGI: One who unites himself scientifically with God. A yogi may be outwardly a man of the world, or may renounce everything. Practice not theory, is important to a yogi.
YOGODA SATSANGA: A non-sectarian organization founded by Yogananada.

SUPER ADVANCED COURSE 1

Lesson 1 /258

Lesson 2 /279

Lesson 3 /287

Lesson 4 /296

Lesson 5 /304

Lesson 6 /320

Lesson 7 /326

Lesson 8 /334

Lesson 9 /344

Lesson 10 /350

Lesson 11 /358

Lesson 12 /367

Super Advanced Course Number 1
Lesson 1
Christian Yoga And The Hidden Truths In St. John's Revelation Interpreted According To Intuitional Experience

The spinal passage and the seven astral doors of escape, including the medullary door through which the soul can fly to the Spirit.

Of all the books in the Bible, *Genesis* and *Revelation* are the two most important. The first chapter of Revelation, which is the basis of this lesson, contains the hidden truths of Christian metaphysics and Hindu Yoga as revealed through the intuition of St. John.

Revelation means "that which has been revealed." How? Not through intelligence but through intuition. This lesson is merely a spiritual forecast; as you proceed to the highest pinnacle of understanding, these truths will be revealed to you by the light of your intuition.

What is the difference between understanding and intuition? Understanding depends upon the senses for knowledge; intuition brings direct perception of truth. When you see a rope in the dark, you may think you are seeing a snake. Your inferences are often mistaken, because your intelligence can reach its conclusions only through the data supplied by the senses. If the senses mislead you, your inferences are necessarily wrong. Intuition, on the other hand, does not depend on intelligence or sense perception. At times you have a feeling that something is going to happen. You do not hear, or see anything on which to base the expectation, but it happens. This is popularly called a "hunch." Try to change your "hunch" to controlled intuition by meditation. Thus it will become a scientific factor.

In the past, Christianity has remained aloof from Hindu religion. Real Christianity is not to be blamed for this; it is "churchianity" which is responsible for paralyzing rational religious thinking.

Attending churches or temples of Godworship is a good thing, but in itself does not prove actual knowledge of God. Actually knowing God is another matter. Christianity will become the stronger for discarding dogmatic beliefs and supplementing its appeal through a study of the universally true, intuitionally received spiritual experiences of the Hindu savants.

Many religious teachers are but "spiritual victrolas." They grind out sermons without experiencing the truths contained in them. St. John did not deliver sermons he did not realize. He wrote what he saw, felt, and learned intuitively during his meditations. Without knowing and practicing some great method of meditation (as the fifth Yogoda lesson), it is impossible to experience the mysteries of life, or to know all the intricacies of the human body, the soul, and the cosmos.

So the hidden truth in *Revelation is* intuition-discovered and will be found to be universally acceptable. Whether you are a Christian, Jew, Buddhist, or Mohammedan-if you study the truths that are interpreted here for you, not only through the intellect but through intuitive meditation, you will find that they agree with the essence of your own religious teachings.

St. John's *Revelation can* be understood and known only by Christian metaphysicians and Yogis. Jesus Christ was an Oriental and a Yogi[1]. A document found in a Tibetan monastery proves that during His unknown life, between His twelfth and thirtieth year, He was in India and conferred with the wise men of the East (India) about the mysteries of the inner life, returning the visit they paid Him at His birth.

A detailed account of Jesus' visit to India can be found in a book entitled *The Unknown Life of Christ, by* Nicholas Notovitch. This Russian having heard of the document regarding Jesus, or Issa[2] in the possession of Tibetan monks or lamas, went to Tibet to verify the report. He definitely established the fact of Jesus' visit to India during the time of His disappearance from Asia Minor. Therefore, Jesus taught the oriental, practical Christianity based on inner realization.

Modern Christianity, in spite of its moral and socio-religious foundation, lacks the expressions which come from Self-realization of truths. Occidental Christians generally want salvation by proxy. The average Christian deems it sufficient to go to church regularly and to read the Christian Bible occasionally, though mechanically, forgetting to practice in daily life what he has heard and read.

Your belief alone does not make you a Christian[3]; it is your realization of the Christian truths that does. If you study these lessons faithfully, you will be reborn spiritually and may call *your*self a Christian Yogodan, or a Christian realist, or a true Brahmin[4].

Intuitional study of the scriptures results in tolerance through realization of the fundamental unity underlying all faiths, whereas arrogant, purely intellectual study of the scriptures is productive of argumentation and dissension. In other words, the latter reveals but the outer shell of truth, whereas the former discloses truth's *inner and* outer aspects simultaneously. Study the scriptures after meditation, when the intuitive state is predominant.

The seven Spirits.

St. John did not read a library full of books in order to write the book on Revelation. Jesus conferred with the Hindu Yogis on the universal art of Yoga (the art of human salvation).

St. John, the beloved disciple of Jesus, received revelation after experiencing contact with the seven reflected spirits of God (Christ Consciousness and the six reflected spirits before the throne of His omnipresence. See *Revelation 1:4* below.) St. John felt Cosmic Consciousness not only in his physical, astral, and ideational bodies, but also in the physical, electrical, and ideational universes before he ventured to write about the revealed truths. Many people try to teach after reading a few occult books. One is qualified to teach only after he has actually experienced metaphysical truths and has felt his consciousness beyond the body.

Super Advanced Course 1

To know truth, you must experience it in your own consciousness. *The Hindu Yogis and Swamis[5] practicing Yoga, or the science of oriental Christian metaphysics, have given almost identical descriptions in Yoga books of all that has been recorded by St. John from his inner experiences. This proves the influence o f Hindu Yoga on the teachings o f Christ.* Besides, there is only one truth, and there can be no fundamental difference among those who have realized it, whether they be Hindus or Christians. The moon presents the same face to all, and the one truth must likewise appear the same to all who have really lived it.

Revelation is the true record of St. John's intuitional experiences

Remember, this *Revelation is* and will be found true not only by Christians, but by all so-called believers and unbelievers who follow the universal path to God. I am speaking from personal experience, and if you practice what you are studying, you will feel what I felt. According to the inner revelation of St. John and the Hindu Yogis, I am giving you a glimpse of the inner meaning contained in some passages in the first chapter of St. John's *Revelation*. We find in the tenth to twentieth verses of this chapter the most important record of spiritual experience and description of inner astral anatomy.

A condensed interpretation of this chapter follows:

Revelation 1:1 *The Revelation o f Jesus Christ, which God gave unto him, to shew unto his servants things which must shortly come to pass; and he sent and signified it by his angel unto his servant John:*

Revelation 1:2 *Who bare record of the word of God, and of the testimony of Jesus Christ, and of all things that he saw.*

St. John wrote only of that which he experienced while he was listening to the Cosmic Sound of Om or the Word of God and of the Christ-or Jesus Consciousness present in the Cosmic Sound. (See *Revelation 1:10* below.)

The *angel* mentioned in *Revelation 1:1* is intuition - a conscious force within St. John - which bore testimony of the truth coming from the vibration of Cosmic *Consciousness*[6] *and Christ Consciousness*[7] *(Word of God)*.

The seven seals or the seven charkas, or the seven golden candle-sticks, or spiritual dynamic centers in the spine as described in the Yoga books.

Revelation 1:4. *. . . the seven Spirits which are before his throne . . . refers to the seven manifestations of God in creating man.*

All creation is divided into three macrocosmic and three microcosmic manifestations. When God brought forth creation, His manifestations took the form of three universal spirits and three macrocosmic objects. The macrocosmic is the whole - the ocean, and the microcosmic represents the unit - the wave. There are six *subjective* manifestations of the Spirit, reflected in its six objective manifestations: Three microcosmic objects: Idea; cosmic energy; physical cosmos :

Three macrocosmic subjects: The ideational Cosmic Architect; the astral Cosmic Engineer; the Builder of the gross cosmos.

Three microcosmic objects: Idea body; astral body; physical body;

Three microcosmic subjects: The ideational-body Creator; the astral-body Creator, and the Creator of the physical human body.

In all of the six macrocosmic and microcosmic objects, the Spirit is present as six subjective forms of consciousness or as one reflected Christ Consciousness. There is only one reflected Spirit, the *only* begotten son, called Christ Consciousness, which is the seventh manifestation, reflected in all, objective creation.

In the six objects the Spirit is reflected as six subjective spirits, and these six, as one reflection in all objective creation, are Christ Consciousness. This is the meaning of the seven Spirits which are *before* his *throne.*

Revelation 1:5 *And from Jesus Christ, who is the faithful witness, and the first begotten of the dead, and the prince of the kings of the earth ...*

Christ or Jesus Consciousness is experienced as the princely supreme force governing all other potent material forces, when one first enters the spiritual kingdom by leaving his vitally suspended physical body. This is what is meant by the first begotten *of* the dead and the *prince* of *the kings of* the earth. Christ Consciousness perpetually witnesses all changeable creation governing all matter - each atom. As you meditate and rest from the astral, physical, and ideational bodies, your first perception is Christ Consciousness. You must rise beyond your several bodies before you can attain Christ Consciousness. St. John, after he experienced the truth by contacting Christ Consciousness lying beyond these three bodies and the six spirits, revealed this truth in this chapter of Revelation. God Consciousness transferred the universal truth through intuition to man.

The Cosmic Sound or the Cosmic Trumpet, or the voice of many waters, or Om, or Amen or the Word.

Revelation 1:10 *I was in the Spirit on the Lord's day and heard behind me a great voice, as of a trumpet.*[8]

Revelation 1:11 *Saying, I am Alpha and Omega, the first and the last: and, What thou seest, write in a book, and send it unto the seven churches ...*

That is very clearly expressed. In the Spirit means within St. John's consciousness. (See the fifth Yogoda lesson.) St. John was approaching the Spirit - leaving the realm of matter, i.e., the body and the material senses. He described vividly the experiences which he had as he entered the Infinite. He perceived his soul behind the ego (described as me) and the material consciousness and sub-consciousness, and through the finer perception of the soul he heard the Cosmic Sound manifesting Itself as trumpet sound, emanating from all vibratory creation. The trumpet was *Saying, I am Alpha and Omega.* Can trumpets speak? Not literally, but the Spirit can signify a meaning through trumpets or vibratory sounds. Whenever you hear that Cosmic-Trumpet Sound, you are hearing the Aum creative -preservative- destructive vibration. This vision and conscious experience of Cosmic Sound urged him to transmit his knowledge to the world through spiritual centers and churches where people seek God and His mysteries.

Revelation 1:12 *And I turned to see the voice that spake with me. And being turned, I saw seven golden candlestick*

St. John said in the tenth verse that he *was in the Spirit;* hence, when he spoke of *being turned,* he did not refer to bodily motions. He fixed his attention upon, and became one with, the voice which *spake* or vibrated within *him,* and as he stayed in that vibratory sphere he perceived the seven golden astral doors of escape which lay within his physical body. The physical and astral bodies are the bodies of energy. How are they connected? The physical body is attached to the astral body by seven candlesticks like vibratory seals. Energy flows into the spine through the physical body. *Just* as electricity flows into the bulb through a wire passage, so the Cosmic Force flows through the medulla into the spine and its seven centres; into the body and its five sense lamps. The astral body of the life force is knotted to the physical body by seven golden candlestick-like burning seals.

Super Advanced Course 1

What is the meaning of candlestick? In this book two terms have been, used, stars as well as candlesticks; the former are the lights and the latter, the receptacles. *Angel* means *star,* and *church* also means receptacle.

The mystery of the seven stars or lotuses.

The seven centers of light for the outgoing current are:

(1) Thousand-petaled lotus star (seat of the beautiful, condensed, lotus-like, thousand-rayed life current performing the thousand-and-one functions in the body) : Bliss-ether in which God and the angels abide; main dynamo. Cosmic energy enters the body through the medulla but is stored in, and distributed by, the whole brain;

(2) Medullary center [seat of the two-rayed lotus star of life force (positive-negative current)]: Super-ether in which thoughts and the life force move;

(3) Cervical center (seat of the sixteen-rayed lotus star of life force): Ether through which sounds and electrons travel;

(4) Dorsal center (seat of the twelve-rayed lotus star of life force): Air (vitality);

(5) Lumbar center (seat of the ten-rayed lotus Star of life force): Fire (inner life energy);

(6) Sacral center (seat of the six-rayed lotus star of life force): Water (circulation);

(7) Coccygeal center (seat of the four-rayed lotus star of life force): Earth (the gross flesh).

The spinal cord may be likened to a wire. In it are located these seven centers of light which are the sub-centers for the conduction and distribution of life current throughout the body. The body is nothing but a condensation of this spinal energy. Just as invisible hydrogen and oxygen atoms can be condensed into visible vapor, water, and ice, so light can be transformed into body which is nothing but frozen energy. You must lose all fear of sickness and accidents; as your body is nothing but energy, it cannot be harmed. When you realize this, you will be free.

The seven centers are the *churches* or *candlesticks, and* the seven *stars* are their dynamic radiating currents. *The Cosmic Energy enters through the medulla -to be stored in the brain, whence it descends into the seven centers, feeding the seven elements*[9] *of which the body is composed.* When *these* seven lights *are withdrawn* from the body *in death,* the body *disintegrates.*

In passing from the consciousness of the body to that of the Spirit, one experiences these seven sub-dynamic doors of energy fixed in the astral cerebrospinal axis. The soul must leave the physical, astral, and spiritual bodies through the seven astral doors in order to reach, and merge into, the Spirit. After it lifts its consciousness from the physical body, it must unlock, and pass through, the seven astral doors in the spine.

The Yogoda student, in the third lesson, first contracts the Cosmic Vibration. This is the first state of meditation. In the next higher state of meditation (see fifth lesson), the Yogi lifts his attention from the body. It is then that he perceives the *seven golden candlesticks* or seven astral doors of escape in the spine and falls as dead as his energy is switched off from the body.

Golden Girdle or astral radiation.

Revelation 1:13 *And in the midst of the seven candle-sticks one like unto the Son of Man, clothed with a garment down to the foot, and girt about the paps with a golden girdle.*

St. John speaks of the form of the astral body as something similar to the *Son* o f man, or the physical body which is born of man, or matter. He describes the astral body as built around *the seven* candlesticks or seven centers of golden life force, describing it as *a garment down to* the *foot* (the entire astral nervous system woven with filaments of nerve currents like a garment). The *golden girdle, about the* paps, or the swelled astral radiation, is the golden halo which surrounds, girdles, or spreads out around, the entire astral body. By looking steadily with unblinking eyes at the entire outline of one's body, one can see a vapor-like astral radiation - an astral aureole.

Revelation 1:14 *His head and his hairs were white like wool, as white as snow; and his eyes were as a flame of fire;*

Revelation 1:15 *And his feet like unto fine brass, as if they burned in a furnace; and, his voice as the sound of many waters.*

The astral head is white like wool and is the thousand-petaled (rayed) super-electric lotus (main dynamo of life force) described in Yoga books.

The origin of all concentrated finer forces which govern the physical body *is* in the head; hence the fine, hair-like filaments of white, fleecy lights in the main cerebral centre are described as *white,* fibrous and fluffy, *like wool.*

The cerebral light of thousand petals or thousand rays, as described in Hindu Yoga books, performing the thousand- and-one functions in the body, is pure and *white as snow.* White is the combination of all colors; and the cerebral astral mother cell, the feeder of the above-mentioned seven life sub-centers of different vibrations and colors, is described as *white. The* seven Sub-centers manifest different colors, according to their rates of vibratory manifestations. *Different thoughts register different states* and *thoughts change colors in the spiritual eye and life force.* The physical eyes proceed from one light centre, just as one switch lights the *two* headlights of an automobile. Thus the physical body has two eyes, but the astral body has only one eye, like *a flame of fire.* It is the one astral *flame of fire* which pours into the two eyes, giving them power and manifesting them as two. For this reason, when the two eye currents are concentrated and thrown back in the medulla by focusing the eyes on the point between the eyebrows, they are perceived as one single spiritual eye of light. (. . . *If therefore thine eye be single, thy whole body shall be full of light.*) When the two physical eyes manifest the single spiritual eye, then one can perceive, by continuous spiritual development, the physical body as filled with the super-lights of the supersensuous astral body.

The astral head is pure white, the astral centers of lesser vibrations are golden, and the astral feet, with the lowest rate of vibration, glow yellow, like melted brass in a furnace.

All vibratory manifestations are accompanied by lights or sounds, whether we register them or not; or rather, vibrations express themselves in us through various lights or sounds. The astral body consists of different rates of vibration, manifesting themselves in different colors and voices, or sounds of many waters, or vibrating elements. Different sounds emanate from the seven elements of the astral medullary super-ether current, ether manifesting cervical current; air, or vitality, dorsal current; fire, lumbar current; water, sacral current, and the earth, coccygeal current. All these-super-ether in the medulla; ether in the cervical plexus; air current in the dorsal plexus; fire current in the lumbar plexus; water current in the sacral plexus, and earth current in the coccygeal plexus-are the different vibrating elements which constitute the human body, and they give forth different sounds. For this reason, this astral body of many lights and colors is spoken of as emanating from elements.

Different astral sounds and the Cosmic Sound (Aum or Om).
St. John heard the astral symphony and the one voice of many waters.

The astral body, besides manifesting the individual specific sounds from the seven different centers, also manifests the one *voice* as *the sound of many waters*, including both macrocosmic and microcosmic physical and astral elements.

Super Advanced Course 1

The Yogi, like St. John, can distinguish, by higher spiritual methods, the different sounds of the astral symphony emanating from the coccygeal sacral, lumbar, dorsal, cervical, and medullary plexuses,[10] respectively. Also the Yogi listens to the one Cosmic Voice or Sound of Om, emanating from *many waters or* elements, constituting the whole physical, astral, ideational macrocosmic and microcosmic universes. Hence, the sound *of* many w*aters* spoken of by St. John is composed of the specific astral sounds of the seven plexuses and the one Cosmic Sound of Om. Both kinds of sounds are intuitively heard by the Yogi who has felt, or has had the vision of, the astral body.

Revelation 1:16 *And he had in his right hand seven stars: and out of his mouth went a sharp two-edged sword: and his countenance was as the sun shineth in his strength.*

Furthermore, the seven astral centers and their seven elements are manifested as seven stars of light. The seven elements, bliss-space (the super-fine medium in which bliss abides), super-ether (the fine semiconscious vibratory medium through which thoughts are transmitted), ether (the fine vibratory medium of energy), air, fire, water, and earth (of which the body is composed) are but the seven lotuses of life force or the seven frozen star-rayed currents.

These seven stars, *burning in* his right *hand* in the proper channel of active force, or *Susumna,* or in the astral cerebrospinal axis, remain as vibrating life currents feeding the seven elements, bliss-space, super-ether, ether, air, fire, water, and the earth elements in the body, keeping them constantly supplied and vibrating.

The Conscious Cosmic Energy first enters through the medulla and remains concentrated in the brain as the thousand-petaled electric lotus. Then it descends into the body through spinal cord and the sympathetic nervous system. If these seven stars were extinguished and with· drawn from the proper channel of spinal vitality into the Spirit, the whole body would begin to decay. The body is frozen life current; therefore, as it decays under the influence of the heat of change, it must be kept frozen and fed by these constantly burning seven starry sentinels of life.

We speak of the **medulla as the *mouth of God*** or the finite opening in the body of man through which God breathes His Cosmic Energy or Life into flesh. This medulla, also called the *mouth of the* astral *body,* emanates a *sharp two-edged sword,* or a powerful, two-edged, doubly serving positive-negative current. The one Cosmic Energy must create through the law of duality and relativity, so it sprouts forth the medullary seed current into two positive-negative currents. The birth of the two astral ganglia chains of the sympathetic system, the ***Ida* current on the left and the Pingala current on the right** side of the spinal cord, is also made possible through the dual (two-edged) creative power of the medulla. The astral and the physical medulla are like two cloven half seeds of the positive-negative forces which give birth to the astral and physical nervous system. The astral medulla seed sprouts forth into the vital tree of life, extending its pairs of branches into the two brain hemispheres, eyes, ears, hands, feet, as well as the two pairs of numerous inner organs. The two astral sympathetic nervous currents *(Ida* and *Pingala)* act in conjunction with the astral main central or spinal *Susumna* current. These two branches of life current emanate from the medulla seed and intertwine themselves with the *Susumna* vital current at the spinal centers. He who knows how to withdraw his life force from the body, muscles, and senses and draw it upwards through the spinal plexuses, opening the astral-physical knots of age-old attachment, can reach the cerebrum and behold the thousand-rayed energy lotus shining there in the astral countenance with the strength of thousand billions of crushed suns.

Do you know why you experience darkness when you close your eyes? The gross light vibrations of the moon, sun, and electricity blind your eyes to the powerful, mellow lights within. The average person's spiritual eye is closed but that of the Yogi is open, and he can see the inner lights at any time during the day or night. With the opening of the spiritual eye, a great light appears beyond the veil of darkness. That was St. John's meaning when he spoke of *the light that shineth behind the darkness.*

Revelation 1:17 *And when I saw him, I fell at his feet as dead...*

St. John realized, like the Hindu Yogis, that when this astral body is perceived as separate from the physical body, the energy being reversed to the Spirit, the physical body apparently consciously relaxes like that of a dead man. In conscious relaxation of the involuntary organs the astral energy goes out of the body, leaving it untenanted like a dark electric bulb from which the electricity has been switched off but can be switched on again at will. Then, beholding the separated astral body, one no longer perceives himself as a part of the perishable, brittle body bulb. When St. John saw him, or the astral body and Spirit above his head, he *fell at his feet as dead, i.e.,* he also perceived, in a conscious trance, his physical body, bereft of life force, lying at the feet or lower end of the floating astral body, apparently dead. Following the switched-off body current from the body bulb the soul perceives itself as an emanation of the immortal conscious Cosmic Ray which is the first Creator and the ultimate Absorber of all materialized objects. The Cosmic Ray is swallowing up all minor forms of energy, and the Cosmic Energy is being swallowed up by Conscious Space or Conscious Omnipresence. Then the soul realizes its immortality and is freed from the consciousness of physical death witnessed in many earthly incarnations. The delusion of death, born of the soul's identification with the body, is gone, and the soul perceives itself as alive forevermore.

These eternally true astral experiences were put in writing by St. John in order that flesh-identified brothers might find redemption from the consciousness of death, earthly changes, etc. One versed in the art of astrally separating the inner body from the physical body knows the causes of mortal bondage, or hell. Such an one also knows how to open the doors of mortal change or death and escape into the kingdom of Changeless Infinity. *These eternal truths and* **seven astral doors of escape** *from the prison of torturing matter are described by St. John to enable the awakened ones to fly to the home of Eternal Bliss.*

Each *angel* occupies a *church;* each starry light occupies an astral *church* or *golden candlestick,* or one of the seven elements in the spine.

The experiences described by St. John can be realized by sincerely practicing the fourth and fifth Yogoda lessons, the Higher lesson on the Super-art of Realization"), and the method given below.

A Yogi who can, as St. John, switch off the current from the body and listen to the Cosmic Vibration can, in an advanced state, experience the *seven golden candlesticks* or seven astral doors of escape from the body to the Infinite.

Remember: Omnipresence was our throne. We became slaves, concentrating on the senses. We must return to Omnipresence. We are not only afraid of our omnipresence, but we even try to forget it. We must transfer the soul's attention from the changing, untrustworthy sense centers to the throne of Omnipresence. Sleep is the greatest messenger of Omnipresence. Every night the soul is given a chance to forget the little body and is enthroned in the vastness within.

It was the master's supreme wish that I pass these truths on to you; now it is "up to you" to apply them in every-day life. You have heard many lectures; what you need is study and practice in order to attain realization. The true spiritual way of studying scripture differs from the intellectual. Dozens of vague, meaningless books have been written on Revelation. Jesus Christ was crucified once, but His teachings are being crucified every day by misinterpretations. When you read this, meditate on it.

Heavenly Father! Transfer our consciousness from the physical body to the spine and from it through the seven centers to Cosmic Consciousness, where Thy glory and light reign in the fullness of Thy manifestation; where the Life Force reigns in all Thy power. Peace!

METHOD: Sit upright and straighten the spine to resemble a straight lightning rod. Concentrate the vision between the eyebrows with eyes half open. (Do not frown while doing this; keep the facial expression serene.) Now slightly move the spine to the left and right by swaying the body, changing the centre of your consciousness from the body and senses to the spine. Feel the astral spine and stop swaying the body. Then let your consciousness travel up and down several times, from the coccygeal plexus at the end of the spine to the point between the eyebrows. Then concentrate on the coccygeal plexus and mentally chant Om. Again, but slowly, travel up the spine, mentally feeling the coccygeal, sacral, lumbar, dorsal, cervical, and medullary plexuses, to the point between the eyebrows, mentally chanting Om in each place. When you reach the central point between the eyebrows, return downward, chanting Om at the point between the eyebrows, the medulla, and the five plexuses, and mentally feeling the centers at the same time. Continue to chant Om at the seven centres, feeling them while traveling up and down the astral spinal *Susumna* passage. Practice the above until you distinctly feel that your consciousness is transferred from the body into the spine.

The practice of the above method will release your soul from the bondage of matter and sense attachment by enabling you to escape through the seven astral doors and become one with the Spirit.

SUMMARY

The soul, having been encaged through ages in the three bodies - physical, astral, and ideational - is unable to cast off its shackles and escape into omnipresent Cosmic Consciousness.

The union of human consciousness with Cosmic Consciousness is impossible through imagination and intellectual study of the scriptural truths alone. Such union is possible only through knowledge of the above-mentioned seven astral spinal doors (the *seven golden candlesticks* and *stars)* and through withdrawing the life force and consciousness from the body into the Infinite and then bringing it back again. The soul, imprisoned in the body, must learn to free itself at will from its bondage. No matter what religion one professes, as he comes closer to real salvation, he is confronted with the necessity of opening the seven seals of energy and flesh in order to free the soul from the bondage of the body and unite it with the Spirit.

Both St. John in the Christian Bible and the Hindu savant Patanjali in his *Yoga Aphorisms* have spoken of this one scientific, psycho-spiritual seven-doored passage in the spine, through which all aspirants for salvation must pass to reach the Spirit consciously.

OUTLINE NOTES ON LESSON No. I

Q. What is Revelation? Ans. Revelation consists of those spiritual truths which were psycho-intuitively revealed to St. John and may be revealed to anyone with his state of super-consciousness.

God Consciousness transferred the spiritual truths to Jesus, the man with Christ Consciousness, who through his angel consciousness, or intuition, revealed them to his disciple John.

Revelation 1.-2 *Who bare record . . . of all things that he saw.* All spiritual experiences were verified by the vibratory manifestation of God and the Christ Consciousness immanent in it.

Revelation 1:4 ... *seven Spirits* ... The seven manifestations of God also testified to the truth of St. John's spiritual experiences.

Revelation 1:5 *And from Jesus Christ, who is the faithful witness* ... [See also Revelation 3:14: ...These things saith the Amen, the faithful and true witness, the beginning of the *creation of God*]; Jesus, the Christ 'Consciousness, and the Vibratory Word are the faithful witnesses of everything and the source of all power and grace (ordered creation). Consciousness and sound accompany 'all vibratory creation, just as the running of a motor is accompanied by a droning, humming sound. The intelligently working Cosmic Motor, planets, electrons, atoms-everything emanates the cosmic roar *of Om*. ... *the first begotten of the dead*...{*the* Yogi's first contact with Christ Consciousness after he is dead, i.e., after he transcends the physical, astral, and ideational bodies by conscious meditation.

...,*prince*... (supervisor) ... of *the kings* ... (forces of the earth or -universe).

Revelation 1:8 *1 am... the beginning and the ending* ... (the vibratory relativity consisting of the beginning and end of all created things).

Revelation 1:9 ... *word of* God ... (vibratory manifestations of diverse true principles emanating from God).

Revelation 1:10 *I was in the Spirit* ...[St. John's ego was contacting the Spirit, and he was not wholly allied with the physical consciousness].

...*on the Lord's day* ... (on the day that the Lord revealed Himself as the Spirit - this can be any day for those who are spiritually awake).

... *heard behind me a great voice* ... [spiritual vibration inaudible to human ears, hence intuitively perceived]. St. John was in the spiritual consciousness, hence he was free from the relativity of the dimensions and beyond the fourth dimension. Therefore, the word *behind* cannot mean direction but signifies that he was beyond the conscious and subconscious and in the super-conscious state, and behind the gross bodily vibrations and the musical finer vibrations of the subtle body. *A great* voice - one great Cosmic Sound of Om emanating from Christ Consciousness and Cosmic Vibration or the Cosmic Motor. The word *voice* signifies vibration coming from a conscious Being. As of *a trumpet* - vibrations with variations. Hear the Om sound like the roar of the sea by the practice of the fifth Yogoda lesson. Om is the manifesting sound of intelligent Cosmic Vibration.

Revelation 1:11 Saying (declaring in the sound), I am Alpha and Omega, the first and the *last* . . . (The Om is the origin and end of everything. As motion causes the rise, momentary suspension, and dissolution of the wave, so the Cosmic Vibration of Om at a certain state creates, then preserves, and ultimately dissolves everything in the Infinite Sea).

Revelation 1:12 And I turned to see the voice that spake with me . . . [St. John turned his attention, to be one with *the voice* (conscious Cosmic Vibration) that was consciously vibrating within, suggesting infinite spiritual meanings}. *And being turned, I saw seven golden candlesticks;* [He saw, i.e., intuitively felt, the seven receptacles (centres) of light- —not the lights themselves].

Revelation 1:13 *And in* the midst ... one like unto the Son *of man* . . . [Around the seven centers as the base, he saw one subtle luminous body like the physical body *(Son of man).*

Revelation 1:14 *His head* and *his* hairs were white *like wool,* . . . [The thousand-petaled lotus of Life Energy is white and is the seat and origin of all colors; wool suggests softness.] . . . his *eyes were as a* flame of fire-(the third or spiritual eye burning as one flame, and not the two gross flames or' life energy which arc - present in the physical two eyes) .

Revelation 1:15 And his *feet* like unto fine brass ... [seat of grosser vibrations of lighter color, as brass (yellow), symbolized as feet] ... and his *voice as the sound of many waters* (Christ

Consciousness and Cosmic Vibration manifested the varying Cosmic Sound of OM).

Revelation 1:16 And he *had in* his right hand[11] seven stars: ...{His subtle body had in the seat of stronger virtuous activity (the spine) seven condensed luminous centers with seven different vibrations-the creators of the seven tattwas or elements.] ... *and out of* his mouth *went a sharp two-edged sword:* ...[Out of the luminous medulla proceeded two currents of optic life current which feed the two eyes and all other organs created in pairs...*and his countenance was as the sun shineth in his strength. [The* head is the seat of concentrated energy.]

Revelation 1:17 And when I saw him, I fell at his feet as dead . . . During the time of the vision of the subtle body and the centers, there was relaxation of energy in the involuntary organs in the body; otherwise the outgoing life current would have kept the mind distracted with gross sensations. The death-like physical body was perceived in a conscious trance as resting under the hovering luminous feet of the astral body.

Revelation 1:20 Seven stars ... [the seven vibratory spiritually visible currents] ...*seven golden candlesticks* ... [seven centers or seats of the subtle energy star lotuses].

---

1. *Yogi: One (man, woman, or child) who unites himself or herself scientifically with God through Yoga methods (art of God•contact).*

2. *Issa: Sanskrit, meaning Lord:*

3. *Christian: One who has Christ Consciousness.*

4. *Brahmin: Originally, one who has been reborn spiritually. The supreme teacher recognized only two castes: the Sudras (those bound to the body) and the Brahmins (those having attained Brahma-or God Consciousness). The four-caste system, which is of comparatively recent origin, recognizes the following castes: (1) Sudras (laborers);   (2) Vaisyas (merchants); (3) Kshatriyas (warriors); (4) Brahmins (priests)*

Under this system, children automatically take the caste of their parents. Originally, caste was based on different qualities.

5. *Swami: One who has achieved self-mastery and is endeavoring to attain perfection through renunciation..,*

6. *Cosmic Consciousness: God, the Father, or the Conscious-ness beyond all creation.*

7. *Christ Consciousness: The Consciousness in all vibratory creation.*

8. Compare *Yoga* Aphorisms of the Hindu sage Patanjali: The symbol *of* Spirit is Aum (Om), the Cosmic Sound.

9. *Bliss-ether, super-ether, ether, air, fire, water, and earth.*

10. i. *Medullary plexus= Om Astral Symphony of all plexuses;*

ii. *Cervical plexus= Roar of ocean; iii. Dorsal plexus= Long drawn out bell sound; iv. Lumbar plexus=Harp; v. Sacral plexus=Flute; vi. Coccygeal plexus =Humming sound, like bumble bee.*

11. *The right hand is the spine through which the Cosmic Current first descends, with full power, into the body, and the left hand is the sympathetic nervous system through which the life force flows comparatively more feebly.*

Super-Advanced Course Number 1
Lesson 2

Developing Response-bring Mental Whispers:
The Easiest And Surest Method Of Rousing The Spirit
In Answer To Your Demands.

Differentiate between **your "needs" and your "wants"**. Your "needs" are few, while your "wants" can be limitless. In order to find freedom and Bliss, minister only unto your "needs"; stop creating limitless "wants" and pursuing the will-o'-the-wisp of false happiness. The more you depend on conditions outside yourself for happiness, the less happy you will be.

Fostering the desire for luxuries is the surest way to increased misery. Don't be the slave of things or possessions; boil down even your "needs." Spend your time in search of lasting happiness or Bliss. The uncharitable, immortal soul is hidden behind the screen of your consciousness on which are painted dark pictures of disease, failure, death, etc. Lift the veil of illusive change, and be established in your immortal nature. Enthrone your fickle consciousness on the changelessness and calmness within you, which is the throne of God; then let your soul manifest Bliss night and day.

Rise above the four mental states

Beware! The mind must be protected from the four alternating psychological states of sorrow, false happiness, indifference, and a deceptive, passive peace which claims the ego for brief intervals, whenever it manages to shake off the other three. Look at any face, and you will be able to tell whether its owner is at the mercy of any one of these. It is but rarely that people's faces remain calm while they are in the grip of the four unstable mental states.

Whenever a desire for anything like health or pleasure is denied an individual, sorrow is born, which changes that person's face. "Prince Smile" is routed, by "King Sadness" who tortures the muscles and distorts the expression.

Whenever a person's desire is fulfilled, he is temporarily "happy." Sorrow is born of unfulfilled desire; "happiness," of fulfilled desire. Sorrow and false happiness, like the Siamese Twins, dwell and travel together. They are the children of desire and are never far apart; if you invite "happiness," sorrow is sure to follow.

When the ego is not buffeted about by sorrow or "happiness," it sinks into the state of indifference. You can look around you and find the faces of many people registering this state of boredom.

You ask a person engrossed in indifference, "Are you sad?"

"Oh no," he replies.

Then you ask him, "Are you happy?" "Oh no," he drawls.

"Well then," you ask, "what is the matter with you?"

"Oh," he cries, "I am just bored."

That is the mental state of many people.

Beyond these other changeable states, sorrow, false happiness, and indifference or mental inertia, lies the neutral state of passive mental peace. It is of a negative, short-lived nature-the aftermath of, and temporary lull in, the first mentioned three states.

Beyond these four states of consciousness is the unconditional, ever-new state of Bliss felt only in meditation.

How earthly desires are born.

The soul, being individualized Spirit, if given a chance to unfold, can manifest all the fulfillment and satisfaction of the Spirit. It is through long-continued contact with changeable matter that material desires are developed.

Desire is an impostor which hampers, and encroaches upon, your ever-joyous soul and lures your ego to dance upon the crests of the four fluctuating, short-lived psychological states.

Super Advanced Course 1

How to become a "Bliss billionaire."

Protect the soul from the disturbance a created within your mind by the mad dance of sorrow-producing desire. Learn to overcome wild, wicked desire. Realize that you do not need the things which create misery, for if you search within your soul you will find there true happiness and lasting peace, or Bliss. Thus you will become a "Bliss billionaire."

What is true desirelessness?

The soul's nature is Bliss—a lasting inner state of ever-new, ever-changing joy, which eternally entertains without changing the one entertained even when he passes through the trials of physical suffering or death. Desirelessness is not a negation; it is rather the attainment of the self-control you need in order to regain your eternal heritage of all-fulfillment lying within your soul. First give the soul the opportunity to manifest this state, by Yogoda meditation, and then, constantly living in this state, do your duty to your body and mind and the world. You need not give up your ambitions and become negative; on the contrary, let the ever-lasting joy, which is your real nature, help you to realize all noble ambitions. Enjoy noble experiences with the boy of God. Perform real duties with Divine Joy.

Play your tragic or comic parts in life with an inner smile.

You are immortals, endowed with or comic parts in eternal joy. Never forget this during your play with changeable mortal life. This world is but a stage on which you play your parts under the direction of the Divine Stage Manager. Play them well, whether they he tragic or comic, always remembering that your real nature is eternal Bliss, and nothing else. The one thing which Will never leave you, once you transcend the four unstable mental states, is the joy of your soul.

Therefore, learn to swim in the calm sea of unchanging Bliss before you attempt to plunge into the maelstrom of material life which is the realm of sorrow, pleasure, indifference, and a deceptive, temporary peace.

Proof of the existence of God as Bliss is felt in meditation.

The wholehearted practice of meditation as taught in the fifth Yogoda *lesson* brings deep Bliss. This ever-new *Bliss is* not born of desire; it manifests itself the moment the above-mentioned four mental states melt away by the magic command of your inner, Intuition-born calmness. Manifest this serenity always. When Bliss comes over you, you will recognize it as a conscious, intelligent, universal Being to whom you may appeal, and not as an abstract mental state. This is the surest proof that God is eternal, ever-conscious, ever-new Bliss.

How to make your prayers effective.

When you are experiencing this ever new Bliss, never doubt that you are contacting God. It is at this time that your broadcasting microphone of prayer demand is ready to transmit your mental whispers to Him.

Prayer vs. demand.

Most people are absent-minded while they pray. Some love God but do not express that love continuously; hence their prayers are not answered. Moreover, a beggar supplicates; a child demands. A beggar's plea is of a fawning, groveling, cringing nature; a child's demand is straightforward, sincere, and lovingly unafraid. Most people beg from God; hence they receive a beggar's pittance instead of a son's share. Those who demand as children receive everything the Father has. A beggar doubts that his plea will be granted; a true son k*nows* that his demand will be fulfilled. You *were* a son, but your own weakness has made you a beggar; you must become a son again before you can claim your birthright. Therefore, demand to be a *son* again before *you* demand *anything* else. First establish your identity with God, as Jesus did, by *realizing,* in *the, joy* of meditation, "I and my Father *are one."* Do not beseech Him beggarwise, but unite your ignorance-separated soul with God by constantly remaining identified with the ever-new Bliss within you.

Super Advanced Course 1

Demand, after you have established your identity with God.

After you have re-established your ever-new, joyous contact with Bliss-God, you may offer your demands for health, prosperity, or wisdom through mental whispers.

It is the purpose of this lesson to show the modern theology-blinded, theory-fed, belief-submerged human brother the way to contact Gad easily, To be able to do that, he must know how to develop dynamic mental whispers.

The world has done enough fruitless chanting and praying. Loud prayers are helpful in congregations if practiced with deep concentration and devotion; but, usually, when a person voices his prayers instead of mentally 'whispering them, they are said in "parrot fashion," while the mind is occupied with something else. God knows this; He does not answer when His name is taken in vain. Moreover, a voiced prayer absorbs the power of attention and is thus prevented from marching God-ward.

Contact God through inner mental whispers.

You know that whenever you want something very much, no matter what you may be doing, no matter where you may happen to be, a constant mentally whispering desire for the object forcibly rotates in the back ground of your mind. This haunting real desire for anything, I call a mental whisper. The mind constantly whispers to itself what it wants. Such mental whisper bears no resemblance to parroted prayers; it is spontaneous and secretly works itself into a dynamic power.

An unceasing demand for anything, mentally whispered with unflinching zeal and unflagging courage and faith, develops into a dynamic power which so influences the entire behavior of conscious, subconscious, and super-conscious powers of man, that the desired object is gained. A mental whisper, to achieve its object, must be undaunted by reverses and unceasing in its inner performance; then it will materialize.

Unknowingly, you have practiced such mental whispering many times, and have obtained results in the fulfillment of your desires.

Do away with the mockery of mechanical, loud praying. Shake off the false satisfaction of believing "just something" about God. You must *know* God. You must know how to rouse Him consciously and tangibly and make Him answer your demands. Do not rest until you have heard His voice *consciously.*

You can ease your conscience by claiming that pressure of business prevents you from praying and meditating, but you can have no excuses for not offering Him deep mental whispers at any time, in the temple of activity or on the altar of silence. No matter what you may be doing, you are always free to whisper your love to God, until you consciously receive His response. This is the surest way to contact Him in the mad rush of present-day life.

To rouse God, to receive His response, you must offer Him your mental-whisper songs unceasingly. No matter what you are doing, offer deep, inward mental-whisper prayer-demands with any of the following thoughts:

A few mental whispers - Make them your own by meditating on their meaning before offering them to God.

i. Father, reveal Thyself.

ii. Beloved Divine Mother, hide no more. Blast the wall of ignorance, and appear unto me in all Thy splendor.

iii. Divine Mother, lift the veil of darkness which hangs before me whenever I meditate on Thee with closed eyes.

iv. Divine Mother, show Thyself in the light of my flaming love for Thee.

v. Divine Friend, with my little arms I want to clasp Thy Omnipresence. Come! I can wait no more. Come!

vi. Beloved Spirit, burst through the opaque firmament of my selfishness-clouded love and embrace me with Thy omnipresent light.

vii. I will burn the door of silence with the fires of my ever-working dynamic inner whispers. O ever-burning Love, show Thyself in my flaming devotion.

viii. May the memory of Thy presence shine forever on the shrine of my whispering devotion. May my love for Thee burn secretly in the temple of Thy heart, and may I be able to awaken Thy love in all hearts.

ix. May Thy love burn forever on the altar of my heart, and may I be able to kindle love for Thee on all heart altars.

Thus, day by day, as you offer mental whispers, a new awakening will come; a new living relation with God will be established. The mist of silence and mystery, which hangs over everything, will slowly vanish before the dawning light of your mental whispers for God.

The blue sky will speak, saying, "Look! Here He is, spread all over my bosom." The flowers will say, "Behold His smile in us!" The dumb stones will declare, "See! He is sleeping in us." The trees will whisper, "He is dreaming in us." The birds will sing, "He is awake and singing in us." Your soul will say, "He is throbbing in me." Your hitherto unmindful, unconscious thoughts will say, "He is awake in thee now, awakened by thy inner whispers. Listen! Through thy soul-stirring whispers He is whispering songs of His love unto thee everywhere."

When your unceasing whispers shall at last dig deep into the soil of Omnipresent Silence, the fountains of His answering whispers will gush forth from your soul and with their life-giving waters refresh thirsting hearts everywhere.

SUMMARY

To receive God's response to your prayer-demands, ask only for that which you really need. The desire for superfluous material possessions ultimately brings misery and retards your spiritual progress.

Before demanding anything of God, first establish your identity with Him through meditation. Then demand, as a child of the Father, knowing that your request will be granted-not with the attitude of a beggar.

Many prayers are said absent-mindedly, consisting of empty words forced from without. When you meet a friend after a long absence, you do not consult books on friendship in order to know how to express your love to him. God is your closest Friend; let your prayer-demands to Him be spontaneous outpourings, welling' up from the depths of your heart.

Whenever you have a real need, the thought of it is in your mind all the time, no matter where you are or what you are doing. Developing such deep, dynamic, inner whispers is sure to bring a response from Him. Constantly, unceasingly, whisper unto Him of your eternal love, of your burning desire to contact Him.

"Offer deep mental whispers in the temple of scientific meditation until you hear His answering whispers everywhere, audibly and distinctly."

Super-Advanced Course Number 1
Lesson 3

Reversing The Searchlights Of The Senses.
Where Is Your Consciousness centered?
In What Slums Is Your Soul Roaming?

What is the ego?

The soul's subjective consciousness of the body and its other material relations is termed the ego. The soul itself, being individualized Spirit, should manifest only its kinship with the Spirit, which is unmanifested, ever-existing, ever-conscious, ever-new Bliss. Hence, as Its reflection the soul, in its true state, is individualized, ever-existing, ever-conscious, ever-new Bliss. The ego, however, being identified with the three bodies-ideational, astral, and physical-(and their normalabnormal conditions), has put on their natures.

It is extremely necessary for the advanced student on the path of meditation to **watch the wanderings o f his ego** in the realms of consciousness-in other words, the wanderings of "King Soul" in the form of matter stricken ego.

The physical, astral, and ideational planes must all be comprehended through consciousness. Therefore, we can safely say that when we are in an undeveloped state the roamings of the ego in the "Kingdom of Consciousness" interest us only during the twenty-four man-made terrestrial hours.

The human ego generally travels in the realm of sensation during the waking state. After the curtain of dreams is drawn, the ego semiconsciously roams in the chamber of dreams. It may be said to be semiconscious while dreaming, because it dimly perceives the dream pictures during their performance and can recall them after waking.

Human Consciousness is never wholly suspended.

During the dream state, the ego is semi-unconscious of the world and of sense experiences-yet it is conscious of suspended. It is also conscious of deep sleep while in that state. The link between consciousness and subconsciousness is unbroken; otherwise dreams could not be recalled when consciousness is fully resumed. It is impossible to be wholly unconscious; the soul's subjective consciousness, or the ego, may be asleep or resting, but this can never be termed "unconsciousness."

During retirement to the subconscious dream chamber, consciousness casts off its garment of the gross sensations of touch, smell, taste, sight, and audition. But though divested of its physical sense instruments of perception, consciousness still retains its intuitive powers of cognition through the sub" conscious, and beholds the dreams resulting from memories, thoughts, and the activity of the subtle senses, the mental reflexes of the physical senses. (For instance, nearly every one can recall vivid dreams of eating ice cream, hot pie, or other foods.) However, when the ego enters the silent chamber of deep sleep or semi-superconsciousness, its experiences consist of the unalloyed enjoyment of real peace. The human consciousness, turned within, here begins to resume its normal state of calmness, peace, and joy. The conscious state is marked by restlessness; the subconscious state, by a mixture of restfulness and activity, but Bliss reigns in the superconscious state.[1]

The ego is peaceful in the realm of semi-superconsciousness, subtly excited or pleased in the dream state, and grossly excited or pleased while experiencing gross sensations.

Ordinarily, during its stay in the chamber of sensations, while in the state of physical consciousness, the ego is linked with subconsciousness through memory and with superconsciousness through the sense of inward peace -manifested or unmanifested.

Determine which "throne" of consciousness your ego occupies, i. e., which consciousness is predominant in your mind.

Determining and changing the pre-dominant state of consciousness.

During waking hours, the conscious state is predominant, the subconscious and superconscious states trailing behind. By the power of concentration, you can make the subconscious or superconscious predominant. The conscious state of restlessness can be changed into the dreamy state of subconsciousness or the supremely peaceful state of superconsciousness. *In poets, the subconscious usually predominates; in business men, the conscious state, and in real Yogis and great Swamis, the superconscious state. Change your centre from conscious to superconscious predominance.*

The average man generally concentrates, and stays, on the plane of physical consciousness. But when he is forcibly (through drugs) or passively (through fatigue) led the subconscious chamber of dreams and quiet sleep, or he enters the semi-superconsciousness of Joyous sleep, his ego generally becomes apparently unconscious or dimly conscious. The ordinary ego can support only one state at a time: the physically conscious state, or the subconscious state, or the semi-superconscious state.

In the untrained ego, sidetracked on the path of upward evolution, the conscious state always predominates. It loves to stay and dream in, and be conscious of, the realm of the senses only. 't forgets that during the night it moves semiconsciously through the chamber of dreams or through deep semi-superconscious sleep toward the Spirit.

Consciousness is manifested through gross sensation; subtle astral subconsciousness is manifested through dreams, quiet negative sleep, and through memory which never sleeps.

This subconscious mind is always awake; it works through memory while consciousness predominates, runs the motion-picture theatre of dreamland, and enjoys serenity during negative sleep.

Consciousness, subconsciousness, and superconsciousness are different degrees or states of Christ Consciousness -they can never be entirely independent of one another, although one state is usually stronger than the other. The ordinary man works with consciousness predominating; in the Yogi superconsciousness predominates. *Ask at different times* during *the day which consciousness is predominant in you.*

Business men, in whom, as a rule, the conscious state predominates, as well as those who stay on the subconscious plane, are unbalanced and one-sided, their happiness depending upon the circumstances in which they find themselves. The superconscious individual is not enslaved in conditions outside of himself; he is free and finds happiness within in spite of all circumstances.

The mind can control the body.

The close relation between the body and mind causes a psychological state to be followed by a corresponding physiological reaction which, in turn, intensifies the psychological state. Be angry and your face will show it. Permit anger to spread through your muscles until you are tense all over, and your anger will increase. The Yogi, by adopting certain psychological states, can produce the corresponding physiological reactions, and vice versa, and by certain physical acts he can instantaneously produce the corresponding psychological states. For instance, during sleep the eyes are closed; so by closing the eyes, the Yogi can produce instantaneous sleep at any time, anywhere. During the waking state the eyes are open - generally leveled; hence, by keeping the eyes level, the Yogi can remain consciously awake for days and weeks. Moreover during the superconscious state and in death, when he soul races toward the superconscious, the eyes automatically go upward; so by lifting his eyes upward and focusing his vision on the point between the eye brows, the Yogi can switch off the motion pictures of dreams or sensations and launch into the sea of luminosity, where electrons and life forces and Bliss reign in the "Kingdom of Spirit"

Becoming king of three kingdoms.

Meditation is the conscious method of entering the subconscious and super-conscious realms. By learning to control your eye muscles and shifting the gaze at will, you can transfer your ego from the conscious world to the tranquility of the subconscious dream world or to the superconscious state of perfect joy. Think of the freedom you gain by learning to shift, at will, from the land of terrestrial horror to the land of beautiful dreams, and when even dream fairies bother you, to float in the ether of eternal serenity or Bliss where dreams dare not tread or disturb. You are the king of three kingdoms. Realize that. Do not remain imprisoned in, and identified with, the little island of the body.

The Yogi has complete control over all forms of consciousness.

The Yogi can do just as he pleases - he can live in the realm of the senses, or fly to the land of dreams, or float in the vast ocean of eternal Bliss. He may choose superconscious serenity or subconscious dreams; or he may give predominance to semi-superconsciousness, superconsciousness, or Christ Consciousness, at will. If he prefers, he may remain half conscious and half dreaming, or half conscious and half asleep yet dreamless, or he may be semi-superconscious and half dreaming or quietly subconscious. If none of these pleases him, he may elect to enjoy, simultaneously, conscious sensations, dreams, tranquillity, subconsciousness, semi-superconsciousness, superconsciousness, and immanent Christ Consciousness. When he can do that, his ego becomes soul, and his soul breaks its bubble walls and becomes the sea of Spirit - then it attains the state of Nirbikalpa Samadhi or transcendental Cosmic Consciousness. In this state he perceives that his "throne" of consciousness rests in the Omnipresent Heart of consciousness, subconsciousness, dream subconsciousness, semi-superconsciousness, superconsciousness, immanent Christ Consciousness, and transcendental Cosmic Consciousness, equally and coexistently, all the time.[2] Then the "throne" of consciousness, instead of resting on a little speck of sensation, or a "diamond-chip" dream, or a little shining ambition, becomes fixed in the sparkling bosom of Omnipresence.

Technique for producing different states of consciousness.

Relax your body in a sitting posture. Lean against the back of a comfortable chair. Close your eyes and forget your *worries*, dismissing all restless thoughts; feel drowsy, become passive and mentally "careless"; in other words, "let go," fall asleep, or at least try to doze. Repeat this several times until the minute you lower the searchlight of your vision, the eyes, closing them and switching off the optical currents, you are instantly submerged in the subconscious.

Then, whenever you are heavy with sleep, quickly tense the whole body and lift your drooping eyes, leveling them in front of you. Keep looking at one object without winking; banish sleep at will. Then close your eyes, relax, and fall asleep again.

Every night, before dropping off to sleep, command your subconscious mind to wake you at a different hour. Continue making this suggestion to the subconscious mind until it obeys. Fall asleep with the thought that a matter of vital importance depends upon your getting up at your appointed hour.

After you have trained your subconscious mind to waken you at will, practice fixing your vision on the point between the eyebrows, and instantaneously go consciously into the state of deep peace, of deep intoxicating joy. The regular practice of the fourth and fifth Yogoda lessons and the higher methods will help you to attain this.

Empty your mind of thoughts. Every time thoughts return, firmly dismiss them. Then meditate on peace; be drunk with it; merge in it; consciously sleep over it.

Remember, to gain dominion over the three kingdoms, you must practice these exercises all the time. Whenever you have a period of leisure, lower and close your eyes and enter the "Kingdom of Dreams" at will. Then return at will, leveling your eyes, and enter the "Kingdom of Consciousness," drinking in the beauties of nature. Then lift your vision up between the eyebrows and enter the superconscious "Kingdom of Bliss."

You can attain complete freedom from worldly cares only after you have learned to shift the searchlight of your attention and energy from the conscious to the subconscious plane, or from the conscious to the superconscious plane, either dreaming or enjoying Bliss at will. Then you can fly from the plane of *sensations* to the plane *of dreams or to* the *realm of* eternal peace, as you choose.

Remember, however, that as you shift your vision from the conscious to the subconscious, the life force and energy must also be switched off from the lamps of the billion-celled muscles and the visual, auditory, olfactory, tactual, and gustatory nerves.

In shifting from the conscious to the superconscious plane, your lungs must be breathless, your heart calm, your cells inactive, your circulation stilled, and you must be listening to the symphony of the Cosmic Vibration of Om.

While in the superconscious state, one experiences complete *cessation* of unrest - fruition of peace - soul-expansion, unhampered by the friction attending sensations in the realm of consciousness.

If anyone claimed that he could sleep while he was running, he would be ridiculed, for healthful sleep is always accompanied by sensory and motor relaxation. Many profess to have attained Cosmic Consciousness, who have not yet learned to relax at will. The first signs of the attainment of Cosmic Consciousness are the fixed gaze, the consciously stilled heart, and breathlessness. If one cannot demonstrate these, he has not attained Cosmic Conscious

Contacting inner entities.

After you have learned to do this at will, you may practise the following exercise, at night: Lean against the back of a chair. Close your eyes and shift your gaze from the conscious level downward to the subconscious level and fall asleep. Then invoke the souls which have passed on, and meet them there in your consciously arranged reception parlor of dreamland.

To invoke Christ-like superconscious souls, however, you must extend a superconscious invitation. Lift your gaze and fix it between the eyebrows. Float away to the region of Bliss. In the chamber of Infinity and Perennial Peace invoke superconscious souls; they will come to you, materializing themselves from the Cosmic Consciousness into distinct saintly forms. The saints who became one with Spirit can be recreated by the Spirit. The Spirit Sea becomes a bubble of saintly life. Then, when this bubble of life knows itself as the Cosmic Sea, it merges with It. The Spirit Sea can reassume any form which It has once occupied and manifested. The Spirit is ever conscious. It has an eternal, unfailing memory. These super-conscious souls sometimes descend from the Cosmic Consciousness, taking various forms of light, as the *Devas, so* that they might float about the astral spheres of million-hued mellow, spiritual lights, worshipping God in the land of super-electrons and love, and after entertaining Him with the astral "super-talkies" they return to the sphere of Cosmic Consciousness and vanish in the one Infinite Love.

High spiritual development increases one's capacity for enjoyment. Color becomes more brilliant, sound more marvelous, feeling more intense the farther one advances along the spiritual path.

Liberate "King Soul" from his bondage to body matter, the senses, and other attachments; lift his searchlight *(atten*tion) upward, from petty things to Infinity; from worldly pleasures to Eternal Joy; from the little body to the Universe; from the limited human consciousness to Cosmic Consciousness.

The little searchlight of attention and the five senses ordinarily are focused on imperfect matter. When thrown back upon the Spirit, they disclose the Infinite Perfect Light forever dancing on God's fountain of Bliss, eternally emanating from Omnipresence and Christ Consciousness.

SUMMARY

Man's attachment to matter keeps the soul confined to the body prison and prevents it from finding freedom with God in the realm of Eternal Bliss. The ego attempts to satisfy the soul's constant, insatiable longing for God through material channels. Far from accomplishing its objective, it increases man's misery. *The soul's hunger can never be appeased by indulgence of the senses.* When man realizes this and masters his ego, i.e., when he achieves *self-control,* life becomes glorified by Bliss while he is still in the flesh. Then, instead of being the slave of material desires and appetites, his attention is transferred to the heart of Omnipresence, resting there forever with the hidden joy in everything.

[1]*The three states of consciousness and the physical and mental reactions produced by them:*
    i. Consciousness= Restlessness.
    ii. Subconsciousness=Restfulness and activity,
    iii. Semi-superconsciousness=Negative peace.
    Superconsciousness=Positive peace or Bliss.

[2]*Traveling by automobile, while on the plane of Cosmic Consciousness, often all at once I perceive coexisting in me, in infinite harmony, the car and the scenery surrounding it; my thoughts; my dreams; tranquility; planets; the inner world of many-colored lights; my glistening feelings; intuition-in short, all forms of consciousness-playing their part in the Cosmic Symphony. My soul has merged into the Infinite, and I perceive my body as a tiny, hardly visible moth of light.*

Super-Advanced Course Number 1
Lesson 4

Art Of Finding True Friends Of Past Incarnations. What Is Friendship?

Friendship is the universal spiritual attraction which unites souls in the bond of divine love and may manifest itself either in two or in many. The Spirit was One; by the law of duality it became two-positive and negative. Then, by the law of infinity applied to the law of relativity, it became many. Now the One in the many is endeavoring to unite the many and make them One. This effort of the Spirit to unify many souls into the One works through our emotions, intelligence, and intuition and finds expression through friendship.

To have friends, you must manifest friendliness. If you open the door to the magnetic power of friendship, a soul or souls of like vibrations will be attracted to you. The more friendly you become toward all, the greater will be the number of your real friends. *Friendship is a manifestation of God's love for you, expressed through your friends.*

Friendship and Cosmic Consciousness.

There are people who do not trust anyone, and who utterly doubt the possibility of ever having true friends. Some, in fact, actually boast that they get along without friends. If you fail to be friendly, you disregard the divine law of self-expansion by which alone your soul can grow into the Spirit. No man who fails to inspire confidence in other hearts - who is unable to extend the kingdom of his love and friendliness into other soul territories - can hope to spread his consciousness over Cosmic Consciousness. If you cannot conquer human hearts, you cannot conquer the Cosmic Heart.

Avoid doing anything which brings harm to yourself or to another. If you are self-indulgent, or if you encourage a friend in his vices, you are an enemy disguised as a friend. By being your own and others' true friend, you gain the friendship of God. Once you make your love felt in others' love, it will expand until it becomes the one Love which flows through all hearts.

Selfish attachment is the canker of friendship.
True friendship is broad and inclusive. Selfish attachment to a single individual, excluding all others, inhibits the development of Divine Friendship. Extend the boundaries of the glowing kingdom of your love, gradually including within them your family, your neighbors, your community, your country, all countries - in short, all living sentient creatures. Be also a cosmic friend, imbued with kindness and affection for all of God's creation, scattering love everywhere. Such was the example set by Christ, Swami Shankara, and my masters (Babaji, Lahiri Mahasaya, and Swami Sriyukteswarji).

Realize your kinship with all mankind.
Consider no one a stranger; learn that everybody is your kin. Family love is merely one of the first exercises in he divine Teacher's course in Friendliness, intended to prepare your heart for an all inclusive love. Feel that the life blood of God is circulating in the veins of all races. How does anyone dare to hate any human being of whatsoever race when he knows that God lives and breathes in all? We are Americans or Hindus, etc., for just a. few years, but we are God's children forever. The soul cannot be confined within man-made boundaries; its nationality is Spirit; its country, Omnipresence.

This does not mean that you must know and love all human beings and creatures *personally and individually. All* you need do is to be ready at all times to spread the light of friendly service over all living creatures which you happen to contact.

This requires constant mental effort and preparedness; in other words, unselfishness. The sun shines equally on diamond and charcoal, but the one has developed qualities which enable it to reflect the sunlight brilliantly, while the other absorbs it all. Emulate the diamond in your dealings with people; brightly reflect the light of God's love.

All this may seem very complicated, but when you touch the Infinite, your difficulties will melt away. Divine Love will come to you; beautiful intuitive experiences of universal friendliness will play like fountains in your mind.

Constant contact with the Infinite in meditation fills one with Divine Love, which alone enables him to love his enemies

The secret of Christ's strength lay His love for all, even His enemies. Far better to conquer by love the heart of a person who hates you than to vanquish him by other means. To the ordinary man such a doctrine seems absurd. He wants to return ten slaps for the one he has received and add twice as many kicks for good measure. Why should you love your enemy? In order that you may bring the healing rays of your love into his dark, hatred-stricken heart. When it is so released, it can behold itself as pure golden love. Thus will the flame of your love burn the partitions of hatred and misery which separate your soul from other souls and all souls from the vast sea of Infinite Love.

How to convert enemies into friends.

*Pra*ctice loving those who do not love you. Feel for those who do not feel for you. Be generous to those who are generous only to themselves. If you heap hatred on your enemy, neither he nor you are able to perceive the inherent beauty of your soul.

You need not fawn on your enemy. Silently love him. Silently be of service to him whenever he is in need, for love *is real only when* it *is useful and expresses itself through action.* Thus will you rend the veils of hate and of narrow-mindedness which hide God from your sight.

If humility and apologies on your part bring out your enemy's good qualities, by all means apologize. The person who can do this will have attained a definite spiritual development, for it takes character to be able to apologize graciously and sincerely. It is the consciousness of his own inferiority which makes a man hide behind a display of pride. *Do not, however, encourage a wrongdoer by being humble and apologetic.*

Service is the keynote of friendship.
Cultivate true friendliness, for only *thus do you* attract true friends to yourself. True friendship consists in being mutually useful; in offering your friends good cheer in distress, sympathy in sorrow, advice in trouble, and material help in times of real need. Friendship consists in rejoicing in your friends' good fortune and sympathizing with them in adversity. Friendship gladly forgoes selfish pleasures or self-interest for the sake of a friend's happiness, without consciousness of loss or sacrifice; without counting the cost.

Never be sarcastic to a friend. Do not flatter him unless it be to encourage him, do not agree with him when he is wrong. Real friendship cannot witness with indifference the false, harmful pleasures of a friend. This does not mean that you must quarrel. Suggest mentally or if your advice is asked, give it gently and lovingly. Fools fight; friends discuss their differences.

Help your friend also by being a mental, esthetic, and spiritual inspiration to him.

Friendship should not be influenced by people's relative positions. Friendship may and should exist between lovers, employer and employee, teacher and pupil, parents and children, and so forth.

Unfailing laws of friendship.
Be neither unduly familiar with, nor indifferent to, a friend. Moreover, do not trademark him by telling him, "I know all about you." Respect and love grow among friends with time.

"Familiarity breeds contempt" between those who are mutually useless, selfish, materially minded, and unproductive of inspiration or self-development. The greater the mutual service, the deeper the friendship. Why does Jesus have such a wide following? Because He, like the other great masters, is unequaled in His service to humanity. Hence, to attract friends, you must possess the qualities of a real friend. Idiots may become friends, but their blind friendship may end in a sudden blind hate. The building of wisdom and spiritual and intuitive understanding by mutual effort alone can bind two souls by the laws of everlasting, universal Divine Love. Human love and friendship have their basis in service on the physical, mental, or business plane; they are short-lived and conditional. Divine Love has had its foundation in service on the spiritual and intuitional planes and is unconditional and everlasting.

How to achieve conjugal happiness.

Unless conjugal love has a spiritual basis it can *never last.* If husbands and wives are to live in friendship and harmony, they must be of spiritual service to each other. It is the "newlyweds" who forget that true (spiritual) love is based on unselfish mutual service and friendship, who soon come to a parting of the ways. When two souls are ideally mated, their love becomes spiritualized and is registered in eternity after death as the one love of God.

Finding friends of past incarnations.

There are people with whom you come in daily contact, yet with whom you do not feel in sympathy. Learn to love them and adapt yourself to them. There are others who give you the instantaneous feeling that you have known them always. *This* indicates that they *are* your friends of previous incarnations. Do not neglect them, but strengthen the friendship existing between you. Be on the lookout for them always, as your restless mind may fail to recognize them. Often they are very near you, drawn by the friend ship born in the dim, distant past. They constitute your shining collection of soul jewels; add to it constantly. In these bright soul galaxies you will behold the one Great Friend smiling at you radiantly and clearly. It is God who comes to you in the guise of a noble, true Friend, to serve, inspire, and guide you.

Ugliness of disposition and selfishness drive away all friends of former incarnations, whereas friendliness draws them toward you. Therefore, be ready always to meet them halfway. Never mind if one or two friends prove false and deceive you.

Each individual has his own standard of physical and mental beauty. What seems ugly to one may appear beautiful to another. *Looking at a vast crowd, you like some faces instantaneously; others do not attract you particularly.* The instant attraction of your mind to the likeable inner and outer features of an individual is your first indication that you have found a friend of the past. Your dear ones whom you loved before, *will* be drawn toward you by a prenatal sense of friendship.

Do not be deceived by physical beauty; ask yourself whether or not a face, the manner of walking - in short, everything about a person——appeals to you. Sometimes overeating and lack of exercise may distort the features of a friend, and thus he may escape your recognition. Sometimes a beautiful woman may fall in love with an ugly man, or a handsome man, with a physically unattractive woman, due to the loving friendship of a past incarnation. A fat, distorted body may harbor a real friend. Therefore, to be sure that your eyes have not deceived you regarding the physical characteristics of your supposed former friend, ascertain whether you are mentally and spiritually congenial. Delve deeply into a person's mind and guard yourself against being prejudiced by little peculiarities, in order to find out whether your tastes and inclinations essentially agree. *Seek your friends o f past incarnations in order that you may continue your friendship in this life and perfect it into Divine Friendship. One lifetime is not always sufficient to achieve such perfection.*

Jealousy is self-love and the death of friendship.

The ennobling effects of friendship.

When true friendship exists between souls and they seek spiritual love and God's love together, when their only wish is to be of service to each other, their friendship produces the flame of the Spirit. Through perfected Divine Friendship, mutually seeking spiritual perfection, you will find the one Great Friend.

When perfect friendship exists either between two hearts or within a group of hearts in a spiritual organization, such friendship perfects each individual. In the heart, purified by friendship, one beholds an open door of unity through which he should invite other souls to enter-those that love him as well as those that love him not.

Friendship is God's love shining through the eyes of your loved ones, calling you home to drink His nectar of all differences-and-selfishness-dissolving unity. Friendship is God's trumpet call, bidding the soul to destroy the partitions which separate it from all other souls and from Him. True friend ship unites two souls so completely that they reflect the unity of 'Spirit and Its divine qualities.

When you behold, assembled all at once beneath the canopy of your perfected universal friendship, the souls of the past, present, and future, the busy stars, the amoeba, the whippoorwill, the nightingale, the dumb stones, and the shining sea sands, then the friendship thirst of your heart will be quenched forever. Then God's creation will ring with the emancipating song of all difference-dissolving celestial friendship. Then the Divine Friend will rejoice to see you come home after your evolutional wanderings and roamings through the pathways of incarnations. Then He and you will merge in the Bliss of Eternal Friendship.

Heavenly Father! Let those that are our own come unto us, and finding them may we find friendship with all, and thus find Thee.

SUMMARY

God's effort to unite strife-torn humanity manifests itself within your heart as the friendship instinct.

Make every effort to rediscover your friends of past incarnations, whom you may recognize through familiar physical, mental and spiritual qualities. Rising above considerations of material or even spiritual gain, perfect your friendship, begun in a preceding incarnation, into Divine Friendship.

When Divine Friendship reigns supreme in the temple of your heart, your soul will merge with the vast Cosmic Soul, leaving far behind the confining bonds which separated it from all of God's animate and inanimate creation.

Super Advanced Course Number 1
Lesson 5
The Divine Magnetic Diet:
Physical And Mental Methods For Rejuvenating The Body Cells And Awakening The Latent Powers Of The Mind And The Inner Forces Of The Soul

Most diseases can be cured by judicious fasting under the guidance of a specialist.

Fasting may be divided into two main groups: *partial fasting and complete fasting.*

Partial Fasting:
In this group, four general subdivisions may be mentioned:
   i. Limiting the diet to certain foods;
   ii. Abstaining from certain foods;
   iii. Limiting the food intake as to quantity;
   iv. Limiting the number of meals to one or two per day.

Some of these forms of fasting may be combined. For instance, to cure disease or reduce weight, a person may abstain from certain foods altogether and limit the intake of other foods, etc.

More specific subdivisions are:
Liquid diet:
   (a) "Liquid" fasting. For one or two days a week, and whenever one does not feel hungry, the food intake may be confined to (i) milk, or (ii) orange juice or any other fruit juice.

Solid diet:
   (b) "Solid" fasting. This diet is confined to (i) raw fruits;[1] (ii) raw vegetables; (iii) half-boiled vegetables, including juice in which they were boiled. Drink plenty of water while on this diet.

"Oxygen" diet:
(c) "Oxygen" fasting. Inhaling and exhaling deeply from six to twelve times every hour, filling the lungs with fresh air down to the lower lobes. This method may be practiced outdoors for twelve hours, while alternately slowly walking and resting. When weather conditions necessitate indoor practice, the windows should be kept wide open. (Of course, warm clothing should be worn during the winter season as a protection against the cold.) This fast aids spiritual growth. It should not be undertaken by weak individuals or invalids.

Complete Fasting :
Complete fasting should not, as a rule, exceed ten days and should not be at tempted even for that length of time except under the supervision of a specialist. However, abstaining from food for one day each week and for three consecutive days each month, has brought beneficial results. Water must be taken in abundance during complete fasting, to replace the fluid lost by evaporation through the pores, etc.

Nine-day diet:
The *Nine-day Cleansing and Vitalizing Diet,* given below, has proved a most effective method for ridding the system of poisons.
1 1/2 grapefruit
1 glass orange juice with a teaspoon Senna Leaves or new Original Swiss Kriss[2]
1 1/2 lemons, 5 oranges
1 cooked vegetable with juice (quantity optional)
3 cups vitality beverage
1 raw vegetable salad (one at each meal)

Vitality Beverage: ingredients for beverage
2 stalks chopped celery
1/2 quart. chopped dandelion
5 carrots (chopped) incl. part of stem or turnip greens or spinach
1 bunch chopped parsley
1 quart. water

No salt or spices

The beverage may be prepared in two ways, the first being preferable:

(1) After putting celery and carrots through meat chopper, lightly boil them in the water for ten minutes. Then add selected greens and parsley and boil ten minutes more. Strain by squeezing through cheesecloth.

(2) Use the same ingredients, but do not cook them. After putting them through meat chopper, strain as above.

Drink one cup of the beverage, prepared by either method, at each of the three meals.

This vitality beverage has been found to be a blood tonic and very effective in rheumatism, various stomach disorders (including acute indigestion), chronic catarrh, bronchitis, and nervous "breakdown."

While on the cleansing diet, strictly abstain from spices, candies, pastries, meat, eggs, fish, cheese, milk, butter, bread, fried foods, oil, beans - in fact, all other foods not mentioned above. If one feels the need of additional nourishment, one may take a tablespoonful of thoroughly ground nuts in a half glass of water or a glass of orange juice.

Following the nine-day diet, one should be especially careful in the selection and quantity of one's food intake the first day and resume a normal diet gradually.

If one is not successful in ridding the body of all poisons during the initial attempt, the cleansing diet may be repeated after an interval of two or three weeks.

While on the cleansing diet, it has been found beneficial every night just before going to bed, to use two pounds of some good bath salts in one-fourth tub of warm water; and, also very helpful to take a bath salts bath every now and then, for several weeks after finishing the cleansing diet.

Super Advanced Course 1

Reducing diet:

One should Practice Exercise B of Yogoda Lesson 1 (re-charging exercise), six times, twice a day, and exercises D and E of the same lesson (stomach exercises), twenty times each, three times a day. Command your will, during tension, to burn up the superfluous tissues. Practice the running exercise 50 to 200 times a day. Eat mostly raw vegetables and one-half of a boiled yolk of an egg a day. Abstain from starchy food, fried foods, and sweets. Do not drink water with meals. Every three days fast one day on orange juice.

Extremely stout people have derived much benefit from fasting on orange juice seven days and then going on the nine-day cleansing diet, a normal diet being resumed gradually thereafter. If there was need for further reduction of weight, this procedure was repeated after an interval of two weeks.

"Fattening" diet:

The following foods are of high nutritive value and have been found beneficial for those who wish to gain weight:

bananas with cream
2 eggs
oatmeal with cream
1 large raw vegetable salad
$1/_4$ glass cream
1 tablespoon olive oil
2 slices whole-wheat bread
$3 1/_2$ oz. butter

Weight has also been gained by eating bananas in abundance, and for one month drinking two glasses of water (moderately hot or cold, *not* iced) with each meal.

Some of the foods from the above list are added to the usual dietary.

General dietary rules:

To have faith in God's healing power through the mind and obey dietary laws, is better than just to have faith in God and mind and disregard dietary laws.

Every day, for beneficial results, eat green-leafed vegetables, including a carrot with part of its stem, and drink a glass of orange juice (including pulp) with a tablespoonful of finely ground nuts. Mix good salad dressings made of thoroughly ground nuts, cream, a few drops of lemon juice, orange juice and honey with all salads. Thousand-island dressing is good. A little curry sauce with boiled egg or vegetables, once in a while, is a good salivary stimulant.

Food combinations:

For best results one should abstain from all beef and pork products. Do not make a habit of eating even chicken, lamb, or fish every day. Once a week or better, once a month is enough, if your system demands flesh foods at all. Nuts, cottage cheese, eggs, milk, cream, and bananas are very good meat and fish substitutes. If you eat chicken, lamb, or fish,[3] have a vegetable salad with them.

Fruit should be eaten with bread or some other starchy food, but without sugar; you may add a little honey if you wish. Eat only nature's candies (unsulphured figs, prunes or raisins).

Do not eat too much white sugar. The ingestion of excessive quantities of sweets causes intestinal fermentation.

Remember, foods prepared from white flour, such as white bread, white-flour gravy, etc., also polished rice and too many greasy fried foods, are injurious to your health.

Try to include in your daily diet as much raw food as possible. Cooked vegetables should be eaten with the juice in which they were boiled.

Catarrh of the alimentary canal often results from overeating at night, also from eating excessively of candy or other foodstuffs which have an irritating effect on the mucous membranes of the stomach, duodenum, etc.

Super Advanced Course 1

Fast regularly, using your best judgment as to proper diet, in accordance with the instructions given above. Eat less, and follow dietary rules when you eat. Make sunshine, oxygen, and energy a part of your regular daily diet.

The daily diet:

Your daily food intake should be chosen from the following list of foods which contain all the elements needed for the proper maintenance of the body"

½ apple
1 baked or half-boiled or steamed vegetable with its juice
¼ grapefruit
1 lemon
1 lime
1 orange
1 raw carrot, including part of green top
1 glass orange juice with tablespoon finely ground nuts
6 leaves raw spinach
¼ heart lettuce
1 small piece fresh pineapple
1 teaspoon olive oil
1 glass milk
6 figs, dates, or prunes[4]
1 handful of raisins
1 teaspoon honey
1/8 glass cream
1 tablespoon cottage cheese
1 tablespoon clabber[5]

Eat at least some of the above foods every day, distributing them over your three meals. For instance, you may take the milk at breakfast, bread and egg and vegetable salad at noon, and the ground nuts and fruits at night.

Individual food habits may be taken into consideration, but if they are bad gradually change them. At any rate, add some of the foods in the above list to what you are used to eating. Omit those foods mentioned above which do not agree with you, eating only very lightly when you feel need of nourishment, and gradually accustoming yourself to a more wholesome diet.

You may increase or decrease the quantities given above, in accordance with your individual needs. It is, of course, obvious that the person doing strenuous muscular work requires more food than the sedentary worker.

Whenever one is hungry one may take a large tablespoonful of thoroughly ground nuts in half a glass of water or in a glass of orange juice. When thirsty, drink a glass of orange juice or water (preferably distilled or boiled). However, nature's distilled water - undiluted fruit juice - is best. Do not drink too much ice water with meals. Ice water should be taken sparingly at any time, but especially during and after meals as it lowers the temperature of the stomach, thus retarding digestion. *Never drink ice water when you are overheated.*

THE MAGNETIC DIET

What distilled water is to a wet battery, food is to the body battery. The life energy in the body battery is derived from Cosmic Energy through the medulla, and from food. The life energy in the body breaks up the foods and converts them into energy also. It is the intricate task of the life force to distil more life force from the nourishment taken into the body. Therefore, one's dietary should be confined to foods which are easily converted into energy, or which are productive of fresh energy. Oxygen and sunshine should have a very important place in people's lives, because of their direct energy producing quality. The more you depend on the will and on Cosmic Energy to sustain you, the less your food requirements; the more you depend on food, the weaker your will and the less your recourse to Cosmic Energy.

The magnetic diet consists of such food substitutes as rays and oxygen which can be easily assimilated and converted into energy by the latent life forces in the body. Magnetic foods give energy more quickly than solids and liquids which are less easily converted into life force.

When you are tired or hungry, take a sun bath, and you find yourself recharged with ultraviolet rays, and revived; or inhale and exhale several times outdoors or near an open window, and your fatigue will be gone. A fasting person who inhales and exhales deeply twelve times, three times a day, recharges his body with electrons and free energy from air and ether. Contact of food and oxygen with the inner bodily system is necessary if the life force is to convert the food and oxygen into energy. The life force can assimilate oxygen more quickly than it can assimilate solids or liquids.

Practice the following exercise three times a day: Exhale slowly, counting from 1 to 6. Now, while the lungs are empty, mentally count from 1 to 6. Inhale slowly, counting from 1 to 6. Then hold the breath, counting from 1 to 6.[6] Repeat eleven times.

Just as electricity passes through a rod made of a conductive substance, and electrifies it, so the body battery becomes fully charged with life force derived from oxygen.

People who perform breathing exercises always have shining, magnetic eyes.

One hour's sun bath is also a part of the magnetic diet.

The ultraviolet rays which one absorbs in one whole day on a bathing beach exert a beneficial vitalizing effect on the body, which lasts about three months. Sores and wounds can be cured by exposing them one-half hour daily to the sunlight.

Treatment with artificially produced ultraviolet and infrared rays also supplies the body with magnetic nourishment. Much benefit may be derived from it if it is taken under the guidance of a specialist.

Ordinary window glass prevents the sun's ultraviolet rays from penetrating into a room.

Living in a sun room enclosed by yellow quartz glass, through which the ultraviolet sun rays penetrate, would supply the human body with magnetic spiritual nutriment and make it in turn spiritually magnetic. A man living in a room enclosed by red quartz glass would find brute force developing within himself.

Each one of the many billions of cells within the human body is a tiny mouth taking nourishment. The life force, identified with the body, creates within us a desire to derive energy from the circulation and from meat and other foods taken into the stomach. The life force must be trained to draw energy from subtler sources. The body's energy requirements can be supplied partly by sunshine and oxygen, which are absorbed by the pores. For this reason, the surface of the skin must be kept scrupulously clean at all times.

Exercising with will and concentration produces excellent results because it creates energy directly, by will development. This energy is quickly absorbed by the muscles, blood, bones, and sinews, for cellular rejuvenation. Therefore, the highest degree of energy accompanied by the least tissue destruction is derived from the Yogoda will exercises (Lessons 1 to 3).

Occasionally charging the body with electricity by holding on to two electrodes of a battery is a good method for supplying the body with free energy. (The electric current should be very weak.) Bathing in sunlight - heated or ultraviolet-ray-saturated water is very beneficial.

Rubbing the whole stripped body vigorously and rapidly with the palms before taking a bath generates life force and is also very beneficial.

If a weak man wrestles or lives in the same room with a strong, vital individual, he absorbs some of the latter's vital and mental magnetism. For this reason young and old people should mingle and thus exchange magnetism. Different people have different kinds of vitality. Always try to discover new methods for getting direct energy qualities from different individuals.

As a rule, the word "food" is used only in connection with material nourishment, but there are other kinds of food: mental energy, or concentration, and Divine Wisdom. The first (material food) recharges the body battery; the second (concentration), the mind battery; the third (Divine Wisdom), the soul battery.

Not only are proper material foods in the right combinations necessary for the sustenance of the body, but they exert a decided influence on the brain. The spiritual brain, the active brain, and the material brain are all affected by food, and can form different combinations: (1) spiritual-active brain, (2) intellectual-active brain, and (3) material-active brain.

All food that is eaten produces a sensation on the palate as well as certain chemical effects in body and brain. Food sensations determine a specific mentality. Foods such as dried meat produce gross material reactions which develop the material brain and animal mind. Likewise, the eating of active, vital foods, such as onions, garlic, fresh (not dried) meat, etc., produces an active brain. Eating raw fruits and vegetables produces spiritual qualities in the consumer and develops a spiritual mind and brain.

The quality of the food's taste and color is all reported to the brain through the nerves of taste and sight, and is experienced as specific pleasant or unpleasant sensations. These sensations are elaborated into perceptions and conceptions. Repeated conceptions about foods form definite mental habits and manifest themselves as material, active, or spiritual qualities.

While we know that material foods supply the body with energy, we must also remember that good thoughts are nourishing food for the mind, and thoughts of any other nature are poisonous to the health of body and mind.

Have you ever analyzed your magnetic mental diet? It consists usually of the thoughts which you are thinking as well as the thoughts you are receiving from the close thought contact with your friends. Peaceful thoughts and peaceful friends always produce healthy, magnetic minds. It is easy to tell whether a person feeds on a quarrelsome or a peaceful environment. Inner disquietude and worries, due to the wrong sort of friends or unappreciative immediate relatives, produce an unwholesome, gloomy mind.

Ridding the mind of worry poisons.

If you are suffering from mental ill health, go on a mental diet. A health giving mental fast will clear the mind and rid it of the accumulated mental poisons resulting from a careless, faulty mental diet.

First of all, learn to remove the causes of your worries without permitting them to worry you. Do not feed your mind with daily created mental poisons of fresh worries.

Worries are often the result of attempting to do too many things hurriedly. Do not "bolt" your mental duties, but thoroughly masticate them, one at a time, with the teeth of attention and saturate them with the saliva of good judgment. Thus will you avoid worry indigestion.

Worry fasts.

Then you must go on worry fasts. Three times a day shake off all worries. At seven o'clock in the morning say to yourself, "All my worries of the night are cast out, and from 7 to 8 A.M. I refuse to worry, no matter how troublesome are the duties ahead of me. I am going on *a worry fast.*"

From 12 to 1 p m., say, "I am cheerful, I will not worry."

In the evening, between six and nine o'clock, while in the company of your husband or wife or "hard-to-get-along-with" relatives or friends, mentally make a strong resolution and say, "Within these three hours I will not worry, I refuse to get vexed, even if I am nagged. No matter how tempting it is to indulge in *a worry feast, I will* resist the temptation. I have been very sick of worries—my heart of peace has been diseased. I have had several worry heart attacks. I must not paralyze and kill my peace-heart by shocks of worries. I am on *a worry fast.* I cannot afford to worry."

After you succeed in carrying out *worry fasts* during certain hours of the day, try doing it for a week or two weeks at a time, and then try to prevent the accumulation of worry poisons in your system, entirely.

Whenever you find yourself indulging in a *worry feast,* go on a partial or complete *worry fast* for a day or a week.

Whenever you make up your mind not to worry, i.e., to go on a *worry fast, stick to your* resolution. You can stop worrying entirely. You can calmly solve your most difficult problems, putting forth your greatest effort, and at the same time absolutely refuse to worry. Tell your mind, "I can do only my best; no more. I am satisfied and happy that I am doing my best to solve my problem; there is absolutely no reason why I should worry myself to death."

When you are on *a worry fast,* you need not be in a negative mental state. Drink copiously of the fresh waters of peace flowing from the spring of every circumstance, vitalized by your determination to be cheerful. If you have made up your mind to be cheerful, nothing can make you unhappy. If you do not choose to destroy your own peace of mind by accepting the suggestion of unhappy circumstances, none can make you dejected. You are concerned only with the untiring performance of right actions for right results; but your whole attention must be on the actions, and not on their results. Leave the latter to God, saying, "I have done my best under the circumstances. Therefore, I am happy."

Joy as a cure for overcoming worry.

The negative method for overcoming worry poisoning is *worry fasting.* There are also positive methods. One infected with the germs of worry must go on a strict mental diet. He must feast frugally, but regularly, on the society of joyful minds. Every day he must associate-if only for a little while-with "joy-infected" minds. There are some people the song of whose laughter nothing can still. Seek them out and feast with them on this most vitalizing food of joy. Continue the laughter diet for a month or two. Feast on laughter in the company of really joyful people. Digest it thoroughly by whole-heartedly masticating laughter with the teeth of your attention. Steadfastly continue your laughter diet once you have begun it, and at the end of a month or two you will see the change-your mind will be filled with sunshine. Remember, specific habits can be cultivated only by specific habit-forming actions.

The courage diet:

Having benefited by the *worry fast,* try the *fear fast* next, going on a courage diet for certain hours, days, or weeks. You must act spiritually in order to be spiritual.

The wisdom diet:

In order to destroy ignorance, go on *a wisdom diet.* Drink the tonic of wisdom from the lips of intuition. You can learn from intuition when you meet it in the chamber of deep meditation. Read good books of a devotional and spiritual nature, taking from them what you need.

Consult a spiritual specialist. If your disease of ignorance is chronic, be guided entirely by him. That patient cannot be cured who depends only on his own judgment which may be affected by his state of mental ill health.

Go on ignorance-elimination fasts. Refuse to be enslaved by ignorant habits and thoughtless actions. Take up intensive spiritual study and intensive spiritual dieting, and refuse to suffer any longer from the infection of ignorance.

Overcoming mental stagnation.

Mental stagnation is "mental T. B." Come out of your closed chamber of narrowness. Drink in the fresh air of others' vital thoughts and views. Drink vitality; receive mental nourishment from materially and spiritually progressive minds. Feast unstintingly on the creative thinking within yourself and others. Take long mental walks on the paths of self-confidence. Exercise with the instruments of judgment, introspection, and initiative. Exhale poisonous thoughts of discouragement, discontentment, hopelessness, etc. Inhale the fresh oxygen of success, and know that you are progressing with God's help. This will recharge your soul battery. By consciously experiencing God's Bliss through meditation, you can consciously destroy mental stagnation and acquire progressive spiritual health and wisdom.

Acquiring Physical, mental, and spiritual perfection.

Thus, day by day, eating spiritual magnetism-producing foods and absorbing vitality-producing sunshine, you will physically reflect God's everlasting youth. Eliminating all mental poisons and partaking of the divine nourishment of determination, courage, continuous, unfailing mental effort and concentration, you will learn to overcome the most difficult problems with ease. Eliminating ignorance by constant meditation on God, and following the precepts of Yogoda and your spiritual teacher, you will attain perfect spiritual health. Once you acquire this spiritual health, you will give your life to and for others, to show them also the way to supreme, intoxicating spiritual health.

Once you learn to eat right foods, think right thoughts, being filled with wisdom and joy, your body, mind, and soul will be spiritualized and perceived as dynamos of magnetic energy.

Your body and mind, purified by this energy, will take on the beauty of the Spirit. Once you realize yourself as a soul, you will know you are of the Spirit, resting every where equally in joy, in all space, in all things, as one with all things.

A body, mind, and soul magnet, recharged with good food, rays, power, wisdom, and Bliss, draws unto itself all material and spiritual souls, spiritually deeply magnetic, like itself. A spiritual magnet is charged with the life of God, and whomsoever it touches it makes God of him.

SUMMARY

Those who think that life depends only on breakfast, lunch and dinner - on solids and liquids - are gross-minded. We can derive energy either from material foods or from the Cosmic Source.

The man of the future will draw nourishment from the ether and from the ocean of invisible Cosmic Energy in which he moves and has his being.

It is the aim of this lesson:

(1) To direct the student's attention to the advisability of drawing his energy requirements, so far as possible, from air and sunlight. The nourishment derived from these two sources can be most easily converted into energy within the body.

(2) To show the student the necessity of choosing only those material foods which emit and lodge spiritual vibrations in man's mind and brain.

Material foods impress the mind with certain good or bad qualities, and people's thoughts, actions, and health generally are determined by the foods they eat.

---

[1] *No bread or other starchy foods or sugar; no meat, eggs, or fish - nothing but the foods mentioned in (1) or (2) or (3), and only one meal per day (at noon).*

[2] *To he taken every night while on cleansing diet, before going to bed. To obtain best results, take 1/2 tsp. at first; later increase to 1 tsp.. Note that for invalids and children one should use proper care and discretion in going on this cleansing diet, and if necessary consult a specialist first.*

[3] *Chicken, lamb, or fish should be thoroughly baked, stewed, or broiled, and eggs should be hard boiled before eating, in order to destroy any harmful bacteria which they may contain.*

[4] *These fruits are wholesome only when they are unsulphured. Ascertain that they are unsulphured before you buy them.*

[5] *Milk which has been allowed to stand in a warm place, preferably in an earthen vessel, for a day or longer, until it has soured or curdled.*

[6] *Never hold breath longer than it takes to count slowly form 1 or 6 or, at most, from 1 to 12.*

Super Advanced Course Number 1
Lesson 6
Installing Habits
Of Success, Health, and Wisdom
In The Mind At Will

In search for success one must concentrate on needs and not on wants. It is well that man does not get every thing he wants, and that the Cosmic Law does not grant the wishes which would result in harm. A child may ask his father to catch him a beautiful poisonous snake, but the father does not fulfill such a dangerous wish. The Divine Law also denies the gratification of harmful, though momentarily pleasurable, desires. Of course, man, as the free-born child of God, can, and often does, persist in his longing for something quite delightful in the beginning but harmful in the end.

The greater the need, the greater the likelihood that it will be filled.

Before you can get that which you want, you must develop the power to get at will that which you need.

How to find true happiness.
What are your real needs? Shelter; food for body, mind, and soul; prosperity; health; the power of concentration; a good memory; an understanding heart; friends; wisdom, and Bliss, are some human needs. Plain living, high thinking, cultivating real happiness within oneself in order to make others spiritually happy, are also real needs. True happiness is lasting, because it is spiritual in nature, whereas the "happiness" based on sense pleasure soon turns to sorrow. Making the senses serve the needs of body and mind leads to true happiness: indulging the senses brings nothing but misery. A desire for a pleasurable sense object is often mistaken for a natural "need" instead of an artificially created "want." "Wants" must not be multiplied;

instead, the whole of concentration must be directed toward the filling of real "needs" or the securing of actual necessities.

As a rule, the attention is absorbed by loosely floating, unnecessary "wants" and constantly increasing desires. All desires for the ratification of needless "wants" must be stamped out.

Focusing the attention on one "need" at a time is the first step in the right direction. Determine your greatest "need," involving all the factors of life and true happiness; then devote all your attention and energy to attaining your objective by the quickest method.

Human lives are governed not by weak resolutions, but by habits. When people are used to good health, prosperity, a high standard of living, writing, lecturing, etc., all these seem to come easily. Likewise, poverty and failure come to those who are used to them.

Actions of habit, good or bad, are performed easily and naturally, bringing about good or bad results. *Success* and *failure are habits.* Therefore, if you are used to poverty or sickness, you must learn how to get used to health and prosperity instead. If failure, sickness, and ignorance are your constant companions, *nothing but* lack of will prevents you from enlisting the aid of success, health, and knowledge to drive and keep them away, definitely and permanently.

The soul's heritage.

Success, health, and wisdom are the natural attributes and habits of the soul. Identification with constantly manifested *weak* habits and thoughts, and lack of concentration, perseverance and courage are responsible for the misery which people suffer due to poverty, ill health, and so forth.

You are paralyzing your faculty for success by thoughts of fear. Success and perfection of mind and body are man's inherent qualities, because *he is made in God's image. In order to be able to claim his birthright, he* must first rid *himself of the delusion of his own limitations.*

God owns everything. Therefore, know at all times that you as God's child own *everything that belongs to the Father.* The whole mental attitude of an individual must be that of a son of God who is fully satisfied and contented, because he knows he has access to all his Father's possessions. Your native endowment is perfection and prosperity, but you choose to be imperfect and poor. This sense of *possessing everything must be a mental habit with* each individual.

Of what use are habits to us?

Habit formation is a device given us for the easy performance of certain actions. Habits are mental mechanisms which enable us to act automatically, leaving our consciousness free for other duties. A habit is formed by several attentive repetitions of an action.

Time required for habit formation can be shortened.

A special mental note should be made about slow or rapid habit formation. Some people require much time to form mental habits of health, prosperity, and the acquirement of wisdom. Actually, the time needed for this purpose can be shortened. Slow or rapid habit formation depends on the general state of health; on the condition of the nervous system, including that of the brain cells; on habit-forming methods, mental imagery, will, etc. When a wholesome mental attitude is a strong habit - strong enough to be unshakable —- no matter how many times you become ill, you will recover. Most people are "half-hearted" in their thoughts and actions; hence they do not succeed.

A mental habit, in order to materialize, must be strong and persistent.

For instance, the health or prosperity habit must be cultivated by health or prosperity thoughts until results are apparent. An unfailingly wholesome, courageous mental attitude is absolutely necessary to the attainment of one's "needs" and "wants." Failure to prosper and be healthy is due unquestionably to weak mental habits of health and prosperity.

Dislodge negative thoughts.

In affirming, "I am healthy," or "I am wise," the positive affirmation must be so strong that it crowds out completely any subconscious, discouraging, negative enemy thoughts which may be whispering to you, "you fool, you will never succeed. You are a failure; wisdom is impossible for you." You must know that whatever you wish strongly, you can materialize in short order.

Disregard the time element while affirming.

In practicing affirmations, the spiritual aspirant must be unfailingly patient. Believe you are inherently healthy when you want good health; believe you are inherently prosperous when you want prosperity; believe you are inherently wise when you want wisdom - then health, prosperity, and wisdom will manifest themselves in you.

Change the trend of your thoughts; cast out all negative mental habits, substituting in their place wholesome, courageous thought habits, and *applying them in daily life*, with *unshakable confidence*.

Remember that while an inattentive, scatter-brained idiot requires a long time for the formation of even a simple habit, an intelligent, purposeful individual can easily form or substatute a good mental habit for a bad one, in a trice, by the mere wish. Therefore, if you have a habit-mental, physical, or spiritual-that impedes your progress, rid *yourself of it now; do not put it off.*

Exercises:

(A) If you are afflicted with a chronic case of indifference, make up your mind at once to "snap out of it." Be gay; think of something amusing until you find yourself bubbling over with laughter. Exercise self-control; learn to substitute, at will, joy for sorrow; love for hate; courage for fear; openmindedness for prejudice.

(B) Know that anything others can do, you can do also.[1]

(C) If you have an inferiority complex, remember that success, health, and wisdom are your rightful heritage. Your difficulty is due to weakness which may have had its inception in one or more factors. It can be overcome by determination, courage, common sense, and faith in God and in yourself.

Therefore, if you are firmly convinced you are a failure, change your mental attitude at once; be unshakable in your conviction that you have all the potentialities of great success. At times you may find it helpful to recall your mental reactions on occasions when you were successful in some undertaking.

Practice the fourth Yogoda lesson faithfully and regularly and consult your spiritual teacher. Y

You may find it necessary also to change your mental and physical environment in order to install the proper habits of thought.

After you begin to experience success, act with wisdom and perseverance, no matter what happens, until you demonstrate that you have succeeded just as you believed you would if you tried.

SUMMARY

It does not take long to develop good mental habits. In fact, by exercising strong will, mental habits of health or success or wisdom may be formed at once. By concentrating with perseverance, courage, and faith in God and oneself on legitimate necessities, one can materialize them at will.

---

[1] *Once I was having dinner with friends. Everything went well until the Roquefort cheese was served. In India we eat only freshly made cheese, so I viewed the little green specks of mold in the cheese with great suspicion.*

Super Advanced Course 1

My soul rebelled against it, and my brain cells warned me to have nothing to do with it. But as I looked at my American friends eating the cheese, I mustered courage and took a lump of it into my mouth. No sooner had it landed there than all the aristocratic delicacies which had preceded it rebelled. There was great clamor and commotion within me, and they served notice on me that if "Mr. Roquefort" joined them they would all leave in a body. And I dared not open my mouth, but just nodded in answer to my host's question whether I liked the cheese! Then, as I looked intently at the faces of my friends eating Roquefort cheese pleasantly, I suddenly made up my mind. Concentrating deeply, I told my brain cells, "I am your `boss'; you are my servants. You shall obey me-this foolishness must stop." The next minute I was enjoying "Mr. Roquefort's" company pleasantly, and now he always receives a warm welcome when he enters my "hall of digestion."

Super Advanced Course Number 1
Lesson 7
Magnetism

What is magnetism?

The definitions of magnetism are, on the whole, quite similar. The following are typical: Magnetism is (1) that property possessed by various bodies... of attracting or repelling each other; (2) the force to which this attraction is due; (3) the science that treats of the laws of this force; (4) personal attraction or charm ...[1] There is also what is known as animal magnetism, hypnotism, and so forth.

Now let us see what can be learned about magnetism by an intuitional, metaphysical study, which differs from the investigations of physical science in its ability to scale dimensional boundaries.

Originally there was nothing but Undifferentiated Spirit. In order to make possible the creation of dualities and multifarious objects, Spirit had to project; that is, fling forth vibratory force. This repulsed force became Cosmic Energy, out of which the universe and all that is in it materialized.

The origin of evil.

After the universal creative force "fell from heaven" - after it was cast out of the bosom of the Cosmic Spirit and became independent - it began creating delusive, finite dualities contrary to the pattern of the Spirit. In the Spirit was perfection when It was divided into the many. The part could not manifest the quality of the whole. This *conscious, independent force is "Satan," or the satanic creator of all evil and misery-producing finite objects.*

Why we are bound to matter.

Satan wants everything to *reincarnate* and remain in its finite state through the laws of material attachment, instinct, desire, and so forth. If this force were not conscious, human beings - in fact, all creation - after a certain interval would be able to cast off Satan's bonds and return to Spirit. Because Satan deludes all creatures with the consciousness of finiteness and unspiritual duality, they must go through the process of evolution. Thus, souls must reincarnate through the law of cause and effect, and the power of desire born of contact with finite matter.

What is spiritual magnetism?

The Spirit, through Its force of universal attraction, is gradually absorbing all objects created out of It by the misguided force of satanic delusion. In other words, living beings and souls have allowed themselves to be lured away from God and become attached to matter through the influence of the creative force projected by God, who is calling His truant children back to Himself.

The tug-of-war of divine and evil forces in man.

Satan is opposing Spirit's emancipating magnetism which expresses itself in all of creation as an urge toward perfection. Each individual feels within himself the tug-of-war between God's attracting, divine magnetism and Satan's outwardly repelling magnetism. Satanic magnetism keeps objects attracted to matter. Through man's discriminating and intuitive faculties he feels and responds to the call of Spirit, while through his senses and mind he is drawn to matter.

KINDS OF MAGNETISM

Electronic magnetism.

Electrons and protons are held together to a nucleus by the power of universal magnetism. This is termed electronic magnetism. Because the Spirit is in everything and possesses this drawing power, all things created out of It also have the individuality of the Spirit and Its drawing magnetic power which pervades every heart, permeates all things.

Solar magnetism.

The sun's power of attraction, which causes the planets to revolve around it, is called solar magnetism.

Atomic and molecular magnetism.

All atoms and molecules have a nucleus which holds their tiny particles together. The cohesive power in atom and molecule is called atomic magnetism and molecular magnetism, respectively.

Chemical magnetism.

The power that holds together the constituents of, say, H2SO4, or sulphuric acid, is called chemical magnetism.

Material magnetism.

The power that holds together the rocks and like natural objects is called material magnetism.

Plant magnetism.

The power within plants, which draws nourishment out of air and sod and keeps plants from disintegrating is termed plant magnetism.

Animal magnetism.

Animal organisms are held together by animal magnetism. Animals also have within themselves the power by which they attract other animals. The snake, for example, charms and draws little animals to itself by its animal magnetic power.

Magnetism in man.

Man, being a rational, esthetic, spiritual animal, possesses intellectual, moral, esthetic and spiritual as well as animal magnetism.

The right kind of magnetic power has expanding, uplifting and spiritual qualities. Some people are so magnetic that they inspire us and expand our consciousness. This is the sort of magnetic power that we all want, not the stupefying kind of hypnotic or animal magnetism.

Hypnotism vs. spiritual magnetism.

Hypnotism is a spiritual crime, as the hypnotist robs his subject of free will, judgment and consciousness. An individual under the influence of hypnotism is unconscious of his surroundings and aware only of the suggestions of the hypnotist. The conscious mind of the hypnotized person is inert. A person upon whom hypnotism is practiced repeatedly for any great length of time be comes weak-willed and loses all natural forcefulness, being guided by enslaving suggestions.

Never permit yourself to be influenced by anyone's animal magnetism or semi-hypnotic power, which differs but slightly from hypnotism. When an individual exercises his animal magnetism over another, his subject is blinded and unable to perceive clearly the danger to which he is exposed. A person so influenced may *seem* to be a free agent, but in reality he is guided entirely by another's instincts and habits.

HOW TO DEVELOP MORAL, ESTHETIC, BUSINESS, SPIRITUAL, AND DIVINE MAGNETISM

As you know, a magnet has a positive and a negative pole through which it draws toward itself pieces of iron or steel within a certain range. When a magnet is rubbed against a piece of non-magnetic iron or steel, the latter also becomes magnetic. People, too, can become magnetized through close association with magnetic personalities to whom they give their deep, loving, respectful attention. They should, however, first decide what kind of magnetism they want and then choose the particular persons who possess it.

Exchanging magnetism in shaking hands.

For instance, if you are a failure and you want success, associate and shake hands as much as possible with those who have attained success in their business, art, or profession. (Of course, it is not always easy to make such contacts, but "where there's a will, there's a way.")

In shaking hands, two magnets are formed: the upper-spiritual—magnet with the two heads, and the lower physical-magnet with the two pairs of feet as poles. The junction of the hands in the handshake forms the common neutral point as well as the curve for the upper and lower magnets.

Let us see what happens when a spiritual man, who is a failure, and a prosperous business man, who is spiritually weak, attentively shake hands. Through the two pairs of feet, forming the two poles of one magnet, they exchange physical qualities; and through the two heads, forming the two poles of another magnet, they exchange mental qualities. If such men come in close mental contact, besides shaking hands frequently and attentively, the business man becomes more spiritual and the spiritual man becomes more prosperous, by virtue of the upper magnet. They exchange their bad qualities also, through the power of the lower magnet formed by the feet. Both the spiritual man and the business man may be affected in their vocational qualities.

We will now take a different case, that of a reformer of weak character who endeavors to influence- a stubborn, confirmed evildoer, by close association and oft-repeated handshaking. It is quite likely that the reformer will become a positive pole, drawing evil qualities, and the evildoer will become a negative pole, passively drawing good qualities in a very limited way. In this case, the reformer would be the one to be changed. Therefore, unless one has grown very strong spiritually, he should not attempt to reform the very wicked.

From the foregoing, it becomes evident that *indiscriminate handshaking may prove detrimental.* It is harmful to associate constantly with undesirable individuals with whom frequent handshaking is unavoidable, though an occasional, handshake is not of much consequence and may be necessary for courtesy's sake.

Young people of opposite sex, living on the material plane, often exchange animal magnetism, blind one another by emotions and passions, and draw unto themselves all kinds of destructive, evil mentalities.

The range of influence of material magnetism is very low except in unusual cases. Successful business men can but rarely influence failures from a distance.

For the purpose of exchanging moral, mental, esthetic, or spiritual magnetism, personal contact is not always necessary. When one visualizes a spiritual man and deeply meditates on his mentality and character, one can attract and imitate his spiritual magnetism.

Developing spiritual magnetism by self-effort.

One who continually lives, thinks and dreams of spirituality and friendship, magnetism contacts the Spirit's own magnetism and feels Its ennobling influence. One who meditates on Om and God day and night and intuitively perceives all-attracting Divine Magnetism, develops spiritual magnetism of limitless range and power and can draw unto himself whatever he wants, uplifting people either by personal contact or from afar, through his powerfully directed concentration. By this power, one is able to draw unto himself his true friends from previous incarnations; he can command the elements to do his bidding; he can draw all creative, luminous forces, and can invite angels, saints and savants who have passed on, to come to him and dance in his joy. Such a person can attract to himself the rays of all knowledge so that they will sparkle and scintillate around his being.

DIVINE LOVE SORROWS

> I have been roaming,
> Forsaken by Thee
> Who have seen me groping,

Hardly ever answering.
I shall be roaming, roaming,
   Bursting all boundaries of heart,
Evermore moving toward Thee,
   To Thy vast unthrobbing heart.

Come, Thou, to me, O Lord!
   Oh, come at last to me.
Centuries and centuries
   I have waited now for Thee.
Through endless incarnations
   I called out for Thy name,
Searching by the streamlets
   Of all my silvery dreams.

I knew that Thou must come at last

To steal the flowers of my heart.
In sorrow thrills I piped my love;
I sadly sang my song to Thee.
And yet I knew my love must reach Thee,
Though many lives I had to wait;
On mountain crags of high devotion,
I sadly sang my song, my song, my song.

THOU AND I, MY LORD

So be Thou, my Lord,
Thou and I, never apart;
Wave of the sea,
Dissolve in the sea.
I am the bubble,
Make me the sea!

FORMULAS FOR THE DEVELOPMENT OF MAGNETISM BETWEEN INDIVIDUALS OF DIFFERENT MATERIAL, MENTAL AND SPIRITUAL QUALITIES

CONTACTING ELEMENTS	PREDOMINATING TRAITS OF THE TWO INDIVIDUALS	Predominant Magnetism Resulting from Frequent Close Contact
GOOD AND EVIL	Strongly positive evil + passively negative good. Weakly negative evil + strongly positive good.	Positive evil. Positive good.
IRASCIBILITY AND TRANQUILLITY	Marked irascibility + negative mildness. Negative calmness + slight irascibility.	Marked irascibility. Tranquillity.
FAILURE AND SUCCESS	Strongly positive failure + less positive failure. Strongly positive success + less positive success. Strongly positive failure + strongly positive success.	Confirmed failure. Confirmed success. Either failure or success.
BUSINESS AND SPIRITUAL WORK	Strongly positive spirituality + strongly positive business success.	Strongly positive business success and spirituality.
INTELLIGENCE AND STUPIDITY	Strongly positive intelligence + marked stupidity. Strongly positive intelligence + negative intelligence.	Either intelligence or stupidity. Str. positive intelligence.

Super Advanced Course Number 1
Lesson 8
Obliterating The Malignant Seeds Of Failure And Ill Health From The Subconscious Mind

The ultimate purpose of man's presence in the world of matter is *the attainment of spiritual perfection.* Once his development reaches that state, he can cast off the shackles of perishable matter and join God in the realm of Eternal Bliss.

Are ill health and failure accidents?

It is man's reaction to his various experiences - the manner in which he passes his tests in the school of life - which indicates how far he has advanced toward perfection. Let us bear in mind that *the consequences produced by his reactions to every-day experiences not only affect his progress toward ultimate eternal freedom, but they also determine his health or sickness, his success or failure for many incarnations.* Like some physical diseases which send their roots deep into his body, the evil effects of man's actions, unless destroyed, become a part of his conscious, subconscious and super-consciousness, and are felt not alone in one lifetime, but in many lives.

What causes good or ill fortune?

The failures and successes of everyday life become rooted in the mind. Unless they come to fruition or are worked out by wisdom, they bear seeds which the soul must carry over into another incarnation as tendencies and traits. These stubborn ghosts of the past are hiding in the recesses of your mind, emerging suddenly to help and inspire or hinder and discourage, according to the circumstances confronting you. It is for this reason that so many people fail in their undertakings, in spite of their conscious efforts.

From the viewpoint of material science, personal traits and tendencies are due merely to the accident of one's birth into a family of which such traits and tendencies are characteristic. This is very limiting and unsatisfactory. Why should *we* be made to suffer for the sins of our forefathers? On the other hand, why should we be blindly endowed with health, wealth, or genius, *without effort on our part? To* an unseeing materialist, disease, health, wealth or genius may appear to be just the results of a physical law of cause and effect, or hereditary weakness or contagion or good fortune. When a physician discovers a tubercular infection in a patient whose history shows that several members of preceding generations of his immediate family died from this disease, he is convinced that the patient has inherited a natural tendency for tuberculosis. The metaphysician, who attempts to trace the deeper causes of diseases and apparently unjust suffering, finds that the so-called hereditary diseases and predispositions do not come to anyone accidentally. Rather, a disembodied soul carrying a tubercular tendency from a previous existence is born into a family in which there is tubercular infection.

How to escape the results of wrong actions.

Of course, tuberculosis can also be contracted by a healthy person who disregards all physical and hygienic laws. However well, good or prosperous one may be, he cannot be sure of his behavior or future unless he has destroyed all seeds of disease-and-failure-producing actions of the past. This is by no means easy, but it can be done. (We shall see presently what means must be taken toward that end.)

The one certain method for escaping the results of a specific action is to destroy it in this life; otherwise, it will be carried over into the next incarnation. The most successful financier, the healthiest of men, the most intolerant self-righteous moralist- all are liable to be humbled by the sudden manifestation of failure tendencies, hidden germ notions of diseases and unsuspected weaknesses.

It has been said that Henry Ford, during the war, nearly lost everything - his whole vast fortune. He had acquired great wealth because he had been prosperous in former lives, but his mind was also filled with fears of failure and the failures of past lives, so, during the war, while conditions at times were unfavorable to certain lines of business, his failure seeds sprouted and almost caused his financial ruin. If he had permitted himself to become truly discouraged he would have lost everything. By a superhuman effort of will, he fought off his brutal business competitors who were bent on destroying the organization he had built up during many years of hard work. His success consciousness of the past was reinforced by his initiative in this life, by his trained business judgment, his knack for choosing the right workers for his organization, his perseverance, and his daring.

To summarize it briefly, financial success, metaphysically speaking, depends on one's earning ability in past lives and one's initiative and painstaking and persevering quality of will in this life. To raise false hopes on the one hand or discourage an ambitious person on the other, is wrong - the real metaphysician determines the exact influence of the prosperity seeds of past actions and the quality and degree of prosperity will-effort during this life.

How our actions of the past and present effect our lives.

If the success tendency from a past life and the efforts to succeed in this life are weak, then the chances of financial success in this incarnation are meagre; in fact, they are almost negligible. If a person's success tendency from a past life is strong, and present life is marked by inactivity and inertia, then he will either be born into a wealthy family or suddenly inherit a fortune. Some individuals who became indifferent to their wealth in the preceding incarnation may be reborn amidst poverty and struggle, only to acquire great wealth by a so-called "stroke of luck," or through a sudden inheritance, or through lucky small investments.

The individual who has a strong prosperity consciousness from a past life and makes a strenuous effort to earn money in this life succeeds in all his ventures; such a person seldom loses an investment and has unfailing business judgment. If one starts out with a poverty tendency from previous lives but makes an earnest effort to overcome it in this life, he finds that he has to struggle uphill in order to succeed. He may either become prosperous late in life or die struggling. But don't think that his efforts have been in vain, for his next incarnation will be dominated by the success Karma resulting from those struggles. Those who "give up" and accept failure as the decree of fate are foolish, for success or failure is the result of acquirement either of the present or of the past. If you did not acquire wealth before, or if you did acquire it and lost it, dying with the consciousness of your loss, you are reborn in poverty. By *putting up a struggle to overcome your handicap, you stimulate all the dormant success consciousness of past lives, until it becomes active and overshadows the influence o f the predominating failure tendencies.*

The will is man's most effective weapon in the battle of life.
A man cannot be an absolute failure unless he permits his cowardly fears of failure to exert their paralyzing influence over him until nothing can convince him that he can ever again succeed.

Friendly success tendencies are ready to help an individual, and inimical failure tendencies to crush him, depending in the first case on his unflinching efforts, and in the second on his attitude o f resignation to "his fate." These are his invisible friends and also his unseen enemies. Let him rouse his will by repeated judicious efforts, and ultimately he is sure to awaken the success tendencies sleeping in the dark chamber of subconsciousness. The will is the weapon by means of which he can vanquish failure. He must, however, make constant use of it; then it will always be sharp and keen-edged and serve him faithfully. The power of a strong will, guided by divine wisdom, is unlimited. To its possessor nothing is impossible.

The complexities of life and man's weakness, which places him at the mercy of the conflicting tendencies within himself, keep him from being successful in all lives.

No one is a financial success or failure in all lives, for success and failure are the results of "heredity" (ie. seed tendencies from past lives) and environment - the latter, of course, being determined by the former, and the influence of both, by the strength or weakness of man's will. Man has erred much and carries within himself the seeds of those errors. We must not forget, however, that he also carries within the seeds of all fulfillment. Under favorable conditions these germinate, and their growth helps to choke the weeds of failure. Hence it becomes evident that real financial success in all lives, until emancipation is achieved, is not impossible to one who knows how to destroy the tendencies of failure by the power of super-concentration.

A Yogi may not have many material possessions, but by his ability to focus his mind he learns to create at will the financial success he needs. (Of course, the Yogi does not entertain selfish desires; his only wish is that "God's love reign in the shrine of his soul forever.") True Yogis pray, "Heavenly Father! May we kindle Thy love in the flaming heart-altars of others."

When Yogis desire financial success for the group of individuals in a spiritual organization or for a single individual, they put on the success and failure tendencies of the past lives of the person or persons involved, and have to struggle like other people to gain their objective. However, the Yogi's good will always quickens the success of others.

The only possibility of abolishing want lies in the willingness of successful people to aid failures by helping them overcome their past Karma and stimulating their discouraged initiative. Some satisfy their craving for wealth by impoverishing their fellowmen; others fail to share their prosperity. Their selfishness is responsible for much suffering in this world. It is deplorable that people who ride ill Rolls Royces often utterly disregard the needs of thousands of mental and physical cripples who have never received the help that would enable them to help themselves.

A wealthy man who has acquired success by overcoming his failure tendencies, becoming lazy or ignoring the agonies and needs of others, may lose his wealth through poor investments or attract poverty to himself in the next life. Heedless rich people who disregard the sufferings of others are reborn with a craving for luxuries but lack the means to satisfy that craving.

The seeds of wrong actions can be burned and the growth of seeds of good actions stimulated by the faithful practice of meditation.

A man striving for permanent success must meditate every morning and night, and when the superconscious peace-and-concentration rays break through the nocturnal blackness of restlessness, he must concentrate these rays stimulated on the brain and mind, scorching out the lurking seeds of past failures and stimulating the success tendencies.

During meditation the Yogi feels the power of concentration in the will centre, i.e., at the point between the eyebrows, and also experiences a feeling of complete peace throughout his body. Whenever he wants to scour from the brain cells the seeds of past failure or sickness, he must turn that peace-and-concentration power on the whole brain. The entire peace feeling of the body as well as the power of concentration felt between the eyebrows must be transferred and felt in the entire brain. In this way the brain cells become impregnated with peace and power, and their chemical and psychological hereditary composition is modified.

The practice of Yogoda exercises, concentration and meditation, destroy the seeds of disease.

For the purpose of burning seeds of Yogoda exercises, lurking and chronic diseases, the body concentration battery recharging Yogoda exercises of and meditation, Lesson 1, Exercises B, must be practiced destroy the seeds with deep concentration and followed *of* disease by Lessons 4 and 5. In practicing Lessons 4 and 5, the consciousness of health, energy, and power must be kept predominating. When this power is felt all over the body as an unquenchable flow of vitality, it must be concentrated on the brain and mind uninterruptedly for a long time. In this way the vital power will destroy all lurking disease tendencies from the past.

There are many types or degrees of health and disease. Let us examine a few of them and trace their past *Karmas,* diagnosing their prenatal and postnatal habits:

The "asbestos" type of health.

Some few people enjoy such perfect glowing health that they may be said to belong to the water-and-fireproof "Asbestos Clan." This is due to the accumulated health habits of many lives (including the last incarnation), and to obeying health laws and exercising regularly in this incarnation. As a rule this type of individual has been a Yogi in many lives and can destroy all seeds of ill health so long as he practices Yoga.[1]

If he confines himself merely to obeying health laws, i.e., if he exercises regularly, eats properly, etc., but fails to practice Yoga, he may retain his health, but stands a chance of losing it late in life. The one who faithfully and correctly practices Yoga concentration and meditation as taught in the fourth and fifth lessons thereby kills the seeds of his little health transgressions. The aspirant for the "asbestos" type of health should not be satisfied to depend merely on the health tendencies of the past and on physical exercise in this life, but should also burn the accumulating seeds of unhealthy actions of this life, no matter how insignificant they may seem.

The "born-healthy" type.

Some people are in good health nearly all the time, but when they are sick they are violently sick. Health of this type is due to accumulated health seed tendencies and to ordinary care and exercise in this life, but not to Yoga practices. Health gives way when that which has been accumulated is used up. At such time the little transgression seeds of life become active and troublesome.

The "medium-health" type.

Individuals of this type are healthy *but* weak. The exercise of will power results in the health seed tendencies which produce "medium health." Physical exercise will prove strengthening.

The "mechanical-health" type.

The health of persons of this type is like the mechanism of a fine watch - excellent with proper care, but trouble- some at the slightest neglect. They are well only so long as they follow rules; as soon as they break them they suffer. So much dependence on law, instead of faith in God and self-reliance, makes people health-law bound. They are victims of the "law complex." Do not permit laws to enslave you; use them to serve you.

The "die-hard" type.

Some continue to exist in spite of a hailstorm of disease. Their health and disease tendencies are evenly balanced; hence they alternate between health and illness. If you have great devotion and are obedient to God's laws, He is much more likely to respond than if you have great devotion but constantly break His hygienic, mental and spiritual laws.

The "convalescent" type.

There are some whose constitutions are as delicate and fragile as that of a flower. They cannot stand the slightest hardship. This is due to their burning the seeds of disease late in the preceding incarnation. In other words, death occurred after the seeds of ill health were destroyed late in life. Such people are born frail, because the circumstances connected with their recovery are still fresh in their memories; yet they *are* healthy.

Why do great souls – those who have attained spiritual perfection – suffer?

Sometimes great teachers suffer ill-health and poverty because of their efforts to free their fellowmen from the clutches of disease and want. They sacrifice their bodies and possessions and devote their minds solely to the task of helping others, escape the fruits of their past errors. Jesus sacrificed His life that He might help suffering, error stricken humanity to spiritual freedom. The Buddha gave up wealth, position, family - in short, all earthly possessions - for the same purpose. Great souls do this of their own accord, for God does not compel them to make this sacrifice.

When all the seeds of evil tendencies have been destroyed, each microscopic brain cell will be filled with wisdom, inspiration, and health, singing and preaching the glory of God to the many billions of intelligent body cells. At that stage of development one is really free, and is born free in succeeding incarnations if he wishes to return to dry the tears of others. Those who have attained this freedom carry halos of invisible healing rays; wherever they go they scatter the light of prosperity and health.

SUMMARY

In order to destroy ill health and failure we must dig beneath the surf ace and get at their roots, which lie buried in the subconscious mind. Health and success or disease and failure are the fruits of our actions not only in this life but in many lives. When the repeated efforts of an intelligent person to gain health or success miscarry, then disease and failure had their inception in past incarnations. Such chronic cases can be cured only by super-advanced methods of intuitional concentration and meditation.

True happiness and safety are realized by those who know how to destroy scientifically the hidden, ungerminated seeds of transgressions against the laws of physical, mental and spiritual health.

---

[1]*Yoga: Communion with God through the practice of scientific meditation.*

Super Advanced Course Number 1
Lesson 9
Unique Concrete Psychological Machines Or Inner Devices For Conquering Fear, Anger, Greed, Temptation, Failure Consciousness And Inferiority Complexes

CONQUERING FEAR

Fear complexes.

When fear overpowers you, realize that nothing worse than physical death can happen to you; and if that does happen, it releases you from the object of your fears. Realize death is not a tyrant but a deliverer: it releases us from all physical pain and mental suffering. Death is the physical, mental and spiritual anodyne which brings relief from all anguish for a period immediately following mortal life.

Do not fear accidents and disease because you have recently encountered them. Such fear will create a disease and accident consciousness, and if it is strong enough you will draw to yourself the very things you most fear. On the other hand, fearlessness will in all probability avert them and minimize their power.

A mental indulgence in fear will create a subconscious fear habit. Thus, when something really upsetting to the regular routine occurs, the cultivated subconscious fear habit will assert itself, magnifying the object of our fears and paralyzing the will-to-fight-fear faculty of the conscious mind. Man is made in the image of God and has all the powers and potentialities of God; therefore, it is wrong for him to think that trials are greater than his divinity. Remember, no matter how great your trials may be, you are able to conquer them. God will not suffer you to be tempted and tried beyond your strength.

When fear comes, tense and relax - exhale several times. Switch on the currents of calmness and serenity. Let your whole mental machinery awaken and actively hum with the vibration of will to do something. Then harness the power of will to the cogwheels of fearless caution and continuous good judgment, which in turn must constantly revolve and produce mental devices for escaping your specific impending calamity.

When something is threatening to injure you, do not throttle the all-producing inner machine of your consciousness by fear. Rather, use the fear as a stimulus to accelerate your inner machine of consciousness to produce some mental devices which will instantly remove the cause of fear. These mental devices to escape fear are so numerous that they have to be specially fashioned by the almighty tool of consciousness, according to the specific and extraordinary needs of an individual. When something is threatening you, do not sit idle - do *something about it* calmly mustering all the power of your will and judgment. Will is the motive power which works the machine of activity.

Fear should not produce mental inertia, paralysis, or despondency; instead, it should spur you on to calm, cautious activity, avoiding equally rashness and timidity.

Fear of failure or sickness is nourished by thinking constantly of all kinds of dire possibilities, until they take root in the subconscious and finally in the super-conscious. Then these fear seeds begin to germinate and fill the conscious mind with fear plants which bear poisonous, death-dealing, fear fruits.

Uproot fear from within by forceful concentration on courage- and by shifting your consciousness to the absolute peace within. After you succeed in uprooting fear psychologically, then focus your attention on methods for acquiring prosperity and health.

Associate with healthy and prosperous people who do not fear sickness or failure.

If you are unable to dislodge the haunting fear of ill health or failure, divert your mind by turning your attention to interesting, absorbing books, or even to harmless amusements. After the mind forgets its haunting fear, let it take up the shovels of different mental devices and dig out the causes and roots of failure and ill health from the soil of your daily life.

Fear aggravates all our miseries. It intensifies a hundred-fold our physical pain and mental agony.

Fear contaminates vivid imagination emotions, influencing the subconsciousness to such an extent that it in turn completely destroys the willing efforts of the consciousness.

Fear develops in an individual a malignant magnetism by which he attracts the very object of which he is afraid, as a magnet attracts a piece of iron or steel.

Fear is poison to both body and mind, *unless it is controlled and used as a stimulus* to calm caution.

Uncontrolled fear destroys business initiative. It paralyzes the desire to repeat success-producing efforts. Fear inhibits the almighty power of the soul. Have fear of nothing but fear itself.

Fear has a very deleterious effect on the heart, nervous system, and brain. It is destructive to mental initiative, courage, judgment, common sense, and to the will.

Fear throws a veil over intuition and robs you of your confidence to master your difficulties.

Kill fear by refusing to be afraid of it.

Know that you are safe behind the battlements of God's eternal safety, even though death knocks at your door or you are rocked on the seas of suffering. His protecting rays can dispel the menacing clouds of doomsday, calm the waves of trials and keep you safe, whether you are in a castle or on the open battlefield of life where bullets of trials are incessantly flying. Remember, without God's protection your life, health, and prosperity are in dire peril, even though you are locked in a scientifically hygienic castle of opulence, surrounded by impregnable moats, manned by all the fire-emitting guns of man.

Super Advanced Course 1

CONQUERING ANGER

Anger makes you surly and contaminates others with the same sullenness. Anger makes you uncomfortable first and then it transmits your discomforts to others. Anger defeats its own purpose; it is not an antidote for anger. Violent wrath may bring suppression of a weaker wrath, but it will never *destroy it.*

Be calm and indifferent to those who deliberately enjoy making you angry.

Show outward anger only to those whom you can momentarily stupefy and thus prevent from doing mischief, but never initiate anger if it actually makes you angry - or, rather, never be angry *inwardly.* Anger poisons your own peace and that of others. Anger poisons calmness and blights understanding; in fact, it is the manna of mis-understanding. Anger is the method by which fools attempt to conquer others. Your anger merely rouses your enemy's wrath, and you make him stronger and more powerful, instead of conquering him.

The antidote for anger.

Love is the great antidote for anger. Do not be demonstrative in your love for an angry person. He is not in the mood to appreciate it, his reasoning faculty and good nature being temporarily paralyzed. All you can do is to give him your good will. The expression of righteous indignation for the purpose of averting evil is, of course, productive of good.

Anger gives birth to jealousy, hatred, spite, vengefulness, destructiveness, "brain storms," temporary insanity leading to horrible crimes, and so forth.

When anger attacks *you, conquer it.* When you are angry, say nothing. Knowing it to be a disease {like a cold, for instance), throw it off by a mental warm bath. Fill your mind, to the exclusion of all else, with thoughts of those with whom you can never be angry, no matter what they do.

When violently angry, douse your head with cold water, or rub the medulla, the temples, the forehead (especially between the eyebrows), and the top of the head with a piece of ice.

Develop metaphysical reason in order to destroy anger. Look upon the anger-rousing agent as a child of God, a little five-year-old baby brother who has unwittingly, perhaps, stabbed you. You cannot wish to stab back this little brother who did not know what he was doing when he injured you. When you become Christ-like and look upon all humanity as little brothers hurting one another - "for they know not what they do" - then you cannot feel angry with anyone. Ignorance is the mother of all anger.

Mentally destroy anger; do not permit it to poison your peace and disturb your habitual joy-giving serenity.

When anger comes, think of love; think that, as you do not want others to be angry with you, you do not wish others to feel your ugly anger.

When anger comes, set in motion your machinery of calmness; let it move the cogwheel of peace, love and forgiveness. And with these antidotes, *destroy anger.*

OVERCOMING GREED

Remember, you eat to live but do not live to eat. Greed is a servant of the palate-and enemy of digestion and health. Greed wants to please itself and the sense of taste at the cost of your happiness.

Greed produces evil habits of eating, utterly disregarding the needs of the body even to the point of death. Greed says: "Let us eat, drink, and be merry, for tomorrow we die!" Self-control in eating, good mastication, plain food and eating only when you are very hungry, develop right habits of eating and destroy greed. Self-control may not seem so alluring as self-indulgence, but it protects your health.

The purpose of self-restraint in eating is primarily the conservation of health, though wholesome food need not be, and certainly should not be, unpalatable. Eat often, eat less, think of your health and digestion, and do not concentrate on your palate, if you want to conquer greed.

Remember, greed for too many possessions is also evil. Greed for an increasingly greater number of material objects causes a person to disregard health, happiness and honest methods of earning a living. A greedy individual shatters his health and destroys his peace of mind by his self indulgence. Such a person is never satisfied.

Concentrating on your *needs is* an antidote for your insatiable greed for money or possessions.

The noble ambition to acquire wealth in order to aid worthy causes is not greed-for it is not insatiable—it is always satisfied when it can help others.

OVERCOMING FAILURE

Uproot the consciousness of business failure. Three out of four business men in America fail: first, because they choose a wrong vocation; next, because they "give up" too quickly; and last, because their products lack quality.

An inferiority complex is born of contact with weak-minded people and the weak innate subconscious mind. A superiority complex results from false pride and an inflated ego. Both inferiority and superiority complexes are destructive to self-development. Both are fostered by imagination, ignoring facts, while neither belongs to the true, all-powerful nature of the soul. Develop self-confidence by conquering your weaknesses. Found your self-confidence on actual achievements, and you will be free from all inferiority and superiority complexes.

Super Advanced Course Number 1
Lesson 10
The Art Of Super Relaxation

Super-relaxation is complete voluntary withdrawal of consciousness and energy from the entire body.

The soul has suffered itself to be lured away from the vast kingdom of the Spirit and to be trapped in the little, physical body. As the soul forsook its vast kingdom of Omnipresence, it passed through many smaller realms of life until it finally entered through the trapdoor of material attachment and found itself imprisoned in the body, unable to get out and return to its home of Omnipresence. The bird of paradise has become the bird encaged behind the prison bars of flesh. Hence, every soul prisoner who has walked through the gates of ideational, astral, and physical confinements into the trap of body consciousness must learn to open these inner prison gates before he can find freedom and return to the Spirit.

Physical culturists and other health enthusiasts, as well as spiritual teachers, often talk of relaxation; but few know how to achieve it.

Have you seen an electric bulb to which a dimmer device is attached? You can operate this device by moving a little rod backwards, thus gradually dimming the light in the bulb until it is almost extinguished. Then, if you return the rod to its first position, the light gradually becomes brighter until it resumes its original brilliancy. Hence, by means of the dimmer device, you can get several degrees of light in the bulb. For instance, starting with the dark bulb, moving the rod slightly each time results in (1) a very dim light, (2) a dim light, (3) a light of medium brightness, and (4) a bright light.

How to switch on, switch off, and dim consciousness and energy in the body.

The body and mind also have dimmer devices. By using the first method, you can relax your mind and switch off energy from the body. This is known as *physical relaxation.* By using the second method, you can shut out mental distractions. This is called *mental relaxation.*

Some people know how to relax physically but not mentally. To keep the mind fixed constantly on the soul after freeing it from all distracting thoughts is called soul *relaxation.*

Mental relaxation signifies complete mental rest. You can achieve this by practicing to go to sleep at will. Relax the body and think of the drowsiness you usually feel just before you fall asleep. Then try actually to reproduce that state. *(Use imagination,* not will, to do this.) Most people do not relax even while they sleep. Their minds are restless; hence they dream. Therefore, conscious mental relaxation is better than relaxation which is the by-product of physical passive relaxation or sleep.[1] In this way you can either dream or keep dreams off your mental moving-picture screen, as you choose. No matter how busy you are, do not forget now and then to free your mind completely from worries and all duties. Just dismiss them from your mind. Remember, you were not made for them; they were made by you. Do not allow them to torture you. When you are beset by the greatest mental trials or worries, try to fall asleep. If you can do that, you will find, on awakening, that the mental tension is relieved and that worry has loosened its grip on you. Just tell yourself that even if you die the earth would continue to follow its orbit, and business would be carried on as usual; hence, why worry? When you take yourself too seriously death comes along to mock you and remind you of the brevity of material life and its duties.

The mind must manifest calmness; where the worries and trials of everyday life are concerned, it must be like water which does not retain any impression of the waves that play on its bosom.

This is no brief for negligence in business, which should be avoided as carefully as the unnecessary concern arising from an inflated sense of responsibility. You are *not* too busy to eat, sleep, and relax. You must remember that material success, without health, peace and happiness, is of little value to you, for what does it avail you when you are seriously ill and die?

Therefore, "let go" of your worries. Enter into absolute silence every morning and night, and banish thoughts for several minutes each time. Then think of some happy incident in your life; dwell on it and visualize it; mentally go through some pleasant experience over and over again until you forget your worries entirely.

Mental relaxation consists in the ability to free the attention at will from haunting worries over past and present difficulties; consciousness of constant duty; dread of accidents and other haunting fears; greed; passion; evil or disturbing thoughts, and attachments. Mastery in mental relaxation comes with faithful practice. It can be attained by freeing the mind of all thoughts at will and keeping the attention fixed on the peace and contentment within.

By the third method you learn *super-relaxation*. Metaphysical super-relaxation consists in freeing the entire human consciousness from its identification with the body, money, possessions, name, fame, family, country, the world, and the human race and its habits. Super.-relaxation consists in disengaging the attention by degrees from consciousness, subconsciousness, the semi-superconscious state of deep, restful sleep, the superconscious state felt after meditation, and Christ Consciousness[2], and identifying it completely with Cosmic Consciousness[3]. Mental relaxation and semi-super-relaxation consist in releasing consciousness from the delusion of duality and resting the mind, keeping it identified with one's own real nature of unity in Spirit. You have hypnotized yourselves into thinking you are human beings, whereas, in reality you are gods.

By the last and most important method, you learn scientifically to disengage your attention and energy from their identification with the world of sensations, muscles, heart, spine etc. There are several kinds of this astral and mental relaxation.

Unconscious muscular relaxation.

This is usually practiced in a very Muscular imperfect manner by moving the limbs. Those who use this method generally keep half of the muscles tensed and possibly the other half relaxed. Some remain completely tensed and only imagine they are relaxed.

Conscious muscular or motor relaxation.

It is the purpose of this method of relaxation to withdraw consciousness and energy completely from the muscles. To achieve this, first gently tense the entire body or a certain body part. Then relax or withdraw all energy from the body or the body part in question and remain relaxed, *without the slightest physical motion.* The complete absence of motion and tension from muscles and limbs is true relaxation. Imagine that the body is jelly like, without bones or muscles. When you can do this, you have attained perfect muscular relaxation.

Passive sensory relaxation or sleep.

In muscular relaxation, the mind and energy are relaxed or withdrawn from the muscles, but not from the sensory nerves or the sense-seats of optical, auditory, olfactory, tactual, and gustatory nerves. During deep sleep the mind and energy are passively and unconsciously withdrawn from the motor and sensory nerves, and even thoughts are banished. When the soul becomes satiated with material contacts during the day, it passively switches off the life force and mind from the senses. Sleep can be induced at will, by suddenly relaxing the body, lying down on the back, dismissing all thoughts, and by closing the eyes. *Try* this until you learn to sleep or dream at will. With closed eyes, visualize a different room from the one in which you are resting and fall asleep thinking of it. In this manner dreams can be induced.

That which can be done passively and unconsciously can also be attained consciously. By practicing the fourth Yogoda lesson one can achieve complete calmness in the heart, lungs, and other inner organs. When the muscles and inner organs are freed from motion by relaxation, the breaking down of bodily tissues and decay are temporarily inhibited. This in turn helps to keep the blood stream pure, for when there is decay going on in the body, the waste products are thrown into, and poison, the venous blood.

When tissues stop decaying, the venous blood ceases to accumulate in the body. This gives the heart a much needed rest, for there is no longer any need of its pumping great quantities of venous blood into the lungs for purification, as the neutralized electrified tissues do not require blood and oxygen. Thus, heart action and breathing become unnecessary. This leads to the release of the enormous quantity of life current which otherwise would have been needed in the heart for the daily task of pumping eighteen tons of blood through the system. Thus, the many billions of cells no longer work and move through inner currents and are no longer dependent on blood and oxygen. They *rest* and depend more and more on this inner sustaining current to enable them to live in a *conscious, suspended, undecaying* state. When the body cells learn the art of living without bread (blood and oxygen), they truly know how to live by the Word of God or the inner energy coming down from the medulla, and on the released currents from the heart and other inner organs.

When this energy is withdrawn from all inner organs, it is switched off scientifically and automatically from the sensory and motor nerves. This simultaneously insures (1) conscious sensory relaxation[4], and (2) conscious involuntary relaxation. When the energy is withdrawn from all the sensory nerves, the five sense-telephones are disconnected. No sensations can reach the brain and intelligence operators. The attention being thus shut off from sensations, it gains" freedom from thoughts which have their inception in sensations, as well as the associated thoughts of the subconscious memory. This leaves the scientifically freed attention unhampered to march Godward. Sensory involuntary relaxation is meagerly possible by the unscientific method of mental diversion. Trying to free the attention by diverting it from sensations has been tried the world over with little or no success.

What is "death"?

Finally, *death is* not annihilation. It is the switching off of the nerve current from the entire body-bulb. Death is a state of passive involuntary relaxation brought on by sudden accidents, disease, or sorrow. The forcible, sudden, and permanent disconnection of life current from the body-bulb is popularly called *death* or complete annihilation of life. In reality it is only a temporary state-it is not the end of things, but merely the transfer from the domain of changeable, ugly matter to the realm of infinite joy and multicolored, flashing lights.

Why not learn the method by which you can switch off the life current from the entire body through conscious will by the steady, conscientious practice of the fourth Yogoda lesson, thus freeing the soul from the bondage of death. Besides, just as electricity does not die with the breaking of the bulb into which it flows but merely retires into the big dynamo behind it, so our real self is not destroyed but retires into the Infinite Omnipresent Self, when our life forces are switched off from the body-bulb. After thoroughly mastering the fourth lesson and attaining the breathless state, the following method will be found very helpful for inducing relaxation at will.

Method for inducing relaxation.

First, close eyes; expel breath; switch off attention and energy from the senses. Feel and mentally watch the heart and circulation and calm it down by the command of will as you stop a watch by gently touching its spring. With calmness you can arrest the activities of the entire physical machinery. Then switch on the current in the spine and brain, disconnecting your current from the five sense-telephones. Convert your brain into a divine radio, catching the Cosmic Sound and the Song of God. Or you may switch off entirely the body and brain bulbs and merge with the Omnipresent Cosmic Dynamo. You can return at will, snatching yourself from the Infinite Omnipresence and switching on life in your body-bulb, thus caging your omnipresence there. Keep switching on and switching off the life current in the body until you know you are a part of the One Light which lights all the heavenly lamps of atoms, stars and all living creatures.

Those who know how to leave the body consciously can return to it consciously. People who die by accidents or are otherwise forced out of the body cannot re-enter it at will, but bodies under suspended animation can be reawakened by physical and mental methods.

Do not leave the body by imagination; learn to do it actually by releasing consciousness (1) from the muscles, and (2) from the senses by withdrawing the life force from the five sense-telephones. After sensory relaxation is achieved the heart calms down, and the consciousness and energy lodge themselves in the spine.

Involuntary relaxation consists in the ability to calm the heart at will and raise consciousness upward through the seven centers and out of the medulla into Infinite Spirit.

PRAYER AND SUMMARY

O Spirit, release my life and consciousness from possessions, from attachments. Release, Thou, my life and mind from the tensed body, dimming consciousness and life-force from the body muscles. Release my consciousness from the senses, then from the breath; then unlock the energy and unconsciousness from the heart.

Then, O Spirit, lodge life and consciousness in the spine. And then release them unto the Spirit into Infinite Spaces. Oh, make me behold Milky Way Spiral Nebulae floating and glimmering in me.

Then, O Spirit, bring the bright Bird of Omnipresence back through its cage door of medulla into the passage of the spine; and then let it fly into the heart and sing vitality there. And then let it flutter its wings of breaths into the two lungs. And then, 0 Spirit, let it flutter at last over the walls of flesh.

Om . . . vibrate in the hands, in the feet, in the body, in the muscles! Om . . . vibrate in the spirit! Om . . . come back to the spine, back to the heart, and back to the muscles again!

---

[1] *Passive sensory relaxation, or sleep, comes automatically when the body is tired. Conscious sensory relaxation is self-induced.*

[2] *Signs of Christ Consciousness: Contacting others' thoughts and feelings instantaneously. Contacting places and their vibrations instantaneously. Contacting several planets and spheres instantaneously. If you want Christ Consciousness, do not look for phenomena, but march steadily on, deepening your meditation and your joy born of meditation. Do not be lured from your goal by psychical phenomena, no matter how marvelous they may seem. Love for everybody characterizes those who have Christ Consciousness. Through Christ Consciousness, others' feelings and different atmospheric and planetary conditions can be projected in your consiousness by merely thinking of them.*

[3] *Signs of Cosmic Consciousness: Beholding your consciousness as the only reality.*

[4] *Conscious sensory relaxation can be attained also by breathing in and out, followed by long, comfortable exhalations. Concentrate on breathlessness. Expel the breath every time you feel the desire to breathe, and rest attention on the breathless, comfortable state. By continuous inhalation and exhalation the blood becomes oxygenized, thus making breathlessness possible.*

Super Advanced Course Number 1
Lesson 11
Converting The Hands Into Healing Batteries Of Life Force: Healing Like Jesus By The Laying On Of Hands. Healing Stricken People From A Distance.

The body's sources of energy.

The human body may be compared to the wet battery of an automobile. Just as the proper functioning of an automobile battery depends upon distilled water from without and energy from within, so the proper functioning of the human body battery depends upon food from without and life force from within.

Will draws energy from the cosmos into the body

This life force is stored mainly in the medulla and distributed through the sub-dynamos in the five plexuses. The medulla is fed by conscious Cosmic Energy which surrounds the body and which is drawn into the body by the power of the will.

Cosmic Energy is converted into life force by the will which is the radio as well as the main dynamo of the body. Very often, however, people become discouraged and permit hereditary inhibitions in the subconscious mind to hamper the will. The suggestions of old age, accidents, diseases, heredity, instincts, etc., demoralize the will in many individuals. During a serious illness, for instance, memories of previous ailments as well as memories of past failures, frustrations, and disappointments which were due to weakness, fill consciousness with the fear that the body cannot recover. Death occurs if one "gives up"; if he refuses to be disheartened, the will produces life force which can repair and remodel all tissues, including bones, organs, etc. Therefore, if one refuses to become discouraged or to take seriously illusive body changes and thoughts of hereditary limitations, bodily disintegration is arrested. Different degrees of will power develop corresponding degrees of sensitiveness to pain or death. Some combat injuries and live; others resign themselves "to their fate" at the slightest indisposition. Thus it becomes evident that the duration of life is dependent upon the will.

Many people die mentally long before they die physically. When one ceases to have ambitions and to be interested in life, the will becomes paralyzed. When this will-radio is untuned or destroyed, Cosmic Energy ceases to supply the reserve dynamo of the medulla, and physical health slowly fails from want of life force. This is the principal cause for the symptoms of old age. *The stronger the will, the greater the flow of energy into the tissues and body parts.*

Will is the life-sustaining factor.

Food cannot rejuvenate the body of individual whose will is weak, for it is the inner energy, or life force, which converts food into energy. Solids, liquids, and gases cannot be assimilated after the supply of life force, which is dependent upon the will, has ceased. When one has a strong, unflinching will, he grows more and more independent of food. He can absorb the consciousness of changelessness and inject it with Cosmic Energy into all the cells, making them neutral and free from decay or growth. Then these cells become electrified and live only by the vibratory power of intelligent Cosmic Energy, or the Word of God (which is God according to the Bible).

Thoughts of fatigue shut off the supply of energy.

Cosmic Energy, through the will, feeds the medulla which in turn feeds the five plexuses. The life force in the plexuses carries on the telephonic work of the five senses through the sensory nerves and of the muscles and joints through the motor nerves. The same life principle charges the circulation, vitalizes each blood cell, and also feeds every nerve, all of which in turn recharge the other cells of the body. As the cells are but condensed will and energy, they can be instantaneously renewed by the power of strong, unflinching will. Therefore, one should never say or think he is tired, for by doing that one becomes twice as tired and paralyzes the will which must be active in order to draw Cosmic Energy into the body.

Acute and chronic diseases result from lack of life force, a faulty diet, overwork, or other bad habits.

Medicine cannot affect the mental behavior and "disease notions" of the somatic cells.

Food and medicine have but an indirect, limited effect on the simple germ cells, and are very slow to change the nature and behavior of the somatic cell and specialized organs. Medicine and the proper food can bring about many cures, but they cannot recreate an organ. Why? The sperm and ovum, drawing nutrition from the mother's body, develop from boneless specks of protoplasm into a baby with hard bones and nerves and organs, etc. Life force and food created all the specialized organs from the sperm and ovum, because they contained the mind-obeying germ cells. However, as the organs were formed, the cells changed. It is because these changed (somatic) cells, constituting the organs, are very unyielding and hard to control that food and chemicals are unable to recreate organs. Originally, mind and life force induce the germ cells to create organs, but once the germ cells change into somatic cells they begin to rule the mind and life force. Hence humanity can regain the power to recreate lost limbs, organs, etc., only by learning to convert the somatic cells back to their original obedient germ-cell state. By freeing life force and mind from bodily slavery, by increasing vitality and mental power, the somatic cells can be made to change into germ cells.

Why do germ cells change into obstinate somatic cells.

The vital organs are maintained and guided by the subconscious mind which contains the record of our experiences and behavior throughout all incarnations. Therefore, though the human body develops from changeable germ cells, subconscious, fixed designers slowly transform these germ cells into somatic cells which make up the specialized organs and limbs of the human body. In other words, the somatic cells are governed by specialized organic designers. These are the result of our past actions, and are born and die with the organs and limbs which they consciously design and build. When one of the lungs or an arm is lost, the specialized designer in that lung or arm dies with it. Therefore, the body is unable to recreate these lost body parts.

Can lost organs, limbs, etc., be recreated?

In order to recreate lost organs, etc., the following is necessary:
> (1) The life force must be made to obey the will instantaneously;
> (2) The will must be changed to all-creating Divine Will;
> (3) The life force must be supplied with psychological designers of human organs when such organs are lost through disease or accident. One must visualize a lost designer until it is born again. To be able to do that, one must know how to materialize thoughts;
> (4) The will must be able to float them in the life force, and the life force must be charged continuously with Cosmic Energy. The will must be kept free from, and unhampered by, discouraging hereditary suggestions;

(5) Lastly, when the will can overcome all hereditary instinctive prejudices regarding the recreation of human organs, and create living psychological designers, then these designers begin to use the extra charge of life energy and condense the semiconscious life force into electrons which are further condensed into gases, etc. Then the designers begin to use the new protoplasm created by condensation of energy, food chemicals, and blood from the body, to recreate and replace a lost organ.

Buried in the human mind is the evil, weak suggestion of powerlessness of millions of years, and it will take years to learn how to put the above methods into practice.

The efficacy of medical healing methods is limited, as other methods are.

Therefore, scientific healing can be effected unfailingly by the development and strengthening of will power and life force. Moreover, this human will power must be impregnated with the invincible, all-creating, unlimited healing power of the Almighty. Neither medicine nor any other material agency has managed to obtain control over the electronic, vibratory force and recreating power of the body cells. If the body is deprived of energy and consciousness,. it cannot live. There is no denying that material *medical* has its uses. However, the more you depend on the limited power of drugs, the weaker your will and access to God's unlimited healing power, and the more you depend on God, the less *need* you depend on drugs. Organic defects and chronic diseases can be dealt with successfully through divinely charged will power and life force, which alone are the almighty creators and rebuilders of all new or decayed body tissues. Bones, blood, marrow, nerves, brain tissues everything in the body is directly materialized out of the sperm by the latent will power and life-force.

Adam and Eve reproduced themselves by materializing will and energy.

Of course, originally Divine Will had to create especially, and materialize, human sperm and ovum, and these contained God's most perfect design. The primeval sperm cells and ova were materialized into the organism of the original man and woman, Adam and Eve, before propagation by the law of cause and effect was instituted. They could re-create their bodies, and propagate themselves, by materializing their vitality and tendencies and clothing them with materialized limbs and flesh. They were in constant communion with the Almighty. Therefore, their will force was in tune with the Infinite Will, and they could create human beings out of the ether in the same manner as God. Only after their will became subservient to the ego and the senses, instead of being guided by wisdom, did they develop sex and sex creation. This was their f all from heavenly powers to earthly ways of creation and living. Their will, no longer guided by wisdom, opposed the Divine Will which is guided by wisdom only. Ever since, misguided, obstinate self-will and satanic ignorance—being concentrated on the change able body instead of the unchangeable, infinite Spirit in the body-have created defective, limited mental designers of bodies and their organs. These defective mental designers, inherited from the original erring parents of all humanity, are thus perpetuated in the countless human sperm cells and ova. In this manner did man lose the power to materialize spiritual children and to create perfect bodies in which any organ or limb, etc., could be recreated at will.

The breaking of bones, the loss of limbs or organs, or even injury or loss of the brain would be of no consequence if they could be restored or recreated painlessly by super-conscious methods and Divine Will, during conscious relaxation or under anesthesia. The territory of the will and energy is the entire human body. The ordinary individual who is a slave to his body finds that he has only imperfect control over the muscles.

First learn to control the muscles and the body by will and life force; then learn to feel the living relation between will and life force and the vital organs by relaxation of the sensory nerves and involuntary organs, i.e., by "switching off" energy from heart, lungs, etc. *The purpose of tension and relaxation is dissociation of life force and mind from the consciousness of the body.* When that is accomplished, the will and life force actually own the whole body and can, through their healing rays, remove chronic defects from any body part.

The astral body, in appearance like a vast nebula or the tail of a comet, charges the physical body with Cosmic Energy through the medulla.

As material science has demonstrated that a piece of chicken heart can be kept alive and growing by the administration of food and chemicals, so Hindu Yoga has shown that the human body and heart can be kept alive in a suspended state, without food, oxygen, or chemicals.[1]

By practicing the exercises given in the second Yogoda lesson, one can learn, with absolute faith in the almighty power of will, slowly, conscientiously, and patiently to tense and relax, i.e., alternately to put forth and withdraw life force, several times, from any body part that is diseased.

A body part may be recharged without tension.
This method is not effective for the involuntary organs which can be recharge only by practicing the fourth Yogoda lesson. In order to heal cardiac or cerebral disorders, one may send energy mentally to the affected area by merely concentrating on it, without tensing. By this method one can send a feeble current of energy to any body part. Actually tensing with will, of course, produces more energy than concentration alone, but very gentle conscious tension and relaxation of the whole body also sends healing energy, vitality, etc., to heart and brain. It must be remembered, however, that in tensing and relaxing the whole body with a view to curing heart or brain disorders concentration must be centered on the affected organ.

There is also another method of healing:
Sit erect. Gently tense and relax the whole body. Calm yourself. Touch the medulla once, in order to make it easier for you to concentrate on it. Then visualize Cosmic Energy surrounding and entering the body through the medulla and at the point between the eyebrows, and pouring into the spine. Feel the energy flowing down the whole length of the two arms into the hands. Continue tensing and relaxing and feeling the life force flow from the medulla and the point between the eyebrows through the spine to the hands. Then stop tensing and relaxing, and firmly rub the entire bare left arm with the right palm (up

and down, several times). Do the same to the right arm with the left palm. Then relax, continuously visualizing and willing Cosmic Energy to descend from the medulla through the arms into your hands. Now, with closed eyes, rapidly but gently rub your palms together about twenty times. Then separate the hands, and lift the arms upward. You will feel the life current *flowing* from the medulla into the spine, especially through both arms and hands, with a pricking, tingling sensation.

Your energy-magnetized hands may be used either for curing any diseased part of your own body or some other person's who need not be in your immediate vicinity, for it is not necessary to touch your patient. This life force passing through your hands has infinite power of projection.

The human will and energy imperfectly control the human body, but the divinely transmitted will can work perfectly, not only in healing your own physical ailments, but also those of others, even though they be far away. You must, however, visualize your patient, and he must have faith in you. You must broadcast the healing force by moving your hands, electrified by the above method, up and down in space while willing the current to pass over your patient's diseased body part. Do this in a quiet room for fifteen minutes until you feel that you have accomplished your object.

Convert yourself into a divine battery, sending out through your hands divine healing rays whenever and wherever they may be needed. Then your hands, charged with divine power, will throw healing rays into your patient's heart and brain. Thus his seeds of ignorance will be destroyed, and he will smile with the health of God-love.

SUMMARY

Learn to convert your hands into healing batteries, so that divine currents will flow through them at will. Through this means when properly administered diseases of body and mind, as well as the malady of soul ignorance, have vanished under this benign touch, whether administered at close quarters or from afar. Thus one becomes the fisher man of souls, that he may catch them in the net of his divine healing wisdom and present them unto God.

'If the heart were stopped and energy distributed throughout the body, the latter would not decompose; but if the heart were stopped and energy withdrawn from the spine, bodily decay would be inevitable. Yogis know how to stop heart and lung action voluntarily yet keep physically alive by retaining some Cosmic Energy in their bodies to sustain the cells in a suspended state.

Super Advanced Course Number 1
Lesson 12
Esthetic Way Of Developing Cosmic Consciousness

Extending the kingdom of heart from your own to others.

In feeling God, you must extend the territory of your feelings. You feel for your own heart; now you must every day begin to feel more and more at one with the hearts of others, their woes, struggles, joys and weal. To feel others' hearts means not only that you must remain absorbed in loving and working for yourself, but you must learn to work and spend for others, protect and love others with the same degree of interest and enthusiasm as for yourself.

See God in those who hate you.

Begin to feel interest and helpfulness and love toward one soul today, another tomorrow, another day after tomorrow. And let these feelings be active, not weakly passive. Try to love and help others actively each day, especially those who love you. Keep on doing this until you can do it even to those who care nothing for you. And at last let the feeling of love and good will and helpfulness go forth to enfold even those who hate you. This is the real, practical way by which the soul can spread its victories from heart to heart, ever enlarging its boundaries, until at last it can recover its rightful kingdom of all the hearts of all creatures.

Feeling all hearts, you will feel the One Heart of God.

Your unceasing love and unselfish readiness to help others without distinction of sex, creed or caste will make your heart big enough to receive all humanity therein. And once the love of all human beings and all living things shall have entered into your heart, your heart will be the One Heart of God. Feeling all hearts as one, you will feel the One Cosmic Heart beating behind all hearts. Recognizing no individual selfish love, feeling the same love for all, you will feel the One Great Love which is everlasting and forever burns as pure white flame on the universal altar of all hearts. Say silently to your own soul: "I shall drink Thy Love alone from all cups, O God! From the gold and silver and crystal cups of the world and from the shining invisible cups of human hearts, I shall drink Thy Love alone!"

Help yourself in the forms of others.
Recognizing the God-love burning in all heart lamps, you will see and feel only God-love flowing through everybody and everything. Every time you meet a receptive human being, demonstrate by actions; and then make him feel your interest in his physical, mental and spiritual welfare. *Never neglect to do whatever you can for yourself in the forms of others.* To know the Spirit, you must become the Spirit and find yourself as manifested through the bodies and minds of others. Make the bubble of ego one with the ocean of Spirit. Make it big, so big that you can behold all the bubbles of living beings floating in it. Break the boundaries of the small selfishness and include in boundless unselfishness all living beings, universes-everything ever created in the past, existing in the present, and to be created in the future.

Chant the Song of Cosmic Consciousness:

> "So be Thou, my Lord
> Thou and I, never apart;
> Wave of the sea,
> Dissolve in the sea !
> I am the bubble;
> Make me the Sea!"
> *(From Whispers From Eternity.)*

Break the walls of selfishness and make your love broad and deep enough to hold all humanity. The transcendental, metaphysical technique of developing Cosmic Consciousness.

But the quicker and more effective way is to add to the above methods of self-expansion the transcendental way of contacting Spirit. Often, during the day or night, close your eyes and peer into the fathomless eternity, above, beneath, on the right, on the left, and all around and say: "I am glad I turned my gaze from beholding and identify myself with the little bubble of my body to the ocean of Infinity, hiding just behind the dark screen of my human vision."

Chant in silence to your soul: "Om . . . Om ... Om!" And sing over and over and over, the Song of Cosmic Consciousness:
    "So be Thou, my Lord,
    Thou and I, never apart;
    Wave of the sea,
    Dissolve in the sea!
    I am the bubble;
    Make me the Sea!"

Keep on mentally racing millions of miles in all directions at the same time, like an Aurora Borealis, until all directions about you become tangibly shining and glimmering with the searchlight rays of Infinite Light and Bliss.

Feel that as the very essence of your being. That is Cosmic Consciousness.

Get out of the little cage of optical illusion of the body with its confining cage bars of sensation.

Little bird of paradise, forget the familiar cage to which you are so attached; behold your vast kingdom of Light and Bliss hidden behind the shade of darkness which temporarily shrouds your spiritual mental eye during the time you have closed your physical eyes.

The Light shines behind darkness.

Daily seeing the material sunlight, you are blinded and unable to see the magic world of eternally spread luminous electrons shining behind the darkness born of closed eyes. Open your eyes, O blind one! See how tiny your bird of ego is. Now close your physical eyes and keep your spiritual eyes wide open in the sunlight of a new understanding. See how big YOU are, spread over Infinity and Eternity.

The hidden Cosmic Sound.

Listening to little, incomplete vibrations, *you* have forgotten to float in the ocean of Cosmic Sound. The Cosmic Song is hidden behind the multitudinous little noises of your own voice and the voices of material noises. The "still, small voice" is never silent, but it cannot be heard for the clamor drowning it. And all about us, everlastingly, night and day, playing the transcendental Music of the Spheres. "Seeing ye see not; hearing, ye hear not."

Lift the veils of light and thought and behold God.

Stop beholding only the little toy show of this world; close your physical eyes and plunge behind the screen of darkness. Lift the veil of silence, and behold the magic of soothing, rolling fires of planets, of trillions of multicolored dancing atoms. Behold life-force dancing in the hall of electrons. Behold one layer of light lying within another. Behold consciousness dancing in the sphere of living light. Behold the Bliss-God and His blessed angels dancing in the thought-fashioned, wisdom-lighted Eternal Chamber of Perpetual, ever-new Bliss. Lift all curtains of light and behold God in the glory of bliss. The Spiritual Eye is the tunnel through all veils of light, leading straight to God.

Good habits versus human habits. No matter how long you have erred, there is hope for you.

Human habits of beholding yourself as the little body and its small playhouse of the world, must be displaced by God habits. Human habit keeps reminding you of the little, unreal happiness of name, fame, territory and tiny, laughably valueless possessions. *Possess* the *Universe,* for the whole Universe is yours, O Prince of all Possessions! For sake the slums of the beggar-ego and its pitiful claims to its tinsel kingdom of material beggary, O Prince-Image of God! Never mind even if you must live for a few incarnations in the slum of matter, becoming attached to its mirage of reality. Never mind what length of time you have spent and must still spend identified with matter. All of the ages past arc as nothing compared to the Eternity of Time before you, that you may spend in the Bosom of God in the full and conscious possession of all His Glory. No matter how long you have erred and side-tracked away from God, you may NOW forsake the no-longer-attractive slums of ego and reclaim your kingdom of Divine Bliss in Eternity.

Taste God honey-combed in everything.

The little centuries of human years are but days, nay, but a few hours in God's consciousness. Awaken! Arise from dreams of littleness to the realization of the vastness within you. You are dreaming you are a big moth, buzzing around the poisoned honey of blossoming sense-lures. Come! I will show you, my beloved, that you are the Eternal Fire which is drinking with countless mouths the Nectar-Bliss hidden in the honeycombs of all hearts and all things. God is honeycombed in everything. Drink Him through all noble experiences.

Revive your Omnipresent habits.

Feed no longer your human habits with delusive human actions. Let them *slowly* starve for want of the food of activity. Now, come! Meditate daily, with earnestness and devotion. Love God without ceasing. Thus may your Omnipresent habit-nature be revived in your consciousness, displacing the body-bound, sense-limited, world-caged human ideas, beliefs, and conscious and subconscious habits of earth life of this and past incarnations.

Love God through all hearts.

Drink the nectar of God-love in all hearts. Poison the veins of body attachments, all small world attachments. Use every heart as your own wine cup from which to drink the fresh ambrosia of God-love. Drink not this Divine Love from one heart only, but drink freely from all hearts the love of *God alone.*

Feel God as joy of meditation. Think of Him in every action.

Learn to love God as the joy felt in meditation. Victory is very near. Only choose good paths before you start the race to the goal of realization. Then think of God as you start on the path of your material or spiritual duty. Then think of God with each footfall of your advancing feet as you make your way carefully and joyously over the broadening road of fulfillment. Then think of Him after you have traveled far on your life's path and finished your progressive action. Ask God to be with you when you, by your own will, choose good action. Then think of God before you eat body nourishing food; then think of Him while you are eating it. Then, when you have finished eating, think of God.

Keep centered in God, instead of in matter.

When you act in the world, forgetting God, you have changed your center from God to matter. And this grafted material nature will throw you into the whirlpool of change and will stifle you with worries and sorrows. Now revert to your own *real* nature. Change your center from material desires to desire for God. These material nature beggaries are only your grafted nature, so the only way you can forget these is to remember God as Peace and Bliss in your heart always. Ask God to make your peace, silence, joy and meditation His holy altars, where your soul may meet and commune with Him in the Holy of Holies. Let your prayer be: "Make my understanding the temple of Thy guidance."

Be silently drunk with God, but lose not your balance.
Invoke God as Power in the temple of consciousness during the day. Let every action and every word that you utter be tinged and tipsy with God-love intoxication. Talk and act sensibly as a man who drinks a lot and yet keeps his senses awake and in command. Be drunk with God and let every action of your daily life be a temple of God's memory. Perform every action to please Him; and in the indestructible shrine of your devotion God will glisten in every thought.

Carry your love of God deep in your heart before you sleep. Cradle it there, so that when you dream you may dream of Him as resting on the fragrant altar of sleep, as Krishna or Christ or Peace or Bliss. In the temple of Sleep or Dreams, feel God as Peace or as ever-new Bliss. Actually, God embraces you on His Bosom its Peace and joy when You go to sleep in your subconscious chamber or your temple of dreams. Then you are sleeping locked in His Arms of Tranquillity. So, before you fall asleep, realize that you are going to embrace Him in sleep and dreams.

And when you are deeply sleeping or meditating, feel Him embracing you as the Omnipresent Bliss. The Great Omnipresence touches you in sleep and in meditation, and through His Bliss-touch He wants to make you forget your little, painful, worrying memories, mental and physical aches and spiritual agonies, which you garnered during your truant stay in the slums of matter.

Enthrone peace and joy in your heart. Feel that joy, no matter whom you meet and no matter what you do. If you can do this, though the universe shatter itself into nothingness or your soul or body be torn by trials, you will find Him dancing in your memory forever and forever. Let pure joy dance in your memory, and God will dance with you.

Hold fast to your once lost spiritual treasure of joy. Now that it is regained, increase it by giving it freely to others and generously investing it in other hearts. Remember that whatsoever we selfishly keep for self is lost ; and whatsoever we freely give in love to others, that treasure cannot be lost but yields its ever-increasing harvest of happiness, world without end. Worry and selfishness are highwaymen on the road ways of life, and they hold us up and rob us of our wealth of joy and peace. So, determine to hold fast to joy, no matter if death shall frown at your doors or your own subconscious mind may tell you that "all is lost." Drown all confusing noises in the silent, sweet harmony of your perfect, invincible joy.

Enthrone joy in the sanctuary of all your aspirations, your noble ambitions, noble actions, noble thoughts. And then you will feel God consciously as joy reigning in the Kingdom Of your Soul, governing every thought, every feeling and every memory, and laying His scepter on the white altar of your dreams to make every thought and every feeling and every memory a flower blooming there.

Remember this, my beloved: With her veil of sleep and peace, Mother Divine wipes away the dark sorrows of her ignorance-besmirched children. Go then to your dreams as a child to its mother's arms. Divine Love will be enshrined in all your memories of past incarnations and present thoughts. And then you will find that evil and misery were only your own imaginary dream-creations. You slept and dreamed a nightmare of evil; you awake in God and feel only joy and good existing everywhere.

And when the divine memory of constant joy shall arise on the Resurrection Day of your soul's return to its inheritance, you will forget forever your self-created nightmares of evil, and will behold with clear eyes the perfect beauty and good ness that exists everywhere, because God is everywhere.

And then you will pray the only prayer that I pray for myself: "Heavenly Father, may Thy love shine forever on the shrine of my devotion. May my devotion for Thee forever burn on the altar of my memory, and may I be able to kindle love for Thee on all altar-hearts."

God-reminding action. New conception of Cosmic Consciousness in daily life.

1. Think of God before choosing all action. Think of Him before performing an action. And think of Him after the action is performed.
2. Feel God as love in all hearts. Feel God in the impartial love you feel for all human beings and in the tender love you feel for all created things.
3. Create God-like habits by thinking of Him as beauty and fragrance in the flowers; color in the rainbow; love, wisdom and power in all human minds; and vastness in the ocean and skies. Think of Him as life in the breeze; vitality in the sunshine; as peace in the moonbeams; reason in the mind; rest in dreams; joy in sleep; perennial, ever-new Bliss in meditation, and as love in all hearts. This is when the real comfort is found.
4. Reason God as energy which has frozen itself into electrons, gases, liquids and solids. Reason, think and act God as frozen Intelligent Energy.
5. Hear in all songs the heart-stirring ecstasy of God's song. Tune in-hear God's radio program of celestial inspirations.
6. Feel God in the temple of each thought that is born within your mind, in every feeling born within your heart, every aspiration born within your soul.
7. Enthrone God in the temple of Bliss in Meditation.
8. Feel the tangible God as that ever-burning Flame of joy which you directly feel within yourself.

Every step of the way, God walks by your side, speaking to you in every breeze that blows, in every rippling river that goes singing to the sea.

O Divine Mother! Why need we ever cry: "Where art Thou?" Thou art eloquent everywhere, and Thy seeking children may glimpse Thee through windows of beauty, if they but lift to seeing eyes a single fragrant petal of a rose!

> Door of my heart
> Open I keep for Thee.
> Wilt Thou come, wilt Thou come?
> If but for once, come to me!
> Come to me, oh, come to me!

ALWAYS SING

> I will sing Thy name,
> I will drink Thy name,
> And get all drunk,
> Oh, with Thy name!
>
> I will sip Thy name,
> I will drink Thy name.
> Oh, thirstily and greedily
> I will drink Thy name.
>
> I will drink Thy name,
> I will give Thy name.
> I will spread Thy name,
> Oh, everywhere.

We will sing Thy name,
We will drink Thy name.
We'll dance and we'll sing
As we drink Thy name.

We'll sing Thy name
And drink Thy name,
And get all drunk,
Oh, with Thy name.

We'll dance through hearts,
We'll dance through lives,
And sing Thy name,
And sing Thy name.

More books from Alight Publications

Breathe Like Your Life Depends On It
Author: *Rudra Shivananda*
Explore the secrets of Life-force control and expansion for self-Healing, strength and vitality. Imagine living a life protected from stress and ill-health, with wisdom and strength. This is the fruit of controlling and expanding the life-force energy called *prana*. Powerful, simple and beneficial practices which utilize the life-force in the breath, to rejuvenate the body and transform our emotional, mental and spiritual being. [208 pages. US$18.5]

Chakra selfHealing by the power of *OM*
Author: *Rudra Shivananda*
A practical workbook on healing and spiritual evolution. Tap into the potential of the primary energy centers of the body, to eliminate depression and fatigue, relieve anxiety and stress, and calm the mind to achieve inner happiness. Learn the effective *yogic* system of tuning, balancing, color healing, rejuvenation, emotional detoxification, energization, and transcendence, with the *chakras*, in a simple, and step-by-step practice.[140 pages. US$15.0]

Dew-Drops of the Soul
Author: *Yogiraj Gurunath*
A unique compilation of poetic gems from a contemporary Himalayan Master, expressing the essence of his inner experience, as a guide and inspiration for all spiritual seekers. [106 pages. US$12.5]

Earth Peace through Self Peace
Author: *Yogiraj Gurunath*
A collection of spiritual talks or *satsangs*, answering the questions from sincere seekers of truth. A Master speaks to the soul through the doorway of the heart, opening the reader to the reality of the true Self, in spite of the limitations of human language. *Yogiraj* speaks from his own direct experience, in his own simple, direct way, clearing away all doubts and irrelevancies. [164 pages. US$16.5]

The Essence of Kriya Yoga
Author: *Paramhansa Yogananda*
Awaken! Arise from dreams of littleness to the realization of the vastness within you. Kriya Yoga is an instrument through which human evolution can be quickened.... This is India's unique and deathless contribution to the world's treasury of knowledge. This is a collection of the works of the most influential Yoga Master who has lived and taught in the West. [336 pages, US$18.5]

Healing Postures of the 18 Siddhas
Author: *Rudra Shivananda*
A clear, concise and easy to follow text on the series of 18 postures widely used in Kriya Yoga. For the first time, the spiritual and mental dimensions have been revealed to supplement the physical and healing benefits of practising these postures. Fully illustrated with clear photos. [108 pages, US$12.5]

In Light of Kriya Yoga
Author: *Rudra Shivananda*
An adept of Kriya Yoga has provided practical guidance to all those interested in expanding their awareness. What you need to know about: Self-Realization, Liberation, The Role of a Guru, Grace and Devotion, Living Joyfully, Living spiritually in a material world, Concentration and Meditation as well as other profound keys to Life. [255 pages, US$18.5]

Surya Yoga
Author: *Rudra Shivananda*
Tap into the awesome, everpresent healing power of our life-giving Sun. Through the sincere and constant practice of the *Surya Sadhana* [solar practice], you will heal the physical body, acquire greater vitality, overcome all negativity, and also come to a greater understanding and realization of your true nature. Illustrated step-by-step instructions. [164 pages, US$16.5]

Time and the Human Condition
Author: *Partap Singh*
An examination of time, perspective, and our ability to understand, will reveal steps we can take to solve some of the more vexing problems of the modern world. To help us to take the first steps to better understand ourselves and the world around us, the author sheds light on the nature of time through the limited but sharp lens of science, how our views of the afterlife affect our conduct in this life, how limited perspective affect education, government, and justice and how our sense of time affect our attitudes on stress and love. [220 pages, $13.5]

Wings to Freedom
Author: *Yogiraj Gurunath Siddhanath*
Mystic Revelations fom the immortal Babaji and other Himalayan Yogis, as experienced by a perfected Master, Yogiraj Gurunath Siddhanath. Follow his footsteps and experience through his words, as he walks his talk in the jungles, temples, ashrams and hidden [to the uninitiated] places of India. Enrich your life with the secret oral traditions revealed for the first time - mysteries of life, immortality and the attainment of Self-Realization. [308 pages, US$18.5]

Yoga of Purification and Transformation
Author: *Rudra Shivananda*
Attain Peace of Mind in this life and Terminate the cycle of suffering caused by the accumulation of negative karma. Learn the 5 yogic restrainsts or yamas which constitute the Yoga of Purification and the 5 yogic observances or niyamas which are the heart of the Yoga of Transformation. An inspiring and informative presentation of the often neglected foundation of all successful spiritual practice. Actual detailed practices are given in addition to relevant examples and parables. [220 pages, US$18.5]

For information on these or other books or to purchase them on-line with credit card, visit our web-site:
htttp://www.alightbooks.com

www.ingramcontent.com/pod-product-compliance
Lightning Source LLC
Chambersburg PA
CBHW060450170426
43199CB00011B/1149